# CATHOLIC SEXUAL ETHICS

## A SUMMARY, EXPLANATION, & DEFENSE

Rev. Ronald Lawler, O.F.M. Cap.
Joseph M. Boyle, Jr. & William E. May

OUR SUNDAY VISITOR, INC.
HUNTINGTON, INDIANA 46750

*Nihil Obstat:*
Rev. Lorenzo Albacete, S.T.D.
Censor Deputatus

*Imprimatur:*
Rev. Msgr. Raymond Boland
Vicar General for the Archdiocese of Washington
January 3, 1985

The Nihil Obstat and Imprimatur are official declarations that a book or pamphlet is free of doctrinal or moral error. No implication is contained therein that those who have granted the Nihil Obstat or Imprimatur agree with the contents, opinions, or statements expressed.

*International Standard Book Number:* 0-87973-805-7
*Library of Congress Catalog Card Number:* 84-62225

Cover design by
James E. McIlrath

Published, printed, and bound in the U.S.A. by
Our Sunday Visitor, Inc.
200 Noll Plaza
Huntington, Indiana 46750

805

# ACKNOWLEDGMENTS

The authors and publisher are grateful to the following for the use of their materials appearing in this work:

The Division of Christian Education of the National Council of the Churches of Christ for Scripture quotations taken from the *Revised Standard Version, Catholic Edition,* © 1965 and 1966 by the Division of Christian Education of the National Council of the Churches of Christ, except for those appearing in quoted sources such as *Vatican II: The Conciliar and Post Conciliar Documents* and in paraphrased material. All rights reserved.

The Costello Publishing Company, Inc., for quotations taken from *Vatican II: The Conciliar and Post Conciliar Documents* and *Vatican Council II: More Post Conciliar Documents,* Austin Flannery, O.P., General Editor. Reprinted with permission of Costello Publishing Co., Inc., © 1975 by Costello Publishing Company, Inc., and Reverend Austin Flannery, O.P. All rights reserved.

A special debt of gratitude is owed those publishers, authors, etc., for the use of excerpts taken from the works cited in the chapter notes of this book, among them:

Sheed and Ward, *Marriage: Human Reality and Saving Mystery*, by Edward Schillebeeckx, © 1965 by Sheed and Ward, Inc., reprinted with permission of Andrews McMeel & Parker, all rights reserved; Harvard University Press, *Contraception: A History of Its Treatment by Catholic Theologians and Canonists*, by John T. Noonan, Jr., © 1965; McGrath Publishing, *Official Catholic Teachings: Love and Sexuality*, by various popes and their encyclicals, ed. Odile M. Liebard, © 1978; U.S. Catholic Conference, *Declaration on Certain Questions Concerning Sexual Ethics*, by the Sacred Congregation for the Doctrine of the Faith, © 1976; Franciscan Herald Press, *The Way of the Lord Jesus: Christian Moral Principles*, vol. 1, by Germain Grisez, © 1983; Daughters of St. Paul, *Original Unity of Man and Woman: Catechesis on the Book of Genesis*, by Pope Paul II, © 1981; Paulist Press, *Sexual Morality: A Catholic Perspective*, by Philip S. Keane, S.S., © 1977; Farrar, Straus, and Giroux, *Love and Responsibility*, by Karol Wojtyla (Pope John Paul II), tr. H.T. Willetts, © 1981; Raymond Collins, "The Bible and Sexuality I" and "The Bible and Sexuality II," in *Biblical Theology Bulletin*, vols. 7 and 8, © 1977 and 1978.

# CONTENTS

Pope John Paul II has frequently urged scholars to show ever more clearly the origins of Catholic sexual morality. Setting an incomparable example, the Holy Father repeatedly offers to the modern world the vision of the beauty, the realism,

*Foreword*

and the bracing strength of the Gospel's teaching about human love.

The fact is that Catholic teaching in this area is not clearly understood by many. Hence the need to show in profound ways how securely Catholic moral teaching about human sexuality is rooted in the Gospel, how supportive it is of persons and of personal values, and how much this teaching supports the ethical ideals most needed in contemporary society.

For this reason I am very pleased to welcome this book, and to urge those who are concerned with teaching the Catholic vision of human sexuality to study it carefully.

*Catholic Sexual Ethics* shows clearly that Catholic teaching on love and sexuality is full of joy and hope. It remembers the liberating power of self-possession made possible by the grace of our Lord, Jesus Christ. It is Christ himself who gives joy and strength in living the life for which we were created in him.

Catholic moral teaching reminds us of where authentic sexual liberation is to be found. Freedom is not found in surrender-

7

ing to inner and outer pressures. It is found by those who achieve self-possession in Christ, and the power to live as the heart longs to, in ways always faithful to lasting love, to life, to every human good.

*William Cardinal Baum*
PREFECT, SACRED CONGREGATION FOR
CATHOLIC EDUCATION

The purpose of this book is to present the teachings of the Catholic Church on questions of sexual morality.

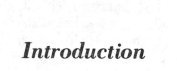

# Introduction

A presentation of Catholic teaching on sexual morality is needed today because many Catholics and non-Catholics alike do not have a clear overall view of this teaching. Even those who know the Church's position on the various controverted issues in sexual ethics do not understand the roots of this teaching and its real human value. Many see it as a set of rules or taboos created by human authorities, or as vestiges of a culture which no longer serves any human needs.

The true character of the Church's teaching on sexual ethics can be understood only if its genuinely personalistic emphasis is grasped. With remarkable uniformity and insistence the Church, over many centuries, has taught that sex is fundamentally a good and wonderful gift of God, and that intelligently ordered sexual activity can be a humanly perfecting and even sanctifying thing. The condemnation of certain kinds of acts, choices, and attitudes bearing on the sexual domain is the result of this conviction about the basic goodness and importance of sexuality, for those things condemned by the Church are the sexual acts and attitudes which harm the human goods at stake in sexual activity. They are treated as gravely wrong because these goods are so central to the person's self-integrity, to the most intimate and fundamental relationships between persons, and to the person's relationship to God.

The Christian view of sexuality stands in stark contrast to many views that have become widely accepted in our culture. Perry London, for example, summarized the change in attitude toward various sexual activities which has occurred over the past few decades. He reported that there have been revolutionary changes in attitude and practice concerning things that have until recently been considered immoral. He concluded that sexual legitimacy is no longer confined to marriage, and that sexual prohibitions might well follow in the way of the now abandoned prohibitions concerning various kinds of food: "If sexual norms were to follow a similar course, then common attitudes and behavior connected with it, like those predominant today with food, might become matters of preference, of health and manners, not of religion and morals."[1] Thus, he says: "It is unclear whether sex will long remain a topic for ethical concerns of any kind in our society."[2]

London, however, is not willing to endorse this trend without some kind of qualification. He believes that there might still be a need to regulate the sex appetite. He argues: "The most important characteristics of sex may finally be that it is so deeply intertwined with affection and that it is still the chief human instrument for making progeny, and these may suggest some limits on its exercise, though they do not reveal the contents of those limits."[3]

From the perspective of Catholic sexual ethics, London's observations are instructive. Intelligent reflection, even from an entirely secular perspective, must acknowledge that sexual activity cannot be treated as a trivial matter, and that the current permissiveness in sexual matters does trivialize sex. Sex is simply too important a part of life to be left as a matter of taste or mere preference.

There are many views about how sexuality is to be regulated so as to avoid its trivialization. Some might wish to see a revival of Victorian prudery or a puritanical denial of the real goodness of human sexuality. Such views, however, involve a denial of what most people correctly see as important human

10

values. A more dominant view nowadays is that sexuality is governed by moral norms, and that these are requirements of its interpersonal character. On this view, the relational character of sexual activity is its most important feature,[4] and thus provides a moral criterion for evaluating sexual behavior. This criterion is the quality of the relationships established and expressed in the sexual activity. By this standard, degrading and exploitive sexual relationships are excluded. Some would add the further condition that the relationship be responsible — that it show care and concern for one's sexual partner, and that it be contraceptive unless a child is expressly desired.[5]

This view of sexual morality might be called the "responsible-relational" view. Besides upholding the conviction that moral norms do bear on sexual activity, this view has the merit of focusing on an undeniably important part of sexual morality, for human beings do establish the most intimate of their interpersonal relationships sexually. However, all human relationships should be responsible and nonexploitive, so this view provides no specific guidance on sexual matters as such. It fails to highlight the special moral responsibilities that flow from concern for the human goods toward which sexuality itself is ordered. It pays insufficient attention to the connection between sexual activity, marital love, and children. It is not surprising therefore that this view tends to approve, in many kinds of circumstances, premarital sex, masturbation, homosexual activity, and so on, and simply has nothing to say about questions of purity of thought. Its view of personal relations is not broad or deep enough to allow a realistic account of what is specifically at stake in sexual activity.

It is surprising therefore to note how much of the responsible-relational view some Catholic writers have accepted. Most of these writers have stated their views in a careful and circumscribed way. But they have denied some teachings very insistently affirmed by the Church, and proposed a view of sexuality more in keeping with the responsible-relational view. Catholic writers, of course, are concerned to preserve the special place of marriage in the sexual domain. But even here some are willing to allow — at least as a possibility — the legitimacy of sexual activity outside marriage.[6] These writers also allow the per-

11

missibility of contraception,[7] and some would count homosexual behavior in some circumstances as morally acceptable or even praiseworthy.[8]

From the perspective of the Church's teaching on sexual morality, the work of these Catholic writers suffers from the same essential shortcomings as that of their secular counterparts. But these writers are Catholic theologians, often priests; and their work — however nuanced in itself — has had the effect of blurring the essential outlines of Catholic sexual morality for many members of the clergy and laity.

For many Catholics nowadays, the clear light of the Church's teaching is not brought to bear on the problems of sexual life. The only moral tempering of the sexual exploitation and hedonism of our culture is provided by the responsible-relational view which can do little to articulate the real grandeur of sexuality or to protect it from the current onslaught. When Catholic moral teachers cannot show clearly what is distinctive about the Christian understanding of sexuality, Catholics are likely to be confused and misled.

In a widely used college textbook on human sexuality, the authors observe that many Catholics disagree with the official teaching of the Church on matters of a sexual nature and are striving to change it. They discuss the case of a devout single woman who has sexual intercourse with a man she loves and plans to marry. If this woman confesses her action to a priest, he will in all likelihood agree that it was a wrongful act, and absolve her if she is repentant. The authors add that the priest may not, nowadays, be faithful to the tradition in regarding the act as wrongful.[9]

It is essential therefore that the Church's teaching on sexual morality be presented in a way that reveals its truth and attractiveness. This book is part of the effort to do this — to fulfill the mandate of Pope John Paul II to reveal "the biblical foundations, the ethical grounds, and the personalistic" appropriateness of the good news about human sexuality which God has commanded the Church to proclaim.[10] Thus, this book will contain an extended exposition of the Church's teaching on sexual morality as well as a theological development of the arguments which support the Church's teaching. This theological argumentation will seek to relate the Church's teaching on sexual morality to the most fundamental concerns of Christian life, and to make clear within the perspective of Catholic faith why the Church's teaching on these matters is important and true.

To achieve these theological and pastoral aims, the book is divided into eight chapters and a conclusion. The first three chapters present a general account of the development of the Church's understanding of human sexuality. The first reviews the scriptural understanding of sexuality; the second the development of the theological tradition; and the third the teaching of the Church's magisterium — the teaching office of popes and bishops. The fourth and fifth chapters deal with general issues of moral theology which lie behind many of the specific issues in sexual morality. The fourth is a brief account of the foundations of moral theology; it provides a critique of the method of moral reasoning used by those Catholic writers who do not accept the received teaching on sexual morality. The fifth is a presentation of the Church's teaching on conscience; it focuses on the relationship between Church teaching and the conscience of the Catholic. The sixth chapter is an account of Christian marriage from a moral theological perspective. The final two chapters consider in some detail the specific requirements of chastity; Chapter 7 considers the requirements of chaste love within marriage; Chapter 8 considers the requirements of chastity for the unmarried. Following the eight chapters the Pastoral Conclusion considers how the Christian message about sexuality is to be presented; it emphasizes both the seriousness of living chastely and the real possibility of living chastely given our union with the risen Lord. His own example of dealing with fallen humankind is proposed as the model for pastoral problems in this area where so much weakness abounds.

This work was begun some seven years ago at the urging of Ronald Lawler, O.F.M. Cap. Many unavoidable delays have prevented its publication until now. It should be noted that these delays have been largely beneficial. Perhaps the greatest of these benefits has been the appearance of the great body of teaching on the issues at hand by the present pope, John Paul II. His statements and analyses have enriched every aspect of our work enormously. Most importantly, his *Familiaris Con-*

*sortio* has made clear beyond any doubt that the received teachings of the Church — what the authors of this work have set out to explain and defend in this book — are indeed the authentic teachings of Christ's Church. Dissent on sexual matters is rejected — firmly and clearly — by the Church in this apostolic exhortation. This statement has exceptional authority, for in it John Paul II — as the authentic pastor of the whole Church and as the leader of the college of bishops — hands on received Catholic teaching. The collegiality of *Familiaris Consortio* is very real, since it is the pope's summary and response to the proposals made by the 1980 Synod of Bishops on the problems of the family.

Originally, the group of people involved in preparing this work was quite large. In addition to the authors, the following persons contributed material which has been used in some way in the development of the final product: Mark Dosh; John Harvey, O.S.F.S.; Frederick Jelly, O.P.; Mary Joyce; John Kippley; James Mohler, S.J.; Henry Sattler, C.Ss.R.; and William B. Smith. The authors thank these friends and colleagues for their irreplaceable help. The authors also thank Germain Grisez, whose insight on the issues addressed and whose work on fundamental moral theology and specific issues in sexual ethics has influenced this book greatly. In addition, the authors thank Barbara Boyle who typed and retyped several versions of a number of the chapters, and Joseph Koterski who entered a number of chapters into a word processor. The authors owe a great debt to the University of St. Thomas in Houston, Texas, and to the Basilian Fathers there, for providing word-processing equipment, hospitality, facilities for the authors' common work, and encouragement.

Finally, a word about the collaboration which led to this book is in order. Boyle and May drafted most of the chapters as they now appear. Drafts of early chapters often made use of materials provided by the collaborators listed above. Revisions were made on the basis of editorial work done by all three authors but primarily by Lawler. The final text therefore is the joint work of all three authors. All have read and agreed to the text as it appears, to the extent that it is very difficult to say who authored any individual sentence or came up with any specific

14

argument or point. The authors hope that this work will prove invaluable to married and single people, to pastors and marriage counselors, and especially to those individuals who are seeking guidance concerning the Church's stand on sexual ethics.

CHAPTER

1

In the *Dogmatic Constitution on Divine Revelation* the Fathers of Vatican II affirmed: "All the preaching of the Church, as indeed the entire Christian religion, should be nourished and ruled by sacred Scripture. In the sacred

# The Biblical Teaching on Sex

books the Father who is in heaven comes lovingly to meet his children, and talks with them. And such is the force and power of the Word of God that it can serve the Church as her support and vigor, and the children of the Church as strength for their faith, food for the soul, and a pure and lasting fount of spiritual life" (*Dei Verbum*, no. 21).

It is appropriate therefore to begin this study of Catholic sexual morality with a review of the scriptural teaching on human sexuality. This review will be based on the work of the best contemporary exegetes and biblical theologians. In it we will sum up what Scripture actually teaches about human sexuality. Of course, such a study of Scripture is not of itself sufficient to communicate the full richness of God's revelation about human sexuality. That requires the full understanding of Scripture by the Church. This understanding develops in the Church's ongoing reflection on Scripture and tradition which is guided by the magisterium, the teaching authority of the Church. This entire work is an attempt to present this Catholic understanding of hu-

16

man sexuality, and this first chapter is the first essential step in that effort.

## I. The Old Testament

The Old Testament is not a textbook either on morality in general or on sexual morality in particular. Nevertheless, as the initial written part of God's revelation, it contains fundamental truths about human life and destiny, for the relationship of friendship with human beings which God establishes in his revelation tells us much about ourselves and how we should live. It is not surprising therefore that the Old Testament articulates fundamental truths about human sexuality and its place in human life and the divine economy. As we shall see, these truths have lasting significance, and remain relevant today.

The proper perspective for understanding the Old Testament teaching on sexual matters is provided by the context of the fundamental concerns of this first stage of revelation. These concerns cluster around the Hebrew awareness of the reality of God and of his covenant with the people of Israel and all humankind. Because of these concerns, the Hebrew people understood human sexuality quite differently than their neighbors. The Hebrews saw sexuality primarily in moral terms, and they understood morality in the light of their faith in God. Morality thus understood was primarily a way of response to the love of God revealed to them in the various covenants God offered them. Thus, the context of morality was religious, and moral requirements were an aspect of worship. All of human life, including sexual life, was seen as a worshiping service of God. This was so because God, who gave to humans the gift of life, wanted his people to be holy, as he was holy. Thus, God was to be worshiped by a life of obedience to his loving call — that is, by the observance of the commandments which God gives out of his love and concern for human beings.[1]

The central message of the Old Testament concerning human sexuality is that it is a good thing. Like other aspects of creation — and of the human person, in particular — sexuality is a gift of the all-good and transcendent Creator. This message is found at the very beginning of Scripture, in the creation narratives of the first chapters of Genesis. Two distinct accounts of creation are presented there: the Yahwist narrative of Genesis 2.4b-24, and the Priestly narrative of Genesis 1.2—2.4a. Although the two narratives were written at different times and with different emphases, some elements are common to both.

First, each was written in a conscious effort to combat the myth of Baal — an account of human life and sexuality which the Hebrews regarded as utterly irreconcilable with the understanding of God and of human life developed through their experience of God's activity among them. This myth and its accompanying fertility cult presented sex as something divine, and sexual union between humans as a participation in the divine. Gods were seen as sexual beings, capable, like men, of the unrestrained passion of lust.[2] Genesis rejects this myth firmly and presents an alternative account of the origins of humankind and of sexuality. On the Genesis accounts, sexuality is not something divine but something human; it is still, however, something very good, since it is the gift of God.[3]

Second, both narratives are stories of the creation of "man" not as an isolated individual but as a personal being made in the image and likeness of God,[4] and sexually differentiated into male and female. Each account contains, in other words, a story of the creation of human sexuality and, indeed, of marriage.[5] This is brought out somewhat differently in the two narratives. The older account in Genesis 2 is more picturesque and anthropomorphic. It portrays God as first bringing the male into being, and then recognizing that it is not good for the male to be alone, for by himself he can never fully be himself; to be this he needs another with whom he can share his life. God sees that none of the other creatures he has created can fill this need. Therefore, God casts the male into a deep sleep and from his body fashions another human, a being equal to the man in human dignity but sexually different from and complementary to him.[6] This being — the woman — is the one for whom the man yearns and to whom he cleaves as "bone of his bone and flesh of his flesh."[7]

According to this narrative, God, in creating "the man," creates mankind — that is, a species sexually differentiated into male and female. This differentiation does not indicate a difference in human dignity but rather points to an inherent com-

18

plementarity and mutuality in the very apex of visible creation. Moreover, this differentiation is intended by God to make possible a special kind of friendship between man and woman. This is indicated by the notion of "cleaving." Raymond Collins explains this notion and its implications as follows:

"Cleaving" (Genesis 2.24) implies a devotion and an unshakeable faith between humans: it connotes a permanent attraction that transcends genital union, to which, nevertheless, it gives meaning. There can be no mistaking the author's intention. He concludes his narrative by interpreting the divinely ordered sexual differentiation and the sexual drive within the perspective of a permanent social union between man and woman.[8]

According to the Yahwist account, therefore, sexuality is central to the reality of human beings. The human species is not composed of sexually undifferentiated persons but of males and females whose sexuality is complementary and ordered to a faithful and intimate sharing of life — that is, to marriage. As Edward Schillebeeckx has observed:

. . . it was in the first Adam [that is, the first human beings, male and female] that God himself constituted the essential structure of marriage between man and woman — the structure that we should expect to encounter in every marriage.[9] To be created by God, or to be named by him, implied a commission to serve him. The whole of the OT [Old Testament] ethic of marriage and the family is based on this. The things of the earth and man received their *hoq* or *huqqah* [their defining characteristics] with their creation; each received, on creation, its intrinsic conditions of existence, its defined limits. This intrinsic reality was none other than God's creative will which called an order, a system, into existence (cf. Gen 1.14; Jer 5.24, 31, 33-36).[10]

The Yahwist narrative in Genesis 2 thus stresses the unitive or life-uniting significance of sexuality and marriage, as well as the fundamental equality and complementarity of the sexes. Its special emphasis is highlighted by the general principle stated in Genesis 2.24 — that God has willed the unity and monogamy of marriage.[11]

In Genesis 2 there is no explicit mention of the procreative

19

nature of the marital union. Nevertheless, the procreative character of the marital union is presupposed in this narrative which forms a literary unit with Genesis 3 and 4. In Genesis 4.1 the Yahwist author states: "Now Adam knew Eve his wife, and she conceived and bore Cain, saying, 'I have gotten a man with the help of the Lord.' " This shows that "the establishment of the first family was the solution to the man's need for social life and for a race to fulfill his commission. Hence the man needed a wife with whom he could beget children and with whom he could establish a family. In creating woman and coupling her with the man, God created one flesh that could be the source of the family."[12] Thus, it would be a significant oversight to miss the reference to family and reproduction which is an underlying motif in the Yahwist narrative.

By way of contrast to the Yahwist narrative, the Priestly narrative of Genesis 1 does not speak of successive creation of humanity but instead portrays the creation of man and woman as simultaneous: "So God created man in his own image, in the image of God he created him; male and female he created them" (Genesis 1.27).[13]

The Priestly account explicitly brings into focus the procreative dimension of human sexuality. The couple, whose sexual complementarity is seen as being "very good" (Genesis 1.31), is blessed by God and instructed to "be fruitful and multiply." As Raymond Collins explains:

> ... human sexuality, although essentially a reality of the secular order, is a sacral value by reason of the blessing which God pronounced upon the sexed humanity which he had created. . . . Progeny is a gift from God, the fruit of his blessing. Progeny are conceived because of the divine power which has been transferred. . . . The blessing . . . indicates that fertility is the purpose of the sexual distinction, albeit not the exclusive purpose of the distinction.[14]

Chapter 3 of Genesis, also from the Yahwist tradition, tells of the primordial sin by the first man and woman. As a result of their sin, the man and woman find themselves at a loss to understand themselves and their sexuality. They experience shame over their nakedness,[15] and the harmony that is meant to exist between them is broken. The man begins to lord it over his wife,

20

and the social and cultural inferiority of women begins. The biblical writers explain the experienced inferiority of women within Hebrew society as the consequence of sin.[16] Genesis 2 and 3 make it clear that this situation is the result of sin and not the Creator's original intention. In his original creation, God intended that man and woman should live harmoniously, in peace and unity. The evil which disrupted the daily lives of men and women in their most intimate aspects was the result of human sin.[17]

The Old Testament provides another important insight into the meaning of human sexuality in the Song of Solomon (or Canticle of Canticles). This sensual and even erotic poem extols the love between the sexes. It portrays human sexuality and sensuality as good in themselves, and sexual union as an occasion for joy and celebration. Certain features of the song merit special attention. First, it appears to be a love song — one particularly fit for a wedding celebration. This indicates that it is in marriage that man and woman are to celebrate their sexuality in an erotic, genital manner. Second, the description of the bride as a "garden locked, a fountain sealed" (Song 4.12) suggests the esteem given to the virginal state of the bride.[18]

The preceding textual considerations taken together make it clear that in the Old Testament sex is viewed as a good thing — a blessing from God. Still, human sexuality must be responsibly controlled; it must not be the controlling dimension of human beings. As Raymond Collins has pointed out:

> ... to affirm the goodness of human sexuality in all its dimensions is not to affirm that human sexuality lies beyond the sphere of human responsibility nor is it beyond the pale of that over which man has dominion as God's vice-regent. Human sexuality was indeed a dimension of human experience which fell within the parameters of Yahweh's hegemony and the covenant relationship. The presence of "Thou shalt not commit adultery" within the covenant clause of the Decalogue (Ex 20.14, Dt 5.18) serves as a clear reminder that the fashion in which man lives his sexuality was not independent of his relationship to Yahweh, the God of his people. . . . Man is responsible for the way he uses his sexuality.[19]

21

Human beings, in other words, are to control their sexuality intelligently and in comformity to God's will. Thus, the Old Testament contains the beginning of divine revelation's teaching on the virtue of chastity: human beings are to integrate their sexuality by understanding its meaning and purpose, and by living out that understanding.

Throughout the Old Testament marriage is presented as something holy; and the sexual relationship within marriage is portrayed as good when it is mindful of God and his covenant. The prophets — beginning with Hosea and continuing through Isaiah, Jeremiah, and Ezekiel — saw in human marriage a fitting symbol of the covenant between God and his people. In using this image, the prophets were more interested in articulating God's love, forgiveness, and mercy than they were in spelling out the nature of loving marriage. Still, as Schillebeeckx has pointed out, the use of this image by the prophets involves a "reciprocal illumination" of the human meaning of marriage. Their use of this image communicates not only the utterly faithful love of God for his people but also the normative reality of marriage — the divinely intended, faithful, and exclusive union of man and woman.[20]

It is true that the understanding of marriage among the Hebrews was imperfect: the husband was permitted to divorce his wife; women were regarded as inferior; there was a double standard for adultery. A married man who had sexual relations with an unbetrothed maiden, harlot, or slave girl was not considered to have committed adultery (Deuteronomy 22.28-29), whereas any sexual relations on the part of a married woman with anyone but her husband were judged adulterous, and she could be subjected to the ordeal for suspected adultery (Numbers 5.11-31).

These inequalities were rooted in socioeconomic factors within Hebrew society, and reflect its patriarchal ethos.[21] It is a mistake to conclude from this, however, that the condemnation of adultery is based simply on the social and familial requirements of a patriarchal society.[22] There is abundant evidence in the Old Testament that the very nature and purposes of human sexuality require that adultery be excluded.[23] The story of Joseph and Potiphar's wife (Genesis 39), the episode of Abimilech

22

and Sarah (Genesis 20), and the Wisdom literature in general show beyond any reasonable doubt the moral basis for the prohibition of adultery.

Moreover, the appreciation of the importance of marital fidelity developed as God's revelation unfolded. An important step in this development is the prophetic teaching that marriage is a sign of God's faithful love for his people: "The fidelity of a covenanted marriage was so highly valued that restrictions were developed so that a wife could not be too easily abandoned by her spouse."[24]

The Wisdom literature repeatedly counsels husbands and wives to be faithful to one another, advises young men to avoid harlots and wayward women, and speaks glowingly of the happiness of a marriage marked by lifelong fidelity. The love of Jacob for Rachel and of Tobit for Sarah became legendary and provided models for the marital relationship as willed by God.[25] The overall thrust of Old Testament teaching is therefore very clear: faithful, lifelong marriage is the normative context for sexual love.

The advice to young men in the Wisdom literature suggests that this overall thrust includes a negative evaluation of fornication or premarital sexual activity. Although there is no explicit condemnation of all fornication in the Old Testament, it "strongly condemns sexual intercourse with a betrothed virgin by someone other than her intended (Deuteronomy 22.23-27)."[26] This strong condemnation, in conjunction with the whole set of values upheld throughout the Old Testament, has the implication — to be drawn more explicitly only later — that all fornication must be excluded.

The Old Testament condemns bestiality and homosexuality as utterly reprehensible and abominable. Since human sexuality is oriented to the personal relationship of marriage and to the good of progeny, no one can properly express his or her sexuality in commerce with a beast. To do so is to be guilty of a most grievous crime (Exodus 22.19; Leviticus 18.23, 20.15-16; Deuteronomy 27.21).

Contemporary Scripture scholars differ as to why homosexuality was so strongly condemned in the Old Testament (cf. Leviticus 18.22, 20.13), and offer different interpretations of

23

such narratives as the Sodom and Gomorrah story (Genesis 19), and the account of Ham's sin with respect to his father, Noah (Genesis 9.20-28).[27] They agree, however, that the Old Testament is unequivocal in condemning homosexual activities as an abomination, a form of idolatry, and a base attempt to gain sexual power. Moreover, the motive for the moral condemnation seems to be the character of homosexual acts themselves.[28] Although there is no explicit distinction made between homosexual orientation and behavior, it is clearly the latter which is at issue in the Old Testament.

This short summary makes it clear that the treatment of human sexuality in the Old Testament is not simply an expression of Semitic culture and social conditions. This teaching is part of the initial stage of God's revelation about the meaning of sex. While it is incomplete and in need of the perspective of the fullness of revelation in Christ, this teaching is, as far as it goes, true, and the relevance of this truth is enduring.

## II. The New Testament

The principal message of the New Testament is that the long-awaited good news, heralded by the prophets, is now at hand. God himself, through Jesus, is establishing his kingdom of justice, peace, and love, bringing his people and all mankind redemption and salvation, and, most wonderfully and unexpectedly, making possible a kind of intimate friendship with himself. This good news brings with it radical moral demands, and puts everything in a new light — including human sexuality. Everything human is to be seen within the perspective of the full revelation of God's saving grace, of the real possibilities for forgiveness and a new form of human existence through Jesus.[29]

This new perspective is shown very clearly in the new evaluation of virginity and celibacy. The Jews of the first century — with the exception of the ascetic Essenes — believed that a life of celibacy was absurd, even sinful. According to the rabbinical schools of the time: "No man may abstain from keeping the Law, 'Be fruitful and multiply,' unless he already has children; according to the school of Shammai, two sons; according to the school of Hillel, a son and a daughter."[30] Yet Jesus was himself a virgin and commended virginity for the sake of the Gospel.[31]

24

Similarly, St. Paul encourages the Christians of Corinth to embrace the life of virginity for the sake of the kingdom, arguing that like marriage it is a great gift from God.[32]

Today, some claim that the prominence given to the virginal state by Paul and other New Testament writers is simply a contingent, culturally conditioned aspect of the apostolic age.[33] But this view is not sustained by a careful examination of the New Testament teachings on virginity. Schillebeeckx, who recognizes that there is a certain measure of cultural influence in these views, presents a fuller analysis of the teachings on virginity. He points out that Paul's views on this matter were, indeed, set in the context of his expectation of an imminent parousia. His overriding concern, however, was to impress on his converts the radical transformation of human life effected by the new life in Christ. Thus, Paul "wanted to encourage Christians to be self-sacrificing enough to embark on the charism of total continence. . . . It is inconceivable that some 'new existential experience,' the discovery of new aspects of marriage which escaped those who experienced it at an earlier period, should make the New Testament vision of Christian celibacy appear relative or incomplete in any respect. . . . Christianity will never be able to close its ears to the authentic biblical call to total abstinence as a possibility that forms an intrinsic and essential part of Christianity itself."[34]

This emphasis on the summons to total abstinence is a useful point of departure for considering the New Testament teaching on sexuality and sexual morality, for it reveals the basic perspective from which the New Testament approaches all the questions of human sexuality. Of course, the New Testament takes for granted the teachings of the Old Testament on the goodness of sexuality and on the greatness and beauty of faithful marriage. But the New Testament is concerned above all with showing how marriage, sexuality, and, indeed, everything human, have been transformed and deepened by the new life brought to us by Jesus, and this is revealed dramatically in the eschatological witness of consecrated virginity.[35]

The Gospels do not explicitly say a great deal about sexuality, but what is found there is very significant. Jesus' teachings on divorce, on the importance of purity of thought and intention, and on the sins which proceed from evil intention and make the person unclean are perhaps the most important Gospel passages dealing specifically with sexual morality.

In his sayings on divorce (Matthew 19.3-9; Mark 10.2-12; Luke 16.18), Jesus first reaffirms the goodness of sexuality and marriage as taught in Genesis.[36] By including in the various Gospel accounts references to both Genesis 1.27 (Matthew 19.4; Mark 10.6) and Genesis 2.24 (Matthew 19.5; Mark 10.7) the sacred authors make it clear that for Jesus the sexual differentiation of male and female is part of the plan of creation, and marriage is the only proper context for genital activity.[37]

Two features of Jesus' teaching on divorce are particularly striking. First, he unequivocally condemns both divorce and remarriage; any "remarriage" after divorce is not a marriage at all but adultery.[38] Second, he clarified and developed the Old Testament teaching on the fundamental equality of woman; he stated that one who divorced his wife and married another committed adultery against his wife. This is particularly clear in Mark's account: "Whoever divorces his wife and marries another, commits adultery against her" (Mark 10.11). Thus, any double standard of the sort tolerated in the Old Testament was firmly excluded: adultery was a very serious evil, and since remarriage after divorce was adultery, it was obviously a serious violation of God's will.[39]

Jesus' gracious dealings with women further illustrate his concern for their human dignity and fundamental equality with men. For example, his treatment of the Samaritan woman at the well reveals an open friendliness not expected in first-century Palestine (John 4.27). And his response to the woman taken in adultery, although it makes clear his firm teaching that adultery is seriously wrong, shows his kindness and mercy in a context in which the expectation was for righteous indignation.[40]

Jesus' condemnation of a man's looking lustfully at a woman indicates that for him sexual morality is not merely a matter of external behavior but of a person's internal disposition and will as well. This focus on the person's heart is characteristic of Jesus' moral teaching. It is not so much an extension of moral rules to cover wider areas of human life as it is a focusing on the true nature of morality, for morality is not directly concerned with external behavior and its effect but with the immediate effects one's choices have on one's self — that is, with the kind of person one makes of oneself by one's own free choices.

This focus on the heart, on the person's disposition and will, is also central to the catalog of vices Jesus presents (Matthew 15.19; Mark 7.21-22). These vices proceed from the human heart and, unlike those things which are taken into the body, defile the human person. In the list provided by Mark there are several sexual sins, among them adultery *(moicheia)*, fornication *(porneia)*, and sensuality *(aselgeia)*. In that given by Matthew are included adultery *(moicheia)* and fornication *(porneia)*. Although it is difficult, according to New Testament scholars, to determine precisely the nature of the sexual offenses designated by some of these terms, in particular those designated by *porneia* (translated here, as in the *New American Bible*, as "fornication") and by *aselgeia* (translated here, as in the *New American Bible*, as "sensuality"),[41] it is nonetheless clear that the authors of these Gospels present Jesus as teaching that adultery (*moicheia*, over which there is no dispute) is not the only act of a sexual nature that ought to be considered sinful. There are many others. Still, the precise meaning to be given *porneia* vexes contemporary exegetes. Nonetheless, no matter what its manifold meanings, it is definitely used in the New Testament to include acts properly designated by the English term *fornication*, or premarital sex.[42]

In addition to the Gospels, the writings attributed to St. Paul provide the most important source of New Testament teaching on human sexuality. In the First Letter to the Corinthians, Paul takes for granted the basic goodness of human sexuality. In Chapter 7 he reaffirms the goodness of marriage and of sexual union within marriage. His primary aim in this discussion is to convey a proper Christian attitude about these matters to his new converts at Corinth. This concern was necessary because Corinth was a center both of licentiousness and of an antisexual Gnosticism, which often presented itself as Christian.[43] The fundamental point Paul seeks to communicate is that for those who have received new life through Christ, everything is to be experienced "in the Lord," including their sexuality and married lives.[44]

27

In 1 Corinthians 6.19 Paul emphasizes that the Christian is one who has become united with Christ in an intimately personal and bodily way. Through baptism, the human person becomes one body with Christ; the human body — that is, the whole human self[45] — becomes a temple of the Holy Spirit. This view of the makeup of the Christian person has immediate implications for sexual morality. Since sexual immorality affects the human person in such an intimate, bodily way, it is abominable — a sacrilegious desecration of the body of Christ and the temple of the Holy Spirit. Other sins are outside the body, but sexual sins are especially perverse because they are within.[46]

Chapter 6 of 1 Corinthians also contains a list of vices similar to those in Mark and Matthew: "Neither the immoral [pornoi], nor idolators, nor adulterers [moichoi], nor homosexuals, nor thieves, nor the greedy, nor drunkards, nor revilers, nor robbers will inherit the kingdom of God" (1 Corinthians 6.9-10). Paul clearly believes that sexual immorality is antithetical to the demands of the kingdom.

Several other Pauline teachings are especially important for understanding the New Testament view of sexuality. The first of these is the discussion of marriage in Ephesians 5. There the marital relationship is likened to the relationship between Christ and his Church. The point of the comparison is to provide a reason for the special love and concern which should exist between spouses. Christ is related to the Church — his own body — just as a husband is related to his wife whom he should regard with the care he has for his own body.[47] So, this important teaching is an aspect of the transfiguration of marriage by the new life made possible through Jesus.

Paul's brief discussion of homosexuality in the first chapter of Romans is also noteworthy. Paul does not argue here that homosexuality is wrong; that is taken as evident. He treats homosexual practices as being both sinful in themselves and part of the punishment for disbelief. Homosexuality therefore is presented as an evil, a distortion of human life which follows from sin (Romans 1.26-27).[48]

To sum up this section: The New Testament summons all people to a new life, made possible by Christ. Within this new life, consecrated virginity has a place of special honor as a way

28

of responding to God's call and witnessing to the reality of his kingdom. Still, this new way of living does not fail to respect the goodness of sexuality, or of any of the good things God created. Rather, all these things are transformed and seen within the true perspective of their proper place in God's salvific plan. Marriage is presented as a lifelong union of shared love open to the blessing of children. Marriage, thus understood, is a great and wonderful reality which images and participates in the love of Christ for his Church. This revelation of the ultimate significance and value of sexuality also makes clear how serious are those acts which fail to respect the integrity of marriage and sexuality. The new life with Christ is defiled and human persons are desecrated when sexual satisfaction is sought outside marriage.[49]

The New Testament, then, teaches that chastity is a virtue required of every Christian, male or female, married or unmarried. Because sexuality is a good gift from God, God shows us in the fullness of his revelation in Jesus that its proper use is to be highly prized and its abuse severely condemned. The Letter to the Hebrews says this well: marriage is to be held in honor by all; the marriage bed is to be undefiled; adulterers and fornicators will be judged by God (Hebrews 13.4).

The relevance of God's revelation in Scripture to the issues of human sexuality and sexual morality cannot be exhausted by a consideration of its explicit teachings on sexual matters, much less by a brief survey of central teachings on these questions. Of the many closely related teachings, the biblical teaching on sin is especially important. A brief consideration of sin will therefore complete this chapter.

As we have already seen, all of God's creation, including mankind, is good. So also are the human body, human flesh, human sexuality, and sexual activity. Still, the peace which God willed to exist between himself and mankind and among human persons was shattered by the sin of the first humans. The story of Genesis 3 recounts the awful havoc caused by sin. Although this story does not use the word "sin," it dramatically reveals the reality and consequences of sin. Adam and Eve enjoyed the friendship of God up to the point of their disobedience. After they disobeyed, they "hid themselves from the presence of the Lord God among the trees of the garden" (Genesis 3.8). They no longer wished to be in the presence of God. As Isaiah put it, ". . . your iniquities have made a separation between you and your God" (Isaiah 59.2). Similarly, the first humans' sin ruptured their relationship to one another; hardly was the sin committed when Adam called his wife a temptress. The inclination to evil followed the first sin, and its effects were felt immediately in the alienation between those created to be the closest of friends.[50]

In the New Testament, Paul, in particular, details the terrible effects of Adam's sin. The power of sin, unleashed by Adam's transgression, possesses every human being. It is the root cause of all the particular sins which can prevent a person from entering the kingdom of heaven.[51] Of course, these particular sins include the sexual sins discussed above. Paul teaches that, because of Adam's transgression, mankind has been sold into the power of sin (Romans 7.23). Thus, Paul finds within himself a "law of his body's members" at war with the "law of his mind," and he finds that he does not do the good he wants to do but rather the evil he hates (Romans 7.15).

This biblical doctrine of sin and its effects is one that Christians have always taken seriously. As we shall see, this is a doctrine of considerable importance in the efforts of the Church through the centuries to understand and deal with human sexuality. Of course, Jesus came to rescue us from the power of sin to which we were enslaved. In dying he destroyed the power of sin, and in rising he made it possible for us to live a new life. It is this saving reality which is the most single important factor in the efforts of Christians to understand their sexuality and to integrate their sexuality into their new lives in Christ, for by this teaching we can see the wonderful goodness of our sexual natures, and by the grace of our new lives we can actually live so as to honor and experience this great blessing.

30

CHAPTER

Catholics are the heirs of a long theological tradition. Over the centuries there has been careful reflection on human sexuality and sexual morality in the light of the Scriptures. From apostolic times to the present, Catholic scholars,

## Sex in the Catholic Tradition

saints, and pastoral leaders have sought to understand, in the light of God's revealing word, the meaning of human sexuality and the norms of sexual morality. During this long history, errors have unquestionably been made; but this history is also a story of the development in doctrine toward a clearer understanding of the nature of sexuality as revealed by God and uncovered by human reflection. The growth in the Church's understanding of human sexuality has not been haphazard but systematic, for it has been directed by an awareness of fundamental truths about human nature and destiny which are grounded in Scripture, proclaimed by the teaching authority of the Church, and gradually refined by the developing theological tradition.

This tradition teaches now, and has always taught, that the union of man and woman in marriage is good, indeed holy. It teaches now, and has always taught, that the virtue of chastity is necessary for all persons, male and female, married and unmarried, so that they might fully have freedom of self-possession and not be controlled by unworthy sexual desire. It teaches now, and has always taught, that some specific sorts of sexual activity — fornication, adultery, contraception, and sodomy, for instance — are simply incompatible with the form of living appropriate to a person who has become one body with Christ through baptism, and whose body is a living tabernacle of God.

It is, of course, impossible in a brief section of a book such as this to provide a detailed history of the developing Catholic theological tradition on sex. A satisfactory history on this subject has never, in fact, been written.[1] Still, it is possible to note the major claims about human sexuality and sexual morality that have been central to this developing tradition, and to specify some of the principal developments that have taken place.

## I. Early Christian and Patristic Thought

To understand the sexual attitudes expressed by the earliest Christian writers one must first of all be aware of the context in which they wrote. They lived in an age of great sexual licentiousness — an age whose similarities to our own are unmistakable. The early Christian writers were keenly aware that the teachings of the New Testament on marriage, virginity, and chastity were radically opposed to the sexual outlook and practice of the pagan world. Thus, their thought must be understood in the context of their interaction with a society in which prostitution was widespread; divorce, contraception, abortion, and infanticide were common; and chastity for males was considered out of the question.[2]

In addition to the debauchery and disregard for human life prevalent in the Greco-Roman world of the time, the early Christians likewise faced a religious challenge in the various Gnostic movements of the day. Gnosticism at times posed as a variant of the Gospel, but it was a mystery religion more influenced by contemporary philosophical ideas than by the Gospel. It claimed a "saving" knowledge quite opposed to the Christian message. The Gnostics were metaphysical dualists, and therefore held that matter itself was evil. Consequently, they held that the human body and sexuality were evil. They despised marriage and, in particular, the procreation of new life through marital union. Although they advocated sexual abstinence for the "elite," they did so not because they thought that such absti-

32

nence might be required by God's will or by a proper regard for the goods of human nature but because they regarded sexual union as defiling. Since total abstinence was difficult for most people, however, some Gnostics conveniently taught that the non-elite could freely engage in all kinds of sexual activities for the sake of the exquisite experience of pleasure that they might bring, as long as they took care to ensure that no new life was generated.[3]

Facing these two evils, the early Christian writers drew on the teaching of the Gospels and Paul to instruct the faithful and to articulate Christian attitudes toward sex. While extolling a virginity that would be chosen for the sake of God's kingdom, they taught that marriage itself was something good because it had been divinely instituted and had been blessed by Jesus' presence at the wedding feast of Cana (John 2). Irenaeus, for example, writing in the second century, repudiated the views of the Gnostics, saying: "Saturninus and Marcion, who are called 'the Continent,' preach abstinence from marriage, frustrating the age-old creation of God and implicitly finding fault with Him who made human beings male and female so that they could reproduce themselves. They introduced abstinence from what they describe as 'animal-like,' ungrateful as they are to Him who made everything, God."[4]

In their desire both to encourage the faithful to live chastely and to repudiate Gnostic dualism, the early Christians stressed the procreative purpose of marriage and of human sexuality. Thus, Justin the Martyr, another second-century apologist, declared that "we Christians either marry with but one thought, to beget children, or, if we refuse to marry, we are completely continent."[5] Similarly, Athenagoras of Athens[6] and Clement of Alexandria wrote that marriage is for the sake of children. Clement, writing from a center of Gnosticism and a city notorious for its sexual licentiousness, appealed to the teaching of the Stoic philosophers in stressing the procreative purpose of marriage. Yet it needs to be said that Clement and other Christians who appealed to Stoic thought were not themselves Stoics. They were Christians, and they had already adopted the view that marriage and sex are meant for procreation from their reading of the Scriptures.[7] Clement, who with other Fathers praised virginity as a preferable state of life for Christians, also noted that married persons have more trials. But these trials could themselves serve growth in virtue.[8]

The great value of virginity and the procreative purposefulness of sex and marriage were also emphasized by the Fathers of the fourth and fifth centuries. Athanasius is typical of them in his encouragement of the young to choose a life of virginity for the sake of the Gospel. All of these writers — including Jerome and Augustine in the West, and John Chrysostom and Gregory Nazianzen in the East — see Christ as the founder of Christian virginity. They teach that the life of the virgin is to be preferred to marriage insofar as those who choose the virginal state rightly have fixed their concern on eternal realities and are already living in the anticipated end time.[9]

While they praised highly a life of virginity, these Fathers nonetheless recognized that marriage too is good, and that proper sexual relations within marriage can be morally good. Like earlier writers, they commonly found marital relations good precisely because they can lead to the procreation of children. In their reading of Genesis they saw the good of procreating children as *the* purpose of marriage. As several of them noted, it was, after all, in view of generating human life that God had given Eve — a woman — to Adam as his helpmate instead of another male.[10]

There was nonetheless in these Fathers an anxiety about sex. This anxiety was caused not only by the sexual depravity they witnessed in the lives of the pagans but also by their understanding of Scripture, in particular the story of the fall of our first parents. In the third chapter of Genesis, Adam and Eve are described as being ashamed of their nakedness after eating the forbidden fruit. The Fathers saw in this a sign that sexual appetite in particular had been wounded by sin.[11]

Some of the Fathers were so suspicious of the sexual appetite that they believed it became operative only after the fall. These Fathers — among them Gregory of Nyssa, John Chrysostom, Theoderet, and John Damascene[12] — believed that God had originally intended to generate life in some nonsexual way. Foreseeing, however, that Adam and Eve would fall, he had providentially endowed them with sexual powers that would be used after the fall. This view, to be sure, was not commonly held, and was vigorously repudiated by many. Still, its presence in some of the Fathers is sufficient to show us the caution with which some of them regarded sexual activity. This caution was not based on the conviction that sexual activity was evil in itself but on the conviction that it had been profoundly wounded by mankind's fall.

These Fathers saw sexuality as lying at the root of the conflict so eloquently spoken of by Paul when he described his inability to do the good he willed, and when he distinguished between the law of his mind and the law of his members. The Fathers blamed the loss of rational control over sexual activity on the impairment brought about by original sin. In sexual matters desires frequently seemed to overpower reason. Thus, even within marriage there is need to make sure that reason dominates, lest man be led to sin by unruly desires. Clement of Alexandria wrote: "The man who has taken a wife in order to have children should also practice continence, not even seeking pleasure from his own wife, whom he ought to love, but with honorable and moderate desire, having but one intention, children."[13] The Fathers were thus led to stress the procreative end, or purpose, of marriage, for this wonderful purpose provides married couples with a reasonable ground for the choice to have sexual relations. With this purpose in mind they can moderate their desires and bring them under reason's rule.

Still, there was in Scripture, particularly in the teaching of Paul on marriage in 1 Corinthians, another purpose of marriage. Paul suggested that marriage could allay the concupiscence experienced by humankind as a result of Adam's sin. Among the Fathers, Lactantius in the West and John Chrysostom in the East explicitly affirm that marital relations for the purpose of avoiding concupiscence are licit.[14] These authors do not expressly affirm that marital relations may be chosen as a way of fostering or expressing love between the spouses, but they do say that marital relations may rightfully be chosen in order to alleviate sexual desire and to avoid fornication.

What all this shows is that it was difficult for these Fathers to articulate a balanced sexual morality within the context provided by the twin evils of sexual licentiousness and Gnostic hatred of matter and marriage. The whole aim of the Fathers was to instruct the faithful in the Gospel of salvation. They saw, and rightly so, that sexual immorality, to which humankind is easily inclined, is a form of idolatry, for it is, as Paul had taught, a desecration of a human person who has become, through baptism, one body with Christ and a living temple of the Holy Spirit. Likewise, the Fathers believed that sex in itself, as created by God, is good, as is marriage.

From the Scriptures they had likewise learned that through Adam's sin all men had been harmed, for now the power of sin enslaved all mankind, disrupting the interior harmony of the human person and rendering humans incapable of ordering their desires — in particular, their sexual desires — as they must be if evil is to be avoided. Thus, in their efforts to combat, on the one hand, sexual immorality, and, on the other, Gnostic contempt for marriage and the generation of human life, they quite naturally found it necessary to stress one important truth about sexuality and marriage, namely that these good gifts of God are intended for the generation of new human life.[15]

*St. Augustine.* The thought of St. Augustine is especially important for several reasons. First of all, Augustine wrote more extensively about sexual and marital issues than did other Fathers.[16] Secondly, his influence, particularly on later theologians in the Western Church, has been and continues to be profound. It is fashionable today to portray Augustine as something of a pessimistic villain in the history of Christian theological reflection on sex, with some even accusing him of a latent Manicheism — that is, of an essentially Gnostic viewpoint which regarded sex as evil.[17] But these charges are unfair. There were, as shall be noted, limitations in Augustine's thought. But they are far from gross errors, and they should not cause us to forget the important contributions he has made to our understanding of human sexuality and of marriage.

Augustine regarded as quite erroneous the view that marriage and the sexual generation of human life would not have existed in Paradise (the Garden of Eden). In rejecting this view he says, "I do not see what could prevent there having been honorable marriage and an immaculate marriage bed in Paradise. . . . God could have arranged that, without any restless burning of sexual desire, . . . children would be born."[18] Obviously Augustine did not believe sex and sexual desire as such to be evil, though some claim that he did.[19] Following the Letter to the Hebrews, Augustine believes that marriage is to be held in honor, but he also shares this epistle's concern that the marriage bed "be undefiled" (Hebrews 13.4). He believes that this defilement occurs when desire is disordered, when it is a "restless burning."

Augustine held that concupiscence is the source of this restless burning. Concupiscence, which exists in us as a result of Adam's transgression, is not the same as original sin.[20] Rather, concupiscence is *caused* by original sin and *inclines* us to sin. Original sin itself, from which concupiscence arises, is clearly distinct from concupiscence because baptism completely removes original sin, whereas its effect and punishment, concupiscence, remains.[21] Augustine clarifies the relationship between concupiscence and actual sins of human beings in his commentary on a passage from the Letter of James in which we are told that "everyone is tempted by being drawn away and enticed by his own concupiscence. Once concupiscence has conceived, it gives birth to sin" (James 1.14-15). "These words," Augustine wrote, "distinguish the thing brought forth from the one giving birth. But concupiscence gives not birth unless it conceives; it does not conceive unless it entices, that is, unless it obtains willing consent to commit evil."[22] Thus, concupiscence may be called sin "by a certain figure of speech" (that is, by metonymy), since it comes from sin and leads to sin.[23] But since sin as such exists only in the will, it is not sin in the strict sense.[24]

According to Augustine, concupiscence distorts all our natural desires. These desires are good in themselves; but, as a result of original sin, they are now prone to seek their own proper objectives in a disordered way. Thus, for Augustine, concupiscence is a privation whereby our natural appetites or desires are bereft of their proper subordination to the rule of reason, and, thus deprived, tend to lead human beings away from God to the pursuit of worldly things in a sinful way.[25]

Augustine taught that, in virtue of our freedom and the grace of God poured forth in our hearts through Christ,[26] we are capable of resisting the enticements of concupiscent desire and of choosing and doing the good. We choose what is good when we "use" created goods, including our natural desires, for the purposes for which they have been created. Such "use" is not to be understood in any narrow utilitarian sense but simply in the sense that things to be used must be treated in a way that recognizes their true worth. The goods of this world are to be used and not "enjoyed" as if they were the final objects of human desire, for these are created and limited goods in which our hearts are not to take final rest. These created goods are ordered among themselves and are ordered ultimately to the Uncreated Good, God. He alone is our end — the one in whom our hearts will find rest. He alone is the Being that is to be "enjoyed" in the true sense of that word.[27]

Augustine explains how the goods of human sexuality are to be properly used in his discussion of marriage, for it is within marriage that these goods can be realized fully and rationally. Marriage, for Augustine, is a very good thing, and the goods of marriage provide the standard for proper sexual activity. His classification of the goods of marriage as the good of offspring, the good of fidelity, and the good of indissoluble unity became a classic source for the Christian discussion of marriage and chastity.[28]

For Augustine, offspring is the first and most obvious good of marriage. "What food is to the health of man, intercourse is to the health of the race."[29] This good does not consist merely in the physical generation of life. "Marriage was instituted so that the chastity of women would make children known to their fathers and fathers known to their children. True, it was possible for men to be born of promiscuous and random intercourse with any women at all, but there could not have been a bond of kinship between fathers and children."[30] The good of offspring, for Augustine, means the giving of life to persons who are called to a life of surpassing joy and friendship with God. Augustine says: "By offspring is meant not merely their begetting, but the receiving of them lovingly, the nourishing of them humanely, and the educating of them religiously."[31]

The great good of marital fidelity required, for Augustine, not only fidelity in sexual intercourse for the sake of procreating children but also mutual service in sustaining each other's weakness so that each may avoid illicit intercourse.[32] It is in conjunction with these two goods of marriage that Augustine discusses the morality of sexual union within marriage. Since procreation is "the primary, natural, and legitimate purpose of marriage,"[33] it is evident that conjugal union chosen to serve this good is completely without any fault. It is, indeed, a "chaste activity."[34]

The good of fidelity requires that spouses be faithful to each other, avoiding fornication and adultery. Augustine, like Lactantius and Chrysostom, is mindful of Paul's teaching in 1 Corinthians that people are to marry if they cannot exercise self-control, for "it is better to marry than to burn [with concupiscent desire]" (1 Corinthians 7.9), and that married couples are "not to deprive each other, except perhaps by consent, for a time that [they] may give themselves to prayer and return together again lest Satan tempt them because they lack self-control. But this I say by way of concession, not commandment" (1 Corinthians 7.5-6). But whereas Lactantius, Chrysostom, and Damascene — in speaking of the rightfulness of marital union "to avoid fornication" — imply that marital union for this purpose is unqualifiedly good, Augustine teaches that a spouse who requests marital relations precisely in order to avoid fornication is guilty of a venial sin. By "venial sin" Augustine means the sort of sin to which all of us are daily susceptible and of which we cannot claim to be free without lying (cf. 1 John 1.8); it is the sort of sin that is forgiven when we recite the Lord's prayer.[35] "In marriage, intercourse for the purpose of procreation has no fault attached to it; but intercourse for the purpose of satisfying concupiscence, provided it is with a spouse, is but venial fault because of fidelity; adultery or fornication, however, is a mortal sin."[36]

Many find this teaching of Augustine distasteful and demeaning to marriage. Yet Augustine's teaching perhaps shows a deeper appreciation of the human reality of marriage than does that of Lactantius, Chrysostom, and Damascene, for in holding that there is some minor fault when spousal relations are sought for the precise purpose of allaying desires and avoiding fornication, Augustine suggests that a basic good of marriage is itself not directly being sought but only indirectly fostered by

39

avoidance of an activity that is seriously disordered. What is being sought in this type of intercourse is precisely the allaying of a desire and the avoiding of an evil to which the desire may lead. It is hardly an act which precisely expresses conjugal fidelity or, in modern terms, conjugal love. Augustine did clearly teach that the spouse who serves the good of conjugal fidelity by consenting to marital relations to meet the need of the spouse seeking relations for this purpose is choosing something perfectly good, for this spouse is choosing to serve the good of marital fidelity. Marital intercourse in the service of a real good is itself good.

Where Augustine can be faulted, it would seem, is in his failure to consider that spouses can choose to have marital relations for the precise purpose of expressing their fidelity, their love. With his predecessors, he sees as the possible purposes of marital union (1) the generation of children and (2) the serving of the good of fidelity when one spouse blamelessly agrees to marital union when the other spouse seeks it, with venial fault, expressly as a way of avoiding illicit intercourse. He does not explicitly entertain the possibility that both spouses might choose marital relations precisely as a way of showing their fidelity, their love.

Nevertheless, there is some evidence that if Augustine had considered this possibility, he would have approved it. For instance, in one place he wrote: "Surely we must see that God gives us some goods which are to be sought for their own sakes, such as wisdom, health, friendship; others which are necessary for something else, such as learning, food, drink, sleep, marriage, sexual intercourse. Certain of these are necessary for the sake of wisdom, such as learning; *others for the sake of friendship, such as marriage or intercourse.*"[37] (Emphasis added.) Obviously, there is here the suggestion, one that will be made explicit in the development of the Catholic theological tradition, that spouses can rightly choose marital union as a way of showing their friendship. This would involve no unworthy motive and no sin.

The third good of marriage discussed by Augustine is the bond of indissoluble unity between husband and wife. Although he did not use his term for this bond — the Latin word *sacra-*

40

*mentum* — in precisely the same sense in which the Church now uses the word "sacrament," Augustine nonetheless attributed to marriage two characteristics which make it a true sacrament. First, he taught that Jesus Christ himself instituted this symbolic representation of his union with the Church,[38] and second, he taught that grace is given to the spouses in virtue of this institution.[39]

In his own understanding of the good of *sacramentum* in marriage Augustine first stressed that it was a holy bond. He based the permanence of marriage on the moral obligation of married persons to honor this sacramental bond, but this holy bond is itself rooted in the sacramental sign which reveals the meaning of marriage. Marriage is a human reality pointing toward the mystery of God's love for man, a love made real by Christ's indissoluble union with his bride, the Church.[40] Marriage symbolizes and draws strength from that union.

Augustine taught that every marriage has a natural bond requiring that it not be dissolved, but the marriage of Christians has more than this natural bond. Its indissolubility is also rooted in something even more profound; for Christians, marriage is a reality profoundly touched by the love between Christ and his Church. Christian marriage must be as indissoluble as this love.[41]

Augustine held that any act of adultery or faithlessness violated the good of fidelity, but such an act could not rupture the indissoluble unity between the spouses. The good of fidelity requires the spouses to be faithful to each other and to abstain from any form of sexual immorality; the good of the *sacramentum* excludes that adultery which would be involved in an invalid marriage after separation.[42]

Augustine's analysis of the goods of marriage has provided the Church with a powerful analytical device for understanding both the human significance and the salvific importance of marriage and human sexuality. Later theologians and the magisterium even till the present time make use of a framework whose full implications Augustine did not grasp.[43] Augustine's study of sexual morality therefore, even though it has limitations, is an important step in the development of the Church's understanding of sexual morality.

41

## II. The Teaching of the Medieval Theologians

Between the death of Augustine in 430 and the flowering of scholarship in the universities of the twelfth and thirteenth centuries, Western Europe experienced great social upheaval and disarray as a result of the fall of the Roman Empire and the migrations of the Germanic, Frankish, and Celtic peoples. During these centuries dedicated communities of monks both preserved the cultural heritage of the past and worked to evangelize the pagan peoples and to instruct the Catholic faithful in the Christian way of life.

These monks, as the penitential books they wrote show, regarded marriage as good and holy. They informed the people of the immorality of nonmarital sex, and instructed couples about the immorality of contraceptive, anal, and oral intercourse and the wickedness of abortion.[44] Some of their views were too rigoristic — for instance, their prohibition of marital intercourse during certain seasons of the year, on holy days, and prior to receiving communion.[45] However, these positions were only peripheral to their central teaching, and can perhaps be understood as a function of the difficult times in which they lived. The core of their teaching on sexual matters was not something specific to their cultural situation but rather a set of admonitions and prohibitions which were already present in patristic and scriptural times. Thus, for example, the condemnation of sexual activity outside of marriage is not unique to the monks and their penitentials but was already the common teaching of the Church and was proposed as such by the monks. The teaching of the Fathers of the Church on sexual matters as well as their understanding of the relevant biblical texts had already become normative for Christian life.

The great contribution of the medieval Church to the developing understanding of human sexuality came during the period of the High Middle Ages when theological activity reached a high point of creative achievement, especially in the works of Doctors of the Church like St. Thomas Aquinas and St. Bonaventure in the thirteenth century. Although their cultural situation was very different from that of the Fathers of the Church almost a millennium before, some of the challenges they faced were quite similar to those the Fathers had to deal with. A new form of Gnosticism developed during the High Middle Ages, particularly in the south of France. Albigensianism, Catharism, and Bogomilism constituted a movement which, like the older forms of Gnosticism, held marriage in contempt. This contempt had the standard Gnostic rationale: matter was taken to be evil, and marriage was bad because it was the basis for the generation of new life.

The great medieval theologians also faced a challenge not unlike that presented to the Fathers in the form of pagan sexual licentiousness. The ideal of "pure" or "romantic" love proposed by some of the troubadours was, in effect, an endorsement of romantic sexual activity separated from marriage and procreation, for these troubadours not only emphasized something very good — the love between man and woman — they also glorified sexual pleasure within the context of romance. Far more important, they showed no appreciation for the good of procreation. In this last respect they were influenced by the Gnosticism of the age.[46] This movement had considerable appeal, especially to the wealthier classes, and had the effect of creating within medieval culture a kind of neopaganism.

These two challenges — of Gnosticism and neopagan licentiousness — form the background for the thought of the medieval theologians on sexual morality. Their creative responses to these challenges led them to develop a body of work that deepened the Church's understanding of human sexuality in a real way, for their response to the anti-humanism of the Cathars and Albigenses required an affirmation of the Church's concern for human values, and their response to the hedonism of the heterodox troubadours required a careful sifting of opinions about what really is good for human beings.

Furthermore, this work of clarification took place within the context of an unprecedented effort to systematize the teaching of the Church and to present it as a coherent whole. Thus, in the great theologians of the Middle Ages, there is not only a creative response to serious challenges to Christian life and teaching but also an attempt to see this response within an overall account of Christian doctrine. This effort was carried out within the context of acceptance of the Church's received teachings on moral matters, and of heavy reliance on the Fathers of the Church, and especially on St. Augustine. Augustine's teaching on sexual morality was particularly influential, and his discussion of the goods of marriage was the framework for thinking about marriage. It is not surprising therefore that the medieval theologians unanimously affirmed the goodness of marriage and the excellence of properly ordered sexual activity, and that they unanimously condemned those acts which attacked the great goods of marriage. They counted all such disordered acts as "unnatural."

*The Evil of Acts Which Attack the Goods of Marriage.* Three principal lines of argument were developed by medieval theologians to show the moral evil of nonmarital and "unnatural" sexual activity. The first was an argument from the authority of the Scriptures and the Fathers. This was advanced, for instance, by the twelfth-century theologian and bishop Peter Lombard, whose *Sentences* were used as a textbook for teaching theology from 1157 until 1550, and were commented on by all the great theologians of the thirteenth century. In discussing the sixth commandment, Lombard observed, citing Augustine, that this commandment required one not to have sexual union except within the marital covenant.[47] He also held that any sexual activity fully contrary to the purpose of marriage and of the sexual differentiation of the species into male and female was a gravely sinful violation of this commandment.[48]

A second line of argument, developed at length by the medieval theologians in their discussion of the natural law written in the hearts of mankind and discernible by right reason, was that the prohibited forms of sexual activity violated not only the law divinely revealed by God but also the natural moral law written in our hearts.[49] Bestiality, sodomy, contraceptive intercourse, and other forms of "unnatural sex" were judged to be wrongful in a special way insofar as they violated the order God had called into being by making humankind a species sexually differentiated into male and female and therefore capable of giving life to new human beings through acts of sexual intercourse.[50] These sins were judged to be unnatural in a stronger sense than other sins, including other sexual sins. All evil actions were held to be unnatural insofar as they are contrary to

44

the order of right reason, that is, to the demands of rationally ordered activity which properly respects the goods of human nature. But unlike other sins, these particular sexual sins were held to be unnatural in a further sense, since they violated the most basic, God-given purpose of human sexuality. For this reason, they were held to be more seriously wrong than acts of sexual intercourse outside of marriage. These latter sins too were judged to be gravely sinful because such acts as adultery and fornication contradicted both God's divine law and the requirements of right reason. But sins of sodomy and the like were judged to be more gravely sinful because their peculiar unnaturalness violated divine and natural law in a radical way.

Thomas Aquinas, in arguing that nonmarital sexual union is contrary to the demands of the natural law insofar as it acts against the good of offspring, provides an argument characteristic of this second line of reasoning: "The end [or purpose] of the exercise of the genital organs is the generation and education of children; therefore, every exercise of these powers which is not properly ordered *(proportionatus)* to the generation of children and the education to which they have a right is of itself disordered."[51] Thus, sexual intercourse outside of marriage is excluded, for it is only in marriage that human life can properly be given, nurtured, and educated in the love and worship of God.

The medieval theologians also taught that nonmarital sexual behavior violated the fidelity spouses owe to each other. Bonaventure presents this teaching in a passage which reveals the growing appreciation by the medieval theologians of the love that is meant to exist between husband and wife: "In matrimony there is indeed a singular kind of love *(amor singularis)* which is not possible to be shared with others; naturally, therefore, a husband is jealous of his wife with respect to this, that she love no one else and that she love him in this act, and similarly the wife is naturally jealous of her husband in this respect."[52]

A third line of argument used by some of the medieval theologians to show that every kind of sexual union outside marriage and every kind of "unnatural" sexual act is morally wicked was based on the nature of concupiscent desire. This argument, which they believed to be rooted in biblical and patristic teaching, focused on the inclination to evil that exists in human beings as a result of original sin. According to this view — one expressed by many authors, including Lombard, Aquinas, Bonaventure, Albert the Great, and the authors of the *Summa of Brother Alexander*[53] — all our desires, good in themselves, have been corrupted by original sin. But sexual desires, they held, have been corrupted and indeed infected by original sin in a special way. Of itself the disorderliness of human sexual desire is not a moral evil, for moral evil can arise only when free personal consent is given to evil. But it is an evil we experience as a penalty. This restless itching for sexual gratification in a disorderly way exists in us as a result of original sin.[54] As a result of this we are tempted to do evil deeds in order to satisfy disorderly desires.

But according to the argument advanced, particularly by writers like Peter Lombard and Bonaventure,[55] God has in his goodness given us a remedy to help us avoid the evil to which we are prone as a result of this restless itching. That remedy is marriage. Before the fall, it had been instituted — as Lombard says — to be an office of nature, something good. Indeed now, as Paul and the Fathers had taught, it exists as a holy sign or sacrament pointing to the mystery of Christ's love for his Church. But in our present state, as Paul taught in 1 Corinthians 7, marriage also serves as a remedy for allaying the burning desires of concupiscence.[56] The great goods of marriage noted by Augustine, and, in particular, the good of offspring, serve to rectify sexual desires.[57] These goods cannot be properly and adequately realized outside of marriage, for children can be conceived but not properly cherished outside of marriage, and a kind of fidelity is possible but not the reality of a firm and unshakable union in a single life. Consequently, this argument continued, any choice to exercise one's sexual powers outside of marriage is morally wrong. Such acts may satisfy strong and natural desires; but they are not the remedy which God has provided.[58]

These three lines of argument advanced by the medieval theologians to explain the Church's received teaching on sexual morality were not meant to provide a rationalistic proof of the immorality of nonmarital and unnatural sexual activity. They do not seek to replace faith by philosophical argumentation. Rather, these arguments were proposed as a way of understanding, from within the faith, the sexual teaching based on Scripture and handed down through the Church. If these arguments are taken on their own terms they are very weighty, even if some of their details must be revised or even rejected. The power of these arguments within the perspective of Catholic faith becomes even clearer when their connection with the Church's affirmation of the goodness of marriage is spelled out.

*The Goodness of Marriage.* As the inheritors of Christian tradition, the medieval theologians unequivocally affirm the goodness of marriage. Like the Fathers they regard this matter as settled in Scripture. God himself instituted marriage by creating humankind as he did; and Christ blessed it at the marriage feast of Cana. This theme is sounded throughout the period. It was clearly articulated by Peter Lombard. When discussing the question of the goodness of marriage, he is content to refer simply to the patristic teaching, ably summed up Hugh of St. Victor, the first medieval theologian to set forth in detail a theology of marriage.[59] Hugh had written:

> That marriage is a good thing is proved not only from the fact that the Lord is said to have instituted it in creating our first parents but also because Christ himself took part in the marriage feast at Cana, commending the nuptials with a miracle by changing water into wine. . . . Therefore it is quite evident that marriage is a good thing.[60]

Thus far the medieval theologians reaffirm and make their own the patristic teaching on the goodness of marriage. Where they go beyond the Fathers is in developing a deeper appreciation for all the goods of marriage and conjugal intercourse.

*The Goods of Marriage and the Meaning of the Marital Act.* Augustine's teaching on the threefold good of marriage — progeny, fidelity, and indissoluble unity — was, as noted already, fully accepted by the medieval theologians. They regarded the indissoluble unity to be the good that marriage is, the good that man and woman bring into being when they freely choose to be husband and wife.[61] The medieval theologians saw the bond of unity not only as a *moral obligation* but also as having ontological significance. This bond is not only a sign of the in-

47

dissoluble unity between Christ and his Church but also a reality within marriage. The marriage really participates in this mystery of divine love. It becomes a union so profound that only death can dissolve it. Moreover, it is accompanied by graces intended to assist spouses in living their marriages faithfully and generously.[62] It is for this reason, the medieval theologians taught, that marriage between Christians is a true sacrament of the Church. Ecumenical councils of the Church also affirmed this teaching.[63]

The other two goods of marriage — fidelity and progeny — were held to be the goods that marriage *intends*, that is, they are goods which the spouses promise to give and honor in their shared lives as they make the free consent that constitutes them as husband and wife and brings into being their indissoluble unity.[64] Adultery and contraceptive intercourse violate the goods of fidelity and progeny by undermining and wounding them. Such deeds violate the good of the indissoluble bond of marriage as well, but since this bond is the very reality of marriage itself, it cannot be broken by them. Marriage itself cannot be dissolved by these or any other sins.[65]

The medieval theologians, with Augustine and the other Fathers, held that marital intercourse for the sake of having children — that is, with the intention of begetting progeny — is completely justifiable. Indeed, they commonly taught the conjugal act ordered to this good was an act of the virtue of religion, insofar as its end was the generation of life that was to be brought up in the love and worship of God.[66]

Likewise, the medieval theologians followed Augustine in teaching that it was a venial sin for a spouse to seek sexual union merely as a way to avoid fornication, while the spouse who consented to marital union for this purpose was free of all sin.[67]

But the medieval theologians developed Augustine's teaching in this matter by focusing on an idea only implicit in his writings — namely, that the spouses could rightly choose to unite in marital coition in order to foster and express the good of fidelity. To choose marital union for this purpose, writers like Thomas Aquinas and Bonaventure maintained, is a truly virtuous act, an act of the virtue of justice.[68] In fact, Aquinas argued that a husband ought to anticipate his wife's desires in this matter and offer to give himself to her in sexual union in order to cherish this good.[69]

There is even, on Aquinas's account, a suggestion that the sexual expression of the good of fidelity by husband and wife participates in the sacramental character of the marriage. Thus, St. Thomas writes: "A human act is good in two ways. In one way, by moral goodness, which the act has from the goods which make it a right act. In the case of the marital act, fidelity and progeny do this. . . . In another way, by sacramental goodness: this factor causes an act to be not simply good but also holy. And the marital act has this goodness from the indissolubility of the union, for in this regard it is a sign of the union of Christ and the Church."[70] It is not surprising therefore that Aquinas regarded sexual intercourse for the sake of fidelity to be a meritorious act.[71]

A procreative intent is not, then, necessary for marital acts to be virtuous, holy, and meritorious. To choose conjugal intercourse for the sake of the good of fidelity is to choose to do something exceedingly good. Of course, Aquinas and other writers who justified marital union as an expression of the good of fidelity regarded it as wicked to act *contrary* to the good of offspring — that is, to act contraceptively. But in the medieval theologians there is clear and explicit recognition of the "non-procreative" purposes of marital sexual union.

It is true that Aquinas, Bonaventure, and other medieval theologians who justified marital union as a way of fostering the good of fidelity taught that the act in question was an act of the virtue of justice, of the justice that husband and wife owe each other. They did not, ordinarily, speak of it as an act of conjugal love, but their thought was clearly open to fuller development in this direction. This is strongly suggested by Bonaventure when he speaks of the "singular love that is meant to exist between husband and wife, a love expressed in that act," namely, in the marital act. In this passage love is explicitly related to marital union. St. Thomas Aquinas speaks in a similar way about the special character of the friendship between spouses. He affirms this to be the highest friendship, and clearly supposes that marital intercourse is integral to it; his concern is to affirm that sexual intercourse is not the whole of marital friendship.[72]

A similar emphasis can be found in the teaching of the *Summa Fratris Alexandri*. This work is specially significant because it is not the work of an individual author (Alexander of Hales, to whom it was attributed) but is rather the compilation of many theologians representing "the spirit of the Franciscan thirteenth-century school of theology at the University of Paris."[73] The authors of this work consider an objection to the appropriateness of the human race's derivation from the first pair of humans by way of sexual intercourse. The objection is that this mode of derivation only serves to increase the intensity of carnal love, which is an "impediment" to spiritual love. To answer this objection the authors of the *Summa Fratris Alexandri* distinguish three types of love: carnal love, natural love, and spiritual love. They maintain that "natural love," which is carnal love purged of all lust, is no obstacle to spiritual love; on the contrary, "spiritual love should come to be through natural love, and natural love is meant in turn to be perfected by the spiritual love toward which it disposes."[74] The authors of this work go on to speak of the loving embrace of husband and wife — obviously a reference to sexual union between spouses — as symbolizing the union of the soul with God "both as to the intensity of that union and its fruitfulness."[75]

It is clear therefore that the medieval theologians enhanced the Church's understanding of the values involved in marriage by their development of the teaching that fidelity was one of the goods of marriage, and by their explicit recognition of the value of marital friendship and its relationship to sexual intercourse.

These developments quite naturally led to a more positive evaluation of the status of sexual pleasure than Christian tradition had accepted, but the medieval theologians did not, for the most part, articulate these implications. Thomas Aquinas, however, did make several points that are important in the development of a more balanced view of the moral status of sexual pleasure. Like the other medieval theologians, Aquinas affirmed the common teaching of the Church that sexual intercourse solely for the sake of pleasure was sinful. He maintained that it would be mortally sinful if one's sexual interest in one's wife would be so exclusively aimed at finding pleasure that he viewed her really as only a sex object or object of lust, not as a wife, as one with whom he was lovingly committed to honoring the great goods of marriage. But he rejected as absurd the more rigorous position that it is better to repudiate or merely tolerate the pleasure of marital intercourse.[76] His view on this matter follows from his realistic and warmly human evaluation of pleasure and its role in human life. With Aristotle, he held that pleasure is a natural accompaniment and perfection of a human action. As such the moral character depends on the moral status of the action it accompanies. Thus, the pleasure of a morally good act is itself morally good and worthy of pursuit as part of a good activity. The pursuit of pleasure becomes morally suspect only if it inclines one to act in ways that are somehow unreasonable or disordered. Aquinas's analysis of pleasure provides the ground for a more realistic appreciation of sexual pleasure.[77]

### III. Post-Medieval Catholic Thought

In this section our purpose is by no means to attempt even a brief history of the development of Catholic theological thought on sexual morality from the Middle Ages to the present. Rather, we hope only to indicate the continuity of the Catholic theological tradition, and to note briefly some of the principal developments that have taken place since the end of the age of high Scholasticism.

The continuity of the Catholic theological tradition from the death of St. Thomas Aquinas in 1274 until the 1960s is remarkable. For nearly eight hundred years Catholic tradition has affirmed unanimously and with one voice that marriage is good; that genital sexual activity outside marriage, whether through adultery, fornication, masturbation, homosexual activity, or bestiality, is gravely sinful; and that within marriage some sexual acts — notably contraception and acts leading to orgasm apart from sexual intercourse — are seriously wrong. Germain Grisez and John Ford, S.J., surveyed forty-two manuals on moral theology in common use during the nineteenth and twentieth centuries for their teaching on contraceptive intercourse. All the authors studied unanimously held that such behavior was gravely sinful.[78] Nor is it surprising that these authors taught as they did, for in branding contraceptive intercourse as

51

seriously wrong they were simply reaffirming the centuries-old teaching of the Church, a teaching which the Fathers, the Scholastics, and their modern successors found rooted in the Scriptures as understood by the Church.[79]

The same authors examined by Ford and Grisez likewise unanimously teach that all forms of nonmarital sexual activity (fornication, adultery, rape, sodomy, masturbation, etc.) are serious moral evils, contrary both to the natural moral law and to the law divinely revealed by God. Again, there is nothing surprising in this teaching.

In the 1960s some Catholic theologians began to question the received teaching on contraception; and in 1966 several prominent moral theologians — in preparing a report for the Papal Commission for the Study of Problems of Population, Family, and Birthrate — urged that contraceptive intercourse could be morally justifiable for married couples.[80] In advocating this view, these authors rejected the claim that the principles upon which they justified contraception for married couples could be used to justify anal or oral intercourse for married couples.[81] These theologians held, in accord with the theological tradition, that nonmarital modes of sexual activity were immoral. Likewise, they agreed that sexual activity between spouses must be directed toward sexual intercourse — that seeking orgasm outside of natural intercourse was seriously wrong even for married couples. They thought that allowing contraception for married couples under narrowly described circumstances would not compromise the rationale for these proscriptions. Recent history shows that they were mistaken, for subsequent Catholic theologians — among them Michael Valente[82] and the authors of *Human Sexuality: New Directions in American Catholic Thought*[83] — were willing to draw the conclusion that the principles justifying contraceptive intercourse for married couples likewise can be used to justify nonmarital sexual activity and deviant sexual activity within marriage. As Charles E. Curran has noted: "History has clearly shown that those who were afraid that a change in the teaching on contraception would lead to other changes [in the teaching on sexual morality] were quite accurate."[84] Curran seems to have recognized that a radical change in principle was needed to justify

52

contraception, and that such a change is bound to have wide effects.

It is not our purpose here to enter into the current dispute concerning the morality of contraception and other types of sexual activity. Subsequent chapters of this volume will be concerned with these issues. What is relevant here is that those contemporary theologians who justify contraception, and with it various other kinds of sexual activity condemned by the received teaching of the Church, themselves recognize that their teaching markedly contrasts with the theological tradition as expressed in the writings of theologians prior to the 1960s. No theologian, from the time of the apostolic writers until the 1960s, even suggested that sexual activities of the kinds justified by these writers could be morally legitimate.

This aberrant development is not, however, the only development in the Church's sexual teaching in recent centuries and decades, for there has been a genuine development in the Church's understanding of the purpose of human sexuality *within* marriage on the part of post-medieval theologians. There has been, throughout the modern period, a deepening appreciation of the significance of marital intercourse as an expression of love. This growing appreciation of marital love in no way contradicts the theological tradition but authentically develops themes which were suggested by the medieval theologians and present in Christian consciousness from the start.

As noted above, the medieval theologians clearly recognized that procreative intent was not necessary for marital intercourse to be morally good, and even meritorious and holy.[85] The medieval teaching that marital intercourse undertaken in order to express the good of marital fidelity developed through the modern period into the explicit recognition that marital intercourse can be rightly chosen as a way to foster and nourish spousal love.

Even before the medieval period came to an end, Nicolas Oresme, a theologian who became bishop of Lisieux, wrote warmly about the love between husband and wife, a love that is displayed in their marital act. The teaching of Oresme, who wrote about the middle of the fourteenth century, has been summarized as follows:

The union between man and woman in marriage is fully natural. It is meant to spring from love and to be grounded upon love — a love that is productive of an intensity of joy and pleasure, that makes equals of man and woman and makes each to be supreme in the other's affections. The marriage act is good if decently and lovingly engaged in. It has purposes beyond generation. . . . Sin may enter into the union, but if the union is of reason and is basically good, there is no need to worry about it. It is only when love becomes 'bestial' — when one is intent only upon his isolated pleasure — that there is cause for concern.[86]

Oresme's conception of the value of sexual intercourse between spouses as expressive of their mutual love is foreshadowed by the work of St. Thomas Aquinas, St. Bonaventure, and other medieval writers. It was to be developed and more fully articulated only in the nineteenth and twentieth centuries in the works of thinkers like Jean Gury and Dietrich von Hildebrand.[87]

Another element in the development of Catholic theologians' appreciation of marital intercourse has been the explicit recognition that spouses may legitimately seek pleasure in the marital act. Here too there is a development anticipated by medieval authors. We have already noted that the principles of Thomas Aquinas are open to this recognition, and his great commentator, Thomas Cardinal Cajetan (1469-1534), explicitly recognized that spouses may legitimately seek pleasure in conjugal union. Like Aquinas, he taught that spouses were obliged to seek conjugal union as spouses, that is, as acting for one or the other of the goods of marriage, and that pleasure is the natural perfection of the act, as beauty is the bloom of youth. But he added that spouses ought to give God thanks for the pleasure that marital union brings, thus suggesting that sexual pleasure was a legitimate object of marital activity.[88] He taught, however, that an explicit or actual intent to foster one or the other of the goods of marriage, such as the aim of nourishing faithful love, also had to be present for the act to be morally good.

Subsequent theologians like Thomas Sanchez (1550-1610) and Alphonsus Liguori (1696-1787) taught that this last condition was too stringent. They held that it was sufficient for the proper respect for these goods, and thus for the moral goodness of marital intercourse, that spouses seek marital union *as spouses*.[89] Their teaching became the common heritage of nineteenth- and twentieth-century theologians. In other words, spouses need not *explicitly* intend their marital act to further either the good of procreation or of marital fidelity. A habitual intent to respect these goods — to seek marital union as spouses — was sufficient, although of course, it would be seriously wrong for them to repudiate either the good of *proles* or the good of *fides*.

In short, there has been development since the time of the Middle Ages in the Church's understanding of human sexuality and the role, within marriage, of conjugal intercourse. As one would expect in the legitimate development of God's revelation, this development has many antecedents in the earlier tradition. The medieval notion that spouses could rightly choose marital union as a way of expressing their marital fidelity was a development of ideas found in St. Augustine. The more modern teachings that marital union is a way of expressing the singular love between the spouses and that it is by no means wicked for spouses to take delight in their conjugal union but that it is rather quite proper for them to seek this pleasure *as spouses* are foreshadowed by and rooted in the teaching of the great Scholastics. Another sign of the real continuity and legitimacy of the post-medieval theological developments in sexual morality is the unwillingness of modern theologians to question or compromise the received teaching that it is seriously wrong to seek sexual union within or outside of marriage in ways that deliberately fail to honor any of the goods of marriage.

In sum, even the briefest of surveys of the theological tradition's developing teaching on sexual morality shows beyond all doubt that there is real continuity and development in the Church's understanding of human sexuality. This development has taken place within a framework of moral norms which are not questioned or rejected but better understood as the moral thinking of the Church unfolds in response to new situations. This framework is never presented as a mere imposition of divine or human authority but as an inherent requirement of authentic human life. One of the most important aspects of the development of doctrine on sexual matters has been the ever-clearer articulation of the connection between the specific requirements of Christian sexual morality and the basic moral principles of Christian living. Today it has become clearer than ever before that Christian sexual morality is no more and no less than the implication of the logic of love — what love of God and of neighbor requires in this area of human life.

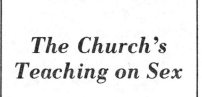

Catholics believe that Christ himself remains always with his Church. He is the one Teacher upon whose word all faith depends (Matthew 7.29, 11.27). In a special way he teaches through the teaching office he has willed to be in the Church, and to which he has given authority to speak in his name. The Second Vatican Council declared that "the task of giving an authentic interpretation of the Word of God . . . has been entrusted to the living teaching office of the Church alone" (*Dei Verbum*, no. 10). This teaching office, first given to St. Peter and the other apostles, is now, by the will of Christ, entrusted to the pope and the bishops who teach in communion with him.

Because Christ and the Holy Spirit dwell within the Church, the Church has unshakable confidence in the words of faith proclaimed in his name. Thus, she teaches infallibly in matters of faith and morals, not only through the solemn definitions of councils and supreme pontiffs but also through her ordinary teaching by the bishops of the Church in union with the pope, when they agree in teaching that something is to be held definitively.[1] This exercise of the ordinary magisterium takes place not only when the bishops arrive at a common position at a synod or council but also when they are carrying out their nor-

The Church's Teaching on Sex

mal task of proclaiming the word of God in their own dioceses. Of course, the teachings of the pope and bishops are not all infallible teachings of the Church; but even when they are not teaching infallibly, the pope and bishops often teach in the name and with the authority of Christ. The faithful have a duty to give internal religious assent to this authoritative teaching of the Church (*Lumen Gentium*, no. 25).[2]

The Church's magisterium therefore is the instrument by which the Spirit of Christ preserves the Church in his saving truth, and prevents the Church from wandering from this truth. The Spirit's work within the Church is not, of course, limited to his guidance of the pope and bishops. The Spirit also guides and instructs the many people within the Church who seek to penetrate God's revelation more deeply. Theologians, philosophers, mystics, and ordinary good people are helped by the Spirit in their attempts to understand and explain the faith. But they can hold and proclaim the faith securely only when they take care to teach in full conformity with the guidance of the teaching office of the Church, for that office alone has been charged with the supervision of public teaching in the Church, and it alone is able to make secure, final judgment in matters of faith and morals. It is for this reason that the Second Vatican Council declares that "in forming their consciences the faithful must pay careful attention to the sacred and certain teaching of the Church. For the Catholic Church is by the will of Christ the teacher of truth. It is her duty to proclaim and teach with authority the truth which is Christ and, at the same time, to declare and conform by her authority the principles of the moral order which spring from human nature itself" (*Dignitatis Humanae*, no. 14).

It is therefore necessary for us to summarize what the teaching office of the Church has said about marriage and sexual morality. This will be done in considerable detail in the last three chapters of this work where we will develop a theological account of the Catholic view of marriage and the concrete requirements of chastity. In this chapter we will summarize briefly what the Church teaches about the goodness of marriage; what the Church teaches about sexual activity within marriage; and what it teaches about the immorality of sexual activity that is not authentically marital. This will be done so as to highlight some of the essential points of Catholic sexual teaching, and to make clear the seriousness, constancy, and nonarbitrariness of this teaching.

## I. The Goodness and Holiness of Marriage

The Church has always taught that the union of man and woman in marriage is a good and holy thing. It is good because, as Scripture makes clear, God himself instituted marriage and gave it its defining characteristics. It is holy because the Lord Jesus made marriage a sacrament of his relation with the Church, and a source of grace.

The Church clearly affirmed the goodness of marriage in the face of the attacks on marriage by the various forms of Gnosticism which appeared through the centuries. As early as 340, a council of bishops meeting in Gangra (in Asia Minor, in what is now modern-day Turkey) stated: "If anyone disparages marriage, shuns a faithful and God-fearing wife who sleeps with her husband, and speaks as though she cannot enter the kingdom of God, let him be anathema."[3] Similarly, the Second and Fourth Councils of the Lateran in 1139 and 1215 defended the goodness of the marital union against the challenge of the medieval neo-Gnostics.[4] In 1208, Pope Innocent III insisted that Catholics "believe that the husband with his wife can be saved."[5]

In 1439, the Council of Florence affirmed that marriage was not only humanly good but also one of the seven sacraments of the new law. This council also affirmed as Catholic teaching the Augustinian doctrine of the threefold good of marriage — that is, that the goods which constitute and perfect marriage are (1) the generation and education of children to the worship of God; (2) the fidelity of husband and wife to each other; and (3) the indissoluble union of the spouses.[6]

The Council of Trent in the sixteenth century was not faced with a challenge to the inherent goodness of marriage but rather with a challenge to the sacramental character and indissolubility of marriage. The response of Trent was a clear and unequivocal affirmation of received Catholic teaching on both points.[7]

In the centuries since Trent there have been many challenges to the Catholic teaching on marriage. None of these is an explicit denial that marriage is a good institution; but many of these challenges involve the belief that marriage is a purely human institution which can be changed by human decision — for example, that marriage need not be regarded as permanent but can be regarded as allowing for divorce and remarriage, or that it can be understood as a relationship between persons with no necessary order to the begetting of children.

In response to challenges of these kinds, popes in recent centuries have reaffirmed the divine origin of marriage and the sacramental character of Christian marriage. They have done this to emphasize that the human meaning and supernatural significance of marriage is threatened by the various proposals to change the character of marriage or to alter sexual morality. Thus, for example, Pope Leo XIII in 1880 affirmed very clearly that marriage was instituted by God, that it was indissoluble, and that as one of the seven sacraments it provided special graces to spouses.[8] Fifty years later these same points were reaffirmed and developed by Pius XI in his great encyclical on Christian marriage, *Casti Connubii*.[9]

The Second Vatican Council reaffirmed these very points in response to the developing modern attitude that marriage is whatever society or individuals may choose to make it. The marriage bond is brought into being by the consent of the spouses, but the character of this sacred bond does not depend on human decisions alone. "For God himself is the author of marriage and has endowed it with various benefits and with various ends in view."[10]

The teaching of Vatican II is affirmed by Pope Paul VI in *Humanae Vitae*,[11] and again by Pope John Paul II in his *Familiaris Consortio*. John Paul II affirms the goodness of marriage as a human reality created by God and takes special pains to explain its special holiness.[12] Because of their baptism, "man and woman are definitively placed within the new and eternal covenant, in the spousal covenant of Christ with the Church" (*Familiaris Consortio*, no. 13). Because of this "indestructible insertion" into the new covenant, married love is elevated and enriched by Christ's redeeming power. As a result:

> ... the marriage of baptized persons becomes a real symbol of that new and eternal covenant sanctioned in the

blood of Christ. The Spirit which the Lord pours forth gives a new heart, and renders man and woman capable of loving one another as Christ has loved us. Conjugal love reaches that fullness to which it is interiorly ordained, conjugal charity, which is the proper and specific way in which the spouses participate in and are called to live the very charity of Christ who gave himself on the cross.[13]

It is important to note in connection with the Church's teaching that marriage is good and holy, that this goodness and holiness are essentially connected with the goods intrinsic to marriage. It is precisely in order to protect and promote these great human goods that God created marriage as he did. And it was in virtue of the real human meaning of these goods that Jesus elevated it to the dignity of a sacrament and was able to use marriage as a sign of his union with the Church. Thus, it is not surprising that, when affirming the goodness and holiness of marriage, the Church has also emphasized the essential ordering of marriage to the procreation and education of children,[14] and to the fostering and deepening of the love between spouses.[15]

The genuine goodness and holiness of marriage is therefore a constant theme of Church teaching, whether in response to Gnostic claims that marriage is evil or in response to modern claims that its meaning is to be determined by human decision. The character of this God-given goodness is especially important today, because those who wish to change the Church's teaching on sexual morality fail to recognize that this morality is necessary to preserve and respect this goodness.

## II. Sexual Activity Within Marriage

The Church clearly teaches that marital intercourse is good and holy when the choice to engage in this act is properly marital. As Vatican II has stated:

Married love is uniquely expressed and perfected by the exercise of the acts proper to marriage. Hence the acts in marriage by which the intimate and chaste union of the spouses takes place are noble and honorable; the truly human performance of these acts fosters the self-giving they signify and enriches the spouses in joy and gratitude (*Gaudium et Spes*, no. 49).

61

As we have seen, this teaching of Vatican II is by no means a new teaching of the Church. The great medieval theologians recognized its truth, and it gradually received greater attention in magisterial teaching over the last few centuries. The need for clearer teaching on this matter was occasioned by the development of modern humanism with its often distorted views about the goodness of sexual pleasure and other forms of human fulfillment. Especially in this century, the popes have seen the need to clarify the genuine goods of marriage in the face of the hedonistic and subjectivist values of secular humanism. The secular humanist view of values has enough truth about it to be very plausible, and it has become dominant in much of modern society; but its shortcomings make it a real threat to the genuine humanism which the Church proclaims.

To stress the authentic goodness of marital love, Pope Pius XI taught that the decision of spouses to engage in sexual intercourse could be a virtuous decision, even when they knew that procreation was physically impossible. He recognized "the cultivation of mutual love" as a worthy purpose in such circumstances.[16] Pius XII taught that spouses may rightly and gratefully seek the pleasure which accompanies their marital intercourse. He carefully dissociates his position from the condemned view that marital intercourse may be properly sought *solely* for the sake of pleasure.[17]

But Pius XII goes on to say:

> The Creator in His goodness and wisdom has willed to make use of the work of the man and the woman to preserve and propagate the human race, by joining them in wedlock. The same Creator has arranged that the husband and wife find pleasure and happiness of mind and body in the performance of that function. Consequently, the husband and wife do no wrong in seeking out and enjoying this pleasure. They are accepting what the Creator intended for them.[18]

Pius goes on to articulate the Church's basic standard for evaluating these pleasures, which is, in fact, the Church's basic standard for evaluating sexual activity: "This, therefore, is the rule to be followed: the use of the natural, generative instinct and function is lawful in the married state only, and in the service of the purposes for which marriage exists. It follows from this that only in the married state and in the observance of these laws are the desires and enjoyment of that pleasure and satisfaction allowed."[19] The purposes to which he refers are, of course, the goods sought in marital activity — the good of offspring and the good of faithful love.

The moral norm stated by Pius has been taken up by the Vatican Council and subsequent popes. Vatican II emphasized that decisions about sexual activity within marriage should be guided by objective criteria. These criteria should be "drawn from the nature of the human person and human action," and should "respect the total meaning of mutual self-giving and human procreation in the context of true love" (*Gaudium et Spes*, no. 51). The Council Fathers continued by stressing that spouses would be able to honor these criteria only by seriously practicing the virtue of marital chastity.

Paul VI makes a similar point in *Humanae Vitae*. He teaches that any marital act which separates the procreative and the unitive significance of marriage is wrong. This separation is wrong because these goods cannot be properly respected and fostered when they are separated. Thus, Pope Paul rejected contraceptive acts because they separate the procreative meaning of marriage from its unitive meaning in a way that is harmful to both of them. He also rejected sexual acts imposed on one's partner without regard for his or her condition or legitimate desires, since they fail to respect the good of marital union.[20] The teaching of *Humanae Vitae* has been strongly reaffirmed by John Paul II, most notably in *Familiaris Consortio*.[21]

Finally, it is worth noting an observation of Pius XII which forms an important part of the evaluation of modern attitudes toward sexuality on the part of recent popes. Pius disputed the popular view "that happiness in married life is in direct proportion to the mutual enjoyment of marital relations." He recognizes, as we have seen, that sexual pleasure adds to the joy of marriage; but he also teaches that it is not basic. Marriage has far greater goods to rejoice in. "Happiness in marital life is in direct ratio to the respect husband and wife have for each other, even in the intimate act of marriage."[22] They respect each other by treating each other as irreplaceable persons, committed to a common life in which each fosters love for each other and the great goods of marriage.

### III. The Immorality of Sexual Activity That Is Not Marital

In proclaiming the norms of sexual behavior rooted in God's law, the magisterium has always taught that it is seriously wrong to choose to engage in any sexual activity that is not authentically marital. From the first days of the Church, pastoral leaders taught, as Scripture had, that those who engage in "fornication, gross indecency, and sexual irresponsibility . . . will not inherit the kingdom of God" (Galatians 5.19-21). Moreover, the magisterium has always proposed its teaching on these matters as being the teaching of God himself, as revealed in Scripture. Thus, for example, the *Roman Catechism*, promulgated after the Council of Trent, in condemning adultery, fornication, prostitution, and homosexual acts, listed them as violations of the sixth commandment — that is, as acts prohibited by Scripture.[23] In addition to these acts, it is clear that the magisterium has from the earliest times regarded masturbation and contraception as among the grossly indecent and sexually irresponsible acts which exclude their perpetrators from God's kingdom.[24]

The reasons for this teaching are difficult to articulate in a brief way, but it is clear that the Church presents this teaching as based on the most serious of reasons. She has received a teaching from God which she must proclaim. This teaching therefore expresses a loving concern to preserve the real meaning and goodness of marital love, and to foster human dignity in intimate personal relations. Pope John Paul II has articulated these considerations as follows:

> The only "place" in which this self-giving in its whole truth is made possible is marriage, the covenant of conjugal love freely and consciously chosen, whereby man and woman accept the intimate community of life and love willed by God Himself, which only in this light manifests its true meaning. The institution of marriage is not an undue . . . imposition of a form. Rather it is an interior requirement of the covenant of conjugal love which is publicly affirmed as unique and exclusive, in order to live in complete fidelity

to the plan of God, the Creator. A person's freedom, far from being restricted by this fidelity, is secured against every form of subjectivism or relativism and is made a sharer in creative Wisdom.[25]

The kind of reasoning exhibited here will be developed further and applied to particular sexual activities in the final chapters of this work. The point here is simply that the Church's teaching on sexual matters is always presented both as the revealed will of God, and also as eminently reasonable. The Catholic vision of sexuality teaches a way of living sexually which is liberating and genuinely good for human beings. Those who reflect carefully in the light of faith can see and experience this for themselves.

# 4

## Patterns of Thinking in Moral Theology

Christian life is not primarily the following of a moral code. It is, most fundamentally, living as adopted sons and daughters of God. This new life is made possible by the redemptive activity of Jesus. It essentially involves participating in God's own life, in living freely in ways that God's grace makes possible. This grace is God's altogether free gift.[1]

Still, it is clear that Christian life involves a morality. Specific ways of living are appropriate for those who live the life of charity, and some ways of living, some choices and actions, are simply incompatible with this life. This is revealed in the covenants which God made with the people of Israel and their ancestors. All the covenants required that God's people keep his commandments. Jesus reaffirms and develops this Old Testament emphasis. He tells us that we must keep his commandments if we are to be saved (Matthew 19.17-19).[2] The moral implications of Jesus' message are so central to it that they appear prominently in the original proclamation of the Gospel; they appear in the heavily moral emphasis of the early Pauline epistles, as they do in all later Catholic teaching.

Jesus did not show his concern with morality only by his teaching. He came to redeem sinners, and their salvation required much more than articulating moral truth. He died and rose for them, to give them power to live a new life. Those who would respond to Jesus' invitation to new life were required to have a change of heart, a conversion. The free cooperation of those who would follow Jesus must include repentance for their sins (Acts 2.38), and a resolve to live unselfish and upright lives, doing all that love requires (1 John 3). Thus, the life of the Christian involves a moral component. The Christian, like Christ himself, must obey the commands of the Father and so live in a way befitting one who has become a new kind of creature.

Christian faith offers important helps toward living as authentic love requires. First, it helps believers to know what God's will is. Then it gives power to live in the good ways in which God wishes us freely to walk.

The Church has always taught the moral vision of Christianity with confidence, for the Church is convinced that authentic Catholic morality is true and good, that this morality serves love, reveres the person, intelligently resolves difficult problems, and faithfully responds to Gospel requirements. In this chapter we cannot provide an exhaustive study of the principles underlying this moral vision.[3] But it is possible — and sufficient for our purposes — to consider the most basic principles of Christian morality in order to reveal their basic soundness and relevance. These principles provide a rationale for understanding the received teaching of the Church on sexual morality. Moreover, they make it plain that the current challenge to this teaching both by various groups outside the Church and by some Catholics is neither rationally defensive nor compatible with basic truths of revelation.

This chapter contains three sections. The first is a discussion of the most basic principles of Christian morality. The second is an account of the human values or goods, recognized by human intelligence and celebrated in Scripture, which are the grounds for moral norms. The third considers how moral norms are based upon the goods discussed in the second section. Since there is considerable debate among Catholic theologians about how moral norms are justified and applied, this section will constitute the bulk of the chapter. In it we will present a critical discussion of the moral theory most often used to justify dissent

67

from the Church's teaching on sexual matters, the theory called proportionalism. We will conclude this section with a discussion of the importance of human actions and choices in the economy of salvation.

## I. The Basic Principles of Catholic Moral Reasoning

To understand Christian morality one must reflect on the reality of free choice and the reality of divine and human love. A correct understanding of these two principles is especially important in a treatment of sexual morality, for mistaken ideas about love and freedom are often at the root of people's distorted views about human sexuality.

*Free Choice.* The word "freedom" has several related senses.[4] Two of these are especially important for the Christian, namely the liberty of the children of God and free choice. The "liberty of the children of God" speaks of God's merciful gifts of grace which enable the Christian to escape from the dominance of sinful desire and selfishness. Free choice is a gift flowing from man's very nature. It is presupposed by the Judeo-Christian notion of moral responsibility. It would be useless to study sexual ethics if human beings were so dominated by irrational forces that they could not come to know and to choose intelligent and good ways to direct their sexual lives, or if God did not provide the power for people to live in these excellent ways. Both kinds of freedom are therefore important. We will focus on free choice in its relation to moral principles.

A person makes a free choice when he or she selects one from a set of practical options. A choice is free when the person's own choosing determines which of the available options the person will select. In other words, all the factors determining the outcome of the choice, other than the person's own choosing, are not sufficient to determine which selection is made. A free choice is made when a person could choose this or that, and the person himself determines which he will select.[5]

The reality of free choice is explicitly affirmed in Scripture: "It was he who created man in the beginning, and he left him in the power of his own inclination. If you will, you can keep the commandments, and to act faithfully is a matter of your own choice. He has placed before you fire and water: stretch out

68

your hand for whichever you wish. Before a man are life and death, and whichever he chooses will be given to him" (Sirach 15.14-17). This biblical teaching has also been explicitly affirmed by the authentic teaching of the Church.[6] Furthermore, free choice is implicit in a number of biblical themes: sin and punishment, conversion and repentance — all presuppose free choice. As St. Thomas Aquinas noted: "Counsels, exhortations, precepts, prohibitions, rewards, and punishments would be in vain" if mankind lacked free choice.[7]

The biblical affirmation of free choice is not opposed to the equally strong biblical emphasis on the importance of God's grace and the inability of fallen human beings consistently to do good without God's help. Human free choice can be exercised for good or for evil, but in the present condition of mankind it cannot be consistently used for good without the help of God's grace. However, the effect of God's grace on human lives does not override or cancel human freedom. God works through human freedom as he does through all the capacities of human nature.

Similarly, the affirmation of free choice in revelation does not involve the denial that many factors affect human behavior and inhibit the exercise of free choice. The work of social scientists in recent decades confirms the commonsense judgment that pressures of various kinds often limit human freedom. The Christian tradition recognizes that not all human behavior is free. Sexual conduct is especially affected by passions and pressures, and often one does not know what measure of freedom was involved in a given act.

Nevertheless, the view that all or most human behavior is determined by factors other than choice has no basis in experience and is irreconcilable with the revealed truth that people are in fact responsible for their acts and the basic direction of their lives. Even in this world of many pressures, God made human beings capable of free choice.

*The Law of Love.* The moral teachings of Christianity express the requirements of love. Both the Old and the New Testaments insist that love is the foundation of all morality. Jesus declared unequivocally that every other commandment flows from the two greatest commands: that we should love God above all things and our neighbor as ourselves (Matthew 22.34-40).

The love commandments play a central part in God's providential plan for mankind, for they direct human beings to a sharing of life and good things with God and with other human beings that is closely related to God's loving purpose in creating mankind. He who is Love itself — sharing divine goodness within the perfect community of the Trinity — wishes to share this love with us creatures by making us his children. This love between God and creatures cannot be realized unless human beings live in such a way as to be open to this wonderful fellowship.

The basic norms of Christian morality are therefore in no way arbitrary. They do not restrict our freedom but are addressed to it.[8] They are proposed to us by a loving God to assist us to live as intelligent love would choose to live.

To make clear the connection between specific moral norms and the love commandments — and thus to reveal the necessity and nonarbitrariness of these specific requirements — we shall reflect on the human goods, the basic perfections of human nature which God desires us to promote and respect.

## II. The Human Good

God loves us and wishes us to flourish in every good. He wishes our lives and actions to be good, for authentic love always wishes the beloved to flourish in what truly enriches and fulfills the beloved. Since this perfection cannot be merely something that happens to intelligent creatures — but rather is something persons must freely and intelligently achieve by their own actions — then God's love for us must include the demand that we show an intelligent concern for what is truly good for us.

Today there is much pessimism about the fundamental roots of a good life. Skepticism and relativism lead many to hold that nothing is really good, or knowable as really good. Christian faith, however, confidently teaches that human beings can know the nature of goodness, even without the help of revelation, and that in principle people can know the real goods that are so precious that they make all moral striving worthwhile.

*The Nature of Goodness.* Difficult moral questions, like those in sexual ethics, cannot be resolved without an under-

70

standing of the most basic ideas, such as "good" and "bad," and without a grasp of the richness of the human values that underlie all our striving. Reflection upon why we call some things, actions, or experiences good and others bad makes clear that the meaning and application of the terms "good" and "bad" are not arbitrary. "Good" does not refer simply to whatever a person prefers or recommends or likes. Most people have asked, or at least can understand, the question, "I like it, but is it good?" This question supposes that the goodness of something is not simply constituted by one's liking it.

Thus, common sense, reflection, and experience support what Christian faith affirms on this matter: there are reasons rooted in reality for calling some things "good" and others "bad." God, the Creator of all, has willed that human beings should be able to participate in his creative activity by their free actions. This is possible only because he has created an intelligible order in which some realities can be recognized as truly valuable and worthwhile. Life, truth, beauty, friendship, peace, and so on are good; what undermines, harms, and attacks them is bad.

Human creativity operates within this divinely established set of values. It cannot create the very goodness of these values. But human beings can grasp the real goodness of these values, and by choosing rightly can create worthy human lives in which the goodness God made accessible can flourish. Thus, human beings can choose to do certain things and to live in a certain way; by their choices they make themselves the kinds of persons they become, but they cannot by their willing it make any kind of action whatsoever to be good.[9] Whatever they choose must have at least some appearance of good; but a good human action, one that tends to make the one who does it a good person, requires, as we shall see, much more.

A good human life therefore is one in which a person is fully perfected in all the dimensions of his or her personality. It is a rich life of human flourishing. Whatever contributes to that flourishing is to that extent good.[10] Being a good person is an essential part of this full human perfection, for one is a good person in virtue of making morally good choices, and this is the part of human flourishing that is most properly human, most properly a form of self-perfection. Moral norms are the standards for choosing well. They are the guidelines for that part of human flourishing that is within our own power to realize. This is why being moral is the same in the end as being good. Being moral is not, in the last analysis, a matter of rules and regulations but of the demands of our own self-perfection, a perfection that God desires because it is good for us.

This general account of the meaning of goodness throws light on the problem of evil. Christian faith believes that all things are made by an infinitely good God who is free and loves our freedom. There are evil deeds, persons, and things, but evil does not have the substantial reality of goodness. Evil in any reality is not a positive and substantial factor in it. The evil in any reality is the lack of proper perfection in it, an absence of the good that should be present. There is evil in the world because things can fail to have the fullness of reality they were meant by their Creator to possess. The worst and most bitter of evils — the evil of deliberate, malicious actions — flows not from God's creative will but from the refusal of the creature to let his or her free acts have the fullness of being that God commands and makes possible but does not force upon the person. It would be a serious mistake to imagine that any sexual sin is evil because sex itself, or pleasure, or passion, is inherently evil or suspect. The things God made are very good. This understanding of the relationship of good and evil is important for Christian ethics generally and for sexual ethics in particular. Any form of Gnosticism which denies the fundamental goodness of physical reality or of human bodily life must be rejected as inconsistent with the basic truth that all of God's creation is very good.

*The Goods of Human Nature.* The human good is that which perfects and completes human nature. Human persons are dynamic, reaching their fulfillment by actively participating in real goods like truth and friendship. This section is concerned with developing an account of those objective values that make up this human good. These values — basic goods of human nature — are revealed by reflection on the basic motives of human action. Some of them are noted in *Gaudium et Spes*, no. 39:

> When we have spread on earth the fruits of our nature and
> our enterprise — human dignity, brotherly communion,

72

and freedom — according to the command of the Lord and in his Spirit, we will find them once again, cleansed this time from the stain of sin, illuminated and transfigured, when Christ presents to his Father an eternal and universal kingdom "of truth and life, a kingdom of holiness and grace, a kingdom of justice, love and peace." Here on earth the kingdom is mysteriously present; when the Lord comes, it will enter into its perfection.[11]

This powerful manifesto of Christian humanism lists as intrinsic components of the Lord's kingdom a number of basic human concerns which are not unique to Christians. All persons and cultures pursue goods like these. Truth, life, justice, love, and holiness are not valued by Christians only but by all men and women. These values are not always properly realized and respected in the individual and social activities of humankind, but they do comprise a good deal of the basic motivation for human action and enterprise. These values motivate us at this basic level precisely because they are the basic components of human perfection. By doing things which realize these values we are perfected and completed as human beings.

Perhaps the most obvious of these basic goods are those realized in the relations between persons and within communities. Such things as love and friendship, justice and peace, are among the most basic concerns of all persons. They are also among the most highly regarded human realities in Scripture.[12] These values are characteristics of persons and communities based on the relationships the persons establish among themselves and with those outside the community and with God himself. It is clear that these goods are realized primarily in the commitments of persons to relate decently to one another and to have good and friendly relationships. It is also clear that these goods can be, and often are, sought not as a means to any further goal but as part of what makes life rich and meaningful. Even those who treat others unjustly by manipulating or oppressing them desire some genuine friends and some real human mutuality. The deep human significance of the charge that one does not really care for another but is merely using the other, shows that people understand that a true human relationship is meant to be a basic, noninstrumental value within human life, precious in itself and

73

not a mere means of pursuing other goals. Clearly, the interpersonal goods perfect a dimension of human nature, for we are by nature social beings; a satisfactory human life without friends and decent relationships is simply unthinkable.[13]

Other human goods perfect other aspects of human nature. Since human beings are complex creatures made up of intellects and wills, minds and bodies, emotions and convictions, it is part of human perfection to harmonize and integrate these elements. This good has a number of aspects, so it is called variously self-integration, authenticity, integrity, practical reasonableness, or, simply, peace.[14] It is the good realized in the cardinal virtues of prudence, temperance, and courage.[15] Consequently, this good is very important for sexual morality, since this good is almost always affected when decisions about sex are made.

Knowing the truth is also a basic human good. Human persons pursue truth not only for pragmatic reasons but also for its own sake, simply because it is good to know; and it is good because the capacity to know is a basic aspect of human nature. Scripture and Church teaching clearly endorse the goodness of knowledge.[16]

Finally, human life itself is a basic good of human nature. Without life the human person does not exist. This does not mean, however, that life has value only as a means or as the context for the realization of other goods. Life is good in itself. To be alive is good, and to flourish in biological life by being healthy and by passing life on to new generations is a perfection of this basic good. The goodness of human life is explicitly and implicitly affirmed in Scripture and in the lives of faithful believers down through the centuries.[17]

This listing of basic human goods is not meant to be exhaustive.[18] It is, however, sufficient for present purposes because it reveals the goods that are most often at stake in sexual activity. Moreover, this discussion makes clear that the human good is not a specific finite goal or achievement but something that is realized in different ways in the actions of individuals and communities. No individual or group can realize all the human goods. That is why choices are necessary. Still, it is possible to make our choices in a way that shows proper regard for all that is humanly good. Moral norms show the way to this proper regard.

*The Goodness of Pleasure.* **Our** discussion of the human goods up to this point is obviously incomplete, for we have not yet considered pleasure. Common experience indicates the basic goodness of pleasure. All human beings desire pleasure in one form or another. Thus, unless human desire is utterly perverse, pleasure must be good. It is unthinkable that God, who created mankind out of love, should have created us with utterly perverse desires.

But common experience also reveals another, darker side of pleasure. For the lure of fleeting, empty, and even destructive satisfactions is an undeniable part of the human condition. Many spouses have deeply hurt those they love, and wounded their own lives, by servile pursuit of adulterous pleasure. The desire for pleasure can lead us away from things we know to be good — even from good things to which we would like to remain deeply committed. Pleasure, in short, can enslave us.

Thus, pleasure has a complex character: it is a good thing but one which — more than other good things — can lead us astray. Consequently, any account of pleasure which implies either that it is essentially a bad thing, or that it is always entirely good, must be rejected as oversimplified.

The tendency in our culture is toward an uncritical overestimation of the goodness of pleasure. This cultural tendency has found a number of theoretical formulations. Perhaps the most important of these is the familiar philosophical doctrine of hedonism. For the hedonist, the point of all human effort and action is pleasure of some sort. Thus, pleasure is not simply the highest good; it is the only thing that is desirable for its own sake. Nothing is counted as good except to the extent that it causes pleasure.

This doctrine correctly emphasizes the goodness of pleasure; but, like all extreme views, it vastly oversimplifies the human experience of this complex phenomenon. As careful students of human motivation from the time of Plato and Aristotle have noted, the goodness of the desirable things in life cannot be explained simply in terms of their capacity to cause pleasure. Some good things are not pleasurable, at least not in most circumstances; and they are good and desirable even when they do not give pleasure, even when they are quite unpleasant. It is

75

good to struggle to protect one's friend, even when the pain and tension of the effort are so great that one cannot enjoy the nobility or praiseworthiness of one's fidelity.

Moreover, other things than pleasure are truly good. Pleasure simply is not the ultimate point of all human action, the basis for all motivation.[19] It is good to pursue and honor truth and justice, even when one's efforts have no pleasurable resonances. Ideally the pursuit and realization of these and other human goods will be pleasant, but they are not recognized as good only to the extent that they lead to pleasure. Trials, hardship, and pain must be endured by one who truly cherishes the goods of human persons. The fidelity of Job and the obedience of Jesus unto death show how good persons pursue what is really good without expecting to taste pleasure in their efforts.

Examples like these show that the direction of Christian thought about pleasure is profoundly anti-hedonist. But being opposed to hedonism is not being opposed to pleasure, for hedonism says that only pleasure is ultimately good, and this is a false theory. It does not follow that pleasure is not fundamentally a good thing.[20] Thus, the Christian evaluation of pleasure is not a rejection of its goodness but a critical, realistic understanding of its complex reality and motivational complexity.

According to this understanding, the good actions and efforts in human life can be and ideally are pleasurable. But they are not good because they give pleasure. Such activities tend to give pleasure because they perfect some dimension of the human person. So, pleasure is a good thing, but it is not the very meaning of goodness nor is it an independent principle of goodness.

This does not mean that actions are always pleasurable in proportion to their goodness, for the amount of pleasure any activity causes depends on many variable conditions.[21] People must work even when they are tired and distracted. Even when the work is noble, they may find no pleasure in it. People must struggle against divided selves — trying to do good when emotion, laziness, or passion is pulling in another direction. So, good activities which under ideal conditions would be pleasant are in fact often not so.

Conversely, activities that are intensely pleasurable can

often be destructive and immoral. The adulterer may take great pleasure in acts he knows are destroying his life. Evil but pleasurable acts do have something good about them. They do fulfill some human potentiality but not in an ordered and integrated way. To the extent that such actions are good, they can be pleasant; but to the extent that they block or destroy the full goodness of persons, the associated pleasures will fail to be deeply and enduringly satisfying.

This evaluation of pleasure is based on an understanding of pleasure as a kind of accompaniment to a good activity which completes and crowns the activity. Pleasure therefore is closely related to what is good, but it is not the primary component in the goodness of humanly good things. The presence of pleasure indicates something good in the activity, though not necessarily total goodness. Its absence does not indicate a lack of real goodness. In determining the goodness of an action, therefore, the emphasis must be on the character of the action itself and not on the quality of the accompanying experiences of pleasure and pain.[22] This is the case in the sexual domain as elsewhere. A morally good sexual act is in no way suspect because of its great pleasure. This pleasure is an appropriate concomitant of the act's overall goodness. Similarly, the pleasure of an immoral sexual act is not itself bad. What is bad is the act itself, and the willingness to yield to disordered desire for gratification, in acts that by striking against the authentic goods of human persons are unreasonable.

### III. From Human Goods to Moral Norms

The good person acts out of love, pursuing what is really good out of love of God, of neighbor, and a right love of self. Since it is possible to pursue good things in evil ways, the task of moral thinking is to discover how to love good things rightly, and to pursue them properly.

The Second Vatican Council urged moral theologians to show more clearly how Christian morality is based upon the Scriptures, and how moral theology throws light on the vocation of Christians and the obligation to bring forth fruit in charity for the life of the world (*Optatam Totius*, no. 16). Thus, the Council Fathers called for a renewal in moral theology which would make clearer its connection with the fundamental realities of Christian life. This call for renewal presupposed a recognition that there were deficiencies in the ways many theologians of recent centuries explained the moral teachings proclaimed by the Church. In the decades and centuries prior to the Vatican Council, the moral teachings of the Church, especially her insistence on moral absolutes, were sometimes presented as legalistic restraints on living which impose merely extrinsic limitations on persons, telling them only the minimum necessary for escaping grave sin.[23]

As the Fathers of Vatican II suggest, the shortcomings of moral theology in the years prior to the Council are not problems in Catholic moral teaching itself but in its presentation and theological explanation. The basic way of overcoming these difficulties is a thoroughgoing recognition that moral norms are, as the Gospel insists, requirements of intelligent love of what is really good. Once this point is accepted, the objection that traditional moral teaching is some form of authoritarian imposition loses its force. At best, such an objection can be addressed to certain theological formulations — not to the substance of Catholic moral teaching.

*Making Good Moral Choices: Two Approaches.* The problem facing us in this section concerns the standards and procedures for arriving at the judgment that a certain choice is morally good or bad. The problem arises because it is not clear how the commandments of love are to be applied to actual human choices. We have already seen that the love commandments require a concern and respect for human goods, but we have yet to see how that concern is translated into practical norms and procedures of moral thinking. This difficulty is a real one in the present situation because Catholic theologians hold strongly opposed views on this matter. With some oversimplification it is possible to classify the opposing views into two broad approaches to moral thinking. They can be called, respectively, "proportionalism" and "the morality of principles." Both of these approaches are attempts to carry out the renewal called for by Vatican II; both seek to escape every kind of legalism and extrinsicism to show that morality is not a set of arbitrary rules imposed without concern for what the human person is and

78

longs to be. Both explain the moral teachings of Christianity in terms of love of persons, and of the great human goods that animate all moral striving — goods like those discussed in the preceding section. Both seek to be faithful to the larger vision of Scripture and Christian tradition, understanding that man was made not simply to keep rules but to serve God creatively as his image, intelligently striving to do what is really good, what love requires.

Proportionalism is so called because of its emphasis on the proportion of good and evil in actions. According to proportionalism, an act which would otherwise be immoral can be justified morally if the overall good or evil involved in doing the action compares favorably with the overall good or evil which the available alternatives would bring about. Thus, its basic principle can be called the principle of the greater good, or more commonly, the principle of the lesser evil. The morality of principles is so called because of its concern for unfailing faithfulness to the first principles of morality, that is, for faithfulness to every person and every human good. Thus, there is no necessary opposition between these approaches concerning the primacy of love or the nature of the human good. They disagree about how love and the human good should shape our choices.

Each of these approaches to moral thinking is, of course, concerned with principles, and each shows real concern about the overall good and evil brought about by actions. But proportionalism emphasizes the overall outcomes of acts, evaluating them in terms of the principle of the lesser evil; and the morality of principles emphasizes loyalty to principles in a way that precludes overriding this fidelity because of the overall good or evil the action brings about. Thus, the designations of the positions are descriptive of their central features.

*Proportionalism.* Proportionalism, as already noted, is a method of moral thinking according to which a person ought to choose that alternative course of action which promises the greater proportion of good over evil.[24] In other words, proportionalists believe that intelligent concern for the human goods requires an assessment of all the good and evil involved in alternative possibilities for action. The purpose of this assessment is to determine, prior to choice, which of the alternatives promises the greater good or the lesser evil. This determination tells us which of the alternatives we morally ought to choose.

The proportionalist method is considered applicable to any moral problem, but the Catholic theologians who make use of it tend to limit its application in various ways. This method is, however, used in an unrestricted form by many secular moralists. These thinkers are usually called "consequentialists," and they tend to treat the principle of the lesser evil as the single basic moral principle. The most widely known form of consequentialism is utilitarianism. In its classical versions this secular form of ethics held that there is really only one good that human action pursues, pleasure; and it taught that men ought always pursue that which leads to "the greatest happiness of the greatest number."

Catholic proportionalists are far from being pure utilitarians. The whole context of their thinking is Christian, not secular. Generally they acknowledge the objective goodness and distinctive reality of each of the kinds of basic goods that we have noted above. Thus, they reject the oversimplified identification of the human good with pleasurable experience.[25] They also rightly reject any suggestion that individual rights can be subordinated to the interests of society. Most importantly, proportionalists acknowledge that there are some moral absolutes — for example, that one should never seek to lead another into sin. Thus, they admit significant limitations on the applicability of the proportionality principle.[26]

But proportionalists distinctively hold that the most common moral absolutes traditionally taught by the Catholic Church — and, even now, insistently taught by the magisterium — are not valid. Ordinarily these moralists hold, against the received teaching of the Church, that not every act of contraception is immoral, that not every act of homosexuality or fornication is objectively wrong, that not every intentional taking of innocent human life is absolutely prohibited.

Proportionalists typically hold that no kinds of acts, when defined in purely descriptive language, that is, language that includes no morally evaluative terms, are *always* wrong, or *intrinsically evil in a strong sense*. If one were to mean by murder an unjust slaying of an innocent person, then they would agree that every murder is indeed wrong, for the characterization of the killing as unjust is sufficient to settle its immorality. But the direct slaying of an innocent person is not held to be absolutely and in every possible circumstance wrong. Such an act does not include evaluative terms in its description, and it is conceivable that in some extreme circumstances such an act would be determined to be the lesser evil. In those circumstances killing would be a morally good act.

Proportionalists recognize, of course, that there are some alternatives for action that, although not excluded because they are by definition morally bad, are likely to cause greater harm in almost all circumstances. To use one of their examples, it would be wrong to force a retarded child to have sexual relations. Such a norm is a "practical absolute" which is "virtually exceptionless." But, as these phrases suggest, the norm here is not absolute in principle. This, or any other act characterized in purely descriptive terms, might under some circumstances we cannot now think of be thought to be the lesser evil, and thus the correct thing to do.[27]

The proportionalist supposes that there is a radical difference between actions characterized evaluatively and actions characterized only in descriptive terms. This difference depends upon one of the most fundamental distinctions in the proportionalist approach — that is, the difference between moral evil and premoral, physical, or ontic evil. Moral evils are essentially morally bad choices and acts. By definition such acts may not morally be done. Thus, proportionalists would not allow the use of their method to justify an action already determined to be morally evil. One important implication is that we should never act deliberately to cause another to commit sin.

Premoral evil refers to the depravation of some good that is due a person or a thing; premoral evils are really bad, but they are not as such immoral. Sickness and death are premoral evils. They are obviously bad, but not as such immoral. The question is whether choices deliberately to cause premoral evils are morally bad choices. The proportionalist answer is that a choice of what is premorally evil can be morally justified if there is a proportionate reason — if choosing or intending that evil is the way to realize the lesser evil in the situation.

81

As a leading proportionalist has put it:

> Where a higher good is at stake and the only *means* to protect it is to choose a non-moral evil, then the will remains properly disposed to the values constitutive of the human good. . . . This is to say that the intentionality is good even when the person, reluctantly and regretfully to be sure, intends the non-moral evil if a truly proportionate reason for such a choice is present.[28]

Thus, we have in the basic logic of the proportionalist method a ground for rejecting much of the Church's received teaching on sexual matters, for much of this teaching is about acts that can appear to affect only premoral goods, and it is possible to think of many situations in which the lesser evil will seem to require that one deliberately harm or fail to respect these goods.

Since recent popes, synods, and episcopal conferences have very frequently reaffirmed the validity and importance of moral absolutes in the Church's traditional sense,[29] it has become characteristic of proportionalists to hold that one need not assent to these teachings of the magisterium in specific moral matters. They hold this, even though the Church has taught these things with such force and in such insistent ways that many theologians believe they have been taught infallibly by the ordinary magisterium.[30] Proportionalists argue that these teachings are proposed only by a fallible magisterium, and that it is licit to dissent from the most insistent teaching of the ordinary teaching authority of the Church, if one has sufficient reasons.

*Arguments for Proportionalism.* Of the many arguments adduced in favor of proportionalism, two seem especially important.

The first is a philosophical argument that the fundamental principle of proportionalism is *evidently true*. Proportionalists argue that if one were not required to choose the greater good, or the lesser evil, the alternative would be that one would be obliged to choose the lesser good or greater evil. This alternative is patently absurd.[31] The self-evidence of the proportionalist principle is said to be confirmed by the fact that it is the natural, obvious way to determine the right course of action, as the actual moral thinking of good people reveals. The good person will

82

certainly concede that he ought not do what leads to a greater balance of evil over good; that is to say, he instinctively judges as a proportionalist. The reason for this conviction is that morally serious persons care about what is really good, and this concern, if it is to be thoroughly reasonable, must justify the principle of the lesser evil.

The second major argument for proportionalism is that just as serious individuals make use of the proportionalist principle in their moral thinking so also does the Church. Thus, the adoption of proportionalism by Catholic thinkers, they claim, is a modest and legitimate development of moral themes already used by the Church, even if only implicitly. This argument is often supported by examples of the role of proportionality in the just-war theory and as one of the conditions of the principle of double effect.[32]

This development of moral teaching is especially appropriate today, so the argument goes, for a variety of reasons. As noted already, Vatican Council II called for a renewal in moral theology. In particular, the Council seems to have called for a more humanistic and less legalistic approach to morality. Proportionalism seems to many to be the proper response to this need in the life of the Church. It seems to be the worst sort of rule worship, the most uncaring legalism for a person to refuse to do an act necessary for avoiding great harms simply because it is prohibited by a moral absolute taught by the Church. Pastoral reasons are also cited in support of the legitimacy of this development. People today will not and cannot accept the moral absolutes that so burden people in the new circumstances of a greatly changed world.

*Difficulties in Proportionalist Arguments.* The claim that the proportionalist principle of the lesser evil is self-evidently true cannot be sustained. This principle supposes that it is possible to determine which alternative has the better or the less bad effects overall. To make this determination it must be possible to "commensurate" in an unambiguous way goods and evils at stake in human actions. It must be possible, in other words, to rank, measure, or compare the goods and evils at stake. One must be able to tell how much harm to one good is offset by the realization of some other good. Unless one can do this, the proportionalist method simply cannot work as a rational procedure of moral decision-making. This commensurating of goods cannot be rationally carried out.

Thinkers within the broad tradition of consequentialism have tried for centuries to show how human goods are commensurable but have never provided an account which is both analytically satisfactory and consonant with the common experiences of deliberation and choice. On the contrary, common experience shows that the goods at stake when a person must make a choice — the very situation in which moral guidance is needed — are not commensurable. It is because the goods between which we must choose are incommensurable that we must in the end settle what we shall do by choosing. Powerful philosophical and theological arguments have been developed which show that the common experience of the incommensurability of goods must of necessity reflect the reality of human motivation and choice.[33]

Moreover, there are other problems with this method, problems about how to determine the consequences, how many consequences to consider, and so on, which have led many non-Catholic moralists to abandon consequentialism altogether.[34] It is somewhat ironic that Catholic thinkers have adopted a method of moral thinking that has been for over a century the centerpiece of secular humanist thinking at the very time when many secular moralists were despairing of its ability to withstand the objections raised against it.[35]

Those who deny the self-evidence of the basic proportionalist principle are in no way proposing that we are ever expected to choose the greater rather than the lesser evil. The claim is that proportionalists have selected an incoherent way to distinguish the greater and the lesser evil. Thus, what a proportionalist might claim to be the lesser evil really is not shown by proportionalist procedures to be the lesser evil.

An example can clarify this. If a woman is considering having a direct abortion, she would, if following the proportionalist approach, list the central good and bad effects of deciding to have the abortion and of deciding to forgo it. Among the bad effects is that she would be choosing to kill directly and deliberately her own unborn child. Among expected good effects

84

might be that she preserves her own mental and physical health, or that she saves the peace, unity, or financial integrity of her family. But how could she objectively add and substract among goods and evils so diverse? Is the acknowledged evil of having the abortion such that it can be outweighed by the goods one anticipates by having it? How could she determine this? Her feelings might lean one way rather than the other, but the need is for a norm that will give rational, objective guidance in such situations.

A leading proportionalist tries to deal with this difficulty as follows: "In fear and trembling we commensurate"; "we *adopt* a hierarchy."[36] This approach seems to concede that there is no rational way to determine the lesser evil. It proposes that one adopt, that one choose for oneself, a hierarchy of goods, as a way of rating the worth of the various goods. One cannot do it objectively; but one *decides* how one will weigh alternatives; then one chooses in the light of the subjective evaluation that one has given. What this means is that one does not discover what is morally good; one decides what one shall call good by an arbitrary assessment.

One can indeed arbitrarily select ways of assigning values to the various incommensurable goods: of holding, for example, that the direct slaying of one's unborn child is an evil, nonetheless is less an evil than the sum of the evils which would follow if one did not have the abortion. However, this is evidently not a serious moral argument; it is a patent act of rationalization. One does not learn or discover that one's moral evaluation is the right one; rather one arbitrarily decides to adopt a standard of evaluation that will make one's preference turn out to be the right course.

This objection to proportionalism does not imply that the phrase "lesser evil" has no use in the moral thinking of decent people, for it surely does play such a role. But "lesser evil" does not have only the one meaning given to it by proportionalists. Some people, for example, think that the morally right course of action is always good, even when it has very sad and tragic consequences. Such persons might express this conviction by saying that the right course of action is the lesser evil, while never for a moment supposing that doing what violated a moral absolute could be the greater good or the lesser evil.[37] What the preceding argument precludes is only the specific use of the notion of lesser evil within the proportionalist method. It is by no means clear that morally decent people make use of this conception of lesser evil in their moral decision-making.

The second argument for proportionalism is also unsatisfactory. Proportionalism is a far more radical position than its defenders acknowledge it to be. It encourages rejections of moral norms that seem to be infallibly taught in the Church, and of positions that certainly cannot be legitimately rejected by Catholics, even if they are not infallibly proposed. Thus, proportionalism cannot be a legitimate development of Catholic moral teaching. The basic problem is that proportionalism leads to the denial that many of the moral absolutes taught by the Church are in fact true moral absolutes. Its history suggests that this is essential to its whole program, for it developed within the Church during the early 1960s as a rationale for justifying some use of contraceptives. This denial of moral absolutes taught insistently by the Church involves a denial of a basic moral principle — namely, that one must not do evil that good might come of it. This principle, as enunciated by St. Paul (Romans 3.8) and taught by the Church over the centuries, excludes the possibility of overturning moral absolutes by appeal to consequences, and this is exactly what proportionalism enjoins us to do.

Thus, it is implausible to maintain that a principle so opposed to what is fundamental in Church teaching can really be a development of that teaching. The precedents cited in favor of this claim are unimpressive. The fact that Christian tradition made use of some considerations about proportionality in some sense does not provide evidence for the claim that Christian tradition implicitly used or endorsed proportionalism, for it is not clear that proportionality was understood as a weighing of values, and even more importantly, such considerations were never used to overturn moral absolutes but only to settle issues in which it was clear that no moral absolute was at stake.[38]

Proportionalism therefore is not authentic development of received Catholic morality but a radical rejection of its central positions. Its claims to be the reasonable way to avoid legalism and to deal with pastoral problems are therefore suspect. Unless one supposes that any approach to morality that holds for moral absolutes must be legalistic, then it is by no means clear that proportionalism is the only way to avoid it. Caring deeply for persons and their goods does not mean attempting impossible ways or calculating and weighing the consequences of acts. Utter fidelity to persons and their goods seems to imply an absolute refusal to do kinds of acts that will harm them by attacking directly basic goods in them. And this refusal implies a rejection of the basic principle of proportionalism. Similarly, pastoral love for the faithful is not shown by encouraging them to reject authentic (and perhaps infallible) Church teaching, and to live in ways that the Fathers and saints have always said would separate one from the love of Christ. Even today it is an "eminent form of charity" to present Catholic teaching fully and persuasively, and to give every assistance to live in accord with its excellent norms.

A final difficulty with proportionalism should also be noted. It is the development of a criticism of consequentialism highlighted by secular moralists — namely, that consequentialist forms of thinking tend to be demoralizing in a number of ways.[39] Pastoral experience confirms the reality of this criticism. When the faithful are told that acts like those of adultery or fornication are not absolutely and always wrong but could be upright acts when proportionate reasons are really present, the faithful are deprived of bracing supports ordinarily necessary to strengthen them in the emotional and intellectual turmoil they experience at the time of temptation. If people are convinced that their own selves, their own moral identities, depend upon unswerving fidelity to moral principles, they have a defense lacking to those who are convinced that there is some way to rationally justify taking a course of action toward which they are inclined, although they know them to be unworthy.

The experience of our time shows how much human rights are threatened when small exceptions to necessary defenses of rights are allowed. For instance, few people wished the massive abortions now overwhelming the world. At first it was urged that some abortions be permitted "for very good reasons." But if abortions are permissible when the calculation of goods and harms permits it (a calculation that cannot be objectively valid; a calculation that will be mightily affected by hopes and fears), then the nonobjective nature of the calculation called for almost certainly leads to the terrible consequences brought about by abortion. Clearly, there can be no inalienable rights when there are no exceptionless duties.

Proportionalism therefore is inadequate as an approach to moral thinking for Catholics. Instead of providing guidance for the care and love of persons and their goods, proportionalism demands that human beings achieve a kind of knowledge only God could have, and undertake a responsibility for the consequences of actions that only God's providence can have. Instead of fidelity to the limited but real commitments we all have and to the moral absolutes which mark the boundaries for proper human participation in God's providence, proportionalism tells us to look farther — to consider all the effects, to put on a scale things that reflect in irreducible ways God's infinite goodness. This may seem noble to some, but it overreaches, taking as our own what we must trust to God's loving concern. Our moral thinking must not suppose that we can extricate ourselves from the tragedies and evils of human life; only God's healing re-creation can do that. But we can be faithful, can have hearts and wills completely faithful to the goodness which God so loves and, in the end, will restore. Proportionalism, sadly, corrupts that fidelity.

*The Morality of Principles.* As noted earlier, we give the name "Morality of Principles" to the broad approach within Catholic moral theology which, on the one hand, seeks to meet the challenge of Vatican II for renewal in moral theology and, on the other hand, seeks to maintain continuity with the received teaching of the Church on moral matters and with the best of the moral thinking in the theological tradition.

The primary way in which the morality of principles maintains continuity with the tradition of Catholic moral teaching is by insisting on the truth and centrality of moral absolutes. This approach holds that the specific moral norms taught by Christian tradition as holding in every instance do indeed have such universal applicability. Such norms as "never directly kill the innocent" and "never commit adultery" are held to be true, always binding, and nontrivial. There can never be any objectively good reasons for violating specific principles such as these.

88

This, of course, is not taken to imply that no moral norms have exceptions. Most norms do have exceptions. "Keep your promises" and "obey all just civil laws" are true general norms, but there are certainly circumstances in which the good person recognizes that they do not apply.

What is new in the morality of principles is its effort to show that the renewal of moral theology called for by Vatican II does not lead to an abandonment of the norms always taught in the Church but rather to a fuller understanding of why these norms are essential to the fabric of authentic Christian living. To reject moral absolutes and the rich tradition of moral thinking developed for applying and refining them would not be to renew Catholic morality but to discard it.

The renewal of moral theology is therefore understood within the morality of principles as an effort of deeper understanding and fuller appreciation of the significance of moral life within the economy of salvation. It is an effort to see how moral activity relates to the saving work of Christ, to the eternal destiny of Christians, and to the true humanism which faith has always held and Vatican II explicitly proclaimed. Thus understood, renewal in moral theology looks deeper into the sources of faith and into Catholic tradition to overcome a presentation of morality either as merely legalistic rules and regulations imposed by God or the Church, or as a set of directives which rationalistic arguments might establish.

The morality of principles therefore does not defend Christian moral teaching, including the teaching on moral absolutes, in a legalistic way. One must not avoid blasphemy or homosexual acts regardless of the consequences of one's faithfulness to the rule simply because one superstitiously venerates rules. Nor is the universality of the rule grounded merely in some command of God, who perhaps inexplicably demands faithfulness, even when more harm than good would appear to follow from faithfulness to the precept in a given situation.

Faith confirms that there are moral absolutes but also insists that moral absolutes are the requirements of love. The morality of principles recognizes that the implications of love are not simply rules but guidelines for authentic Christian life. Hence, proponents of the morality of principles point out that it

89

is always wrong to do such deeds as faith has proscribed absolutely because acts such as these are incompatible with the goods of persons which God calls us to love and absolutely respect. To do such acts is always to act in ways contrary to the full perfection of human persons and communities, and so it is to act in ways unworthy of persons created in God's image and called to act as he does — never willing evil, never harming love, and always respecting the dignity of persons. Human goods are not ideals that dwell apart; they are the fulfillment of human persons, and flourish only in persons. Hence, to act so as deliberately to harm a basic human good is to act against the fulfillment of a human person. And that is incompatible with loving the person.

The preceding argument in defense of moral absolutes is characteristic of the approach taken by those who hold for the morality of principles. But since this is a broad approach and not a single theory, not all who take this approach would develop the argument in exactly this way. Some would emphasize the dignity of persons, and how this dignity cannot be respected unless certain absolute rights and obligations are honored. Others would perhaps focus more on the precious human relationships and meanings that will be distorted unless these absolutes are accepted. But all versions of the morality of principles hold that moral absolutes protect what is most precious, lasting, and valuable in human life. In this sense they are all profoundly humanistic; all are variations on the theme that genuine love requires a care and respect for persons which absolutely excludes certain kinds of actions, namely those that harm persons, manipulate them, or disregard their true dignity.

The contrast between proportionalism and the morality of principles is perhaps sharpest at this point, for while both are concerned for human persons and their goods, this concern is understood very differently by each. Unlike proportionalism, the morality of principles does not suppose that the demands of love can be captured by a single simple moral principle, like the principle of the lesser evil. More important, the morality of principles does not require the mistaken assumption that the goods of human persons can be calculated and measured on a single scale. The tradition's concern with a hierarchy of values was never construed as a scale on which one could calculate the lesser evil as a ground for moral judgment.

The recognition that human goods are not calculable in the way proportionalism supposes does not mean that there can be no rational way to honor and respect them. Quite the contrary. We do not truly honor the precious goods of human persons when we are willing to harm them because doing so would, as we think, bring about the lesser evil. The morality of principles is serious about not harming human goods, and demands that in our acts we respect and honor each of them. Of course, we cannot in a given act immediately promote and pursue all that is humanly good; but we can always do acts in such a way that all the goods of human nature are respected and honored. Our fidelity to the whole good of human persons is often revealed not so much by the goods we seek but how we respect the goods that are not our immediate concern. The basic principle of the morality of principles can be formulated therefore as a principle of respect for the entire human good. We must always act in such a way as to be open to integral human fulfillment.[40]

Concern for the goods of persons is not therefore realized by trying, as it were, to create a world in which the maximum possible amount of good is realized but in making ourselves persons who humbly cherish and respect all that is good. This is not an attitude of contempt for the harms and tragedies which befall human beings, nor is it an attitude of self-righteousness that cares only for moral rectitude and not at all for human problems. It is, rather, realism about the multifarious character of the human good and our limited ability to make the world good. It is humility which recognizes that the solution to the problem of evil is not human action but God's healing re-creation. It is confidence that God will restore all that is really good and that we shall be part of the re-creation if only we cooperate by maintaining the steadfast loyalty revealed by Jesus and his saints, even in the face of failure and tragedy.

The morality of principles therefore is a form of humanism; but it is one in which the true good of man is seen in its full and proper perspective — the perspective of the kingdom of God made possible by Jesus' human acts and God's loving response to them. Thus, it is an approach to moral thinking which is fully

91

open to the larger and deeper meaning of human existence made possible by the revelation of Jesus. In this respect, it compares favorably with the rather narrow, secular, and this-worldly emphasis of proportionalism.

Moral absolutes are only one ingredient in a morality of principles; but they have always had a distinctive place in Catholic moral thought. Even the most corrupt societies have known that adultery is generally harmful, and that divorce is destructive of the basic human community. But Christian thought has been distinctive in teaching that one should not commit adultery, slay the innocent, or seek divorce and remarry even for the most splendid reasons, even to avoid the most bitter consequences. Christian faith has seen that there are in fact evil kinds of deeds, deeds that always involve assaults upon the love of persons. Such deeds must never be done; there can be no "proportionate reason" for doing them. We must not do evil that good may come of it. We must not do even a small evil because a great good seems destined to come of it, or because a great harm can be avoided by doing it. (St. Thomas More was right in judging that he should not affirm by oath false statements already so affirmed by virtually all the religious leaders of England, even though it seemed that little harm and slight additional scandal would come of it, and even though his own life, his family's hopes, and the possibility of influencing the king for the better might be salvaged by doing the evil.)

The morality of principles respects the rich complexity of serious moral thinking. It realizes that a good moral act involves more than doing a good kind of deed, or avoiding a perverse kind. It involves more than having good intentions in what we do, and more than seeking to avoid harmful consequences. St. Thomas Aquinas articulated what might be called a "principle of completeness" for evaluating human actions which required that good actions (like good persons and good realities of every kind) must be complete in their goodness.[41] According to this principle, every aspect of the act must be morally good: a single moral flaw, whether in the kind of action one does, or in the intentions with which it is done, or in the consequences of other circumstances with which it is done, is sufficient to render the act morally bad.

This principle does not prohibit actions because they have a tragic or unfortunate aspect to them; that would make most actions in this fallen world impossible. The integrity required is the integrity of a wholly upright will, of one who is unwilling to do whatever is contrary to a complete and intelligent respect for what is really good. Acts and other realities are morally bad to the extent that they lack any essential trait needed for their integrity and fulfillment. Thus, for example, if an act promises so much harm, and to do little good, in its outcomes, one who respects the Golden Rule will not do the act even if it be of a good kind and done with a good intention. One cannot merge these factors together and judge that one may do a bad kind of act, or approve an act done for a perverse intention, if one perceives that the act, considered in all its features, will have a greater balance of good consequences or aspects over bad ones. *Each* of the moral determinants must be good, or the act will not be a good one; it will not otherwise be faithful enough to what love requires.

*Good Deeds and Good Consequences.* Christian faith has always been more concerned that the faithful do excellent actions and so live morally excellent lives than that they produce many good effects in the world, or have wonderful things occur in their lives. Our lives are constituted far more by what we do than by what happens to us.

Many people in today's world find this aspect of Christian faith to be very puzzling. Modern secular humanists and, in particular, secular consequentialists reject it altogether, for consequentialists believe that it is not actions but the overall effects of actions that are morally most important. Christian ethics, of course, does not deny that we have some responsibility for the predictable effects of our actions but maintains that our actions themselves are the center of moral life.

Classical Catholic thought stresses the centrality of action because our free actions are the existential center of our lives. In our freely chosen acts we not only affect the world and other persons but also shape our own personalities and character. By choosing to do certain actions we determine ourselves to be one kind of person rather than another; we make ourselves to be friends of God by responding to his grace and freely loving all that is good, or we choose actions incompatible with love of God and fellowman.

Of course, we do not choose only actions in the narrow sense. We also make large-scale choices that tend to establish the broader outlines of our lives: our vocations, our professional identities, and our basic relationships with other persons. And the measure of the responsibility we have for the wide range of consequences of our actions varies with the ways we relate ourselves to those consequences. What we deliberately choose to do and the ends we deliberately make our own have an especially great importance. Clearly we do not, in every free choice and action, deliberately choose all that flows from such choices and acts: all the side effects, all the other things left undone, and so on. What is foreseen to come about as a result of our choices — but is not itself chosen — is voluntary in a way; but it is not itself freely chosen. It is accepted or permitted but not positively willed. The voluntary acceptance of side effects is not self-determining in the way free choices of the objects and ends of our acts are.[42]

This difference is the basis for the crucial distinction in Catholic morality between what is directly willed or intended and what is indirectly willed or outside the person's intention. To deny the moral significance of this distinction, as proportionalists often do, is to deny something fundamental to Catholic morality.[43] For if one rejects this distinction, and holds that there is no major difference between directly willing or doing evil and indirectly causing it, one would have to concede that it is permissible at times to do evil, and that there really are no moral absolutes. For it is scarcely deniable that even good people do, and cannot escape doing, acts from which bad effects flow. A parent who saves his or her child from the violent assault of an attacker may be able to do this only by a protective act that causes great harm or death to the assailant, however unintended that harm may be. But if every act that causes harm is morally indistinguishable from an act in which the harm is directly done or intended by the agent, then the absolute moral prohibition of directly doing evil would be meaningless.

To deny the moral significance of the distinction between directly doing and indirectly causing (or permitting) evil is un-

94

reasonable. Anyone can see how different is the personal attitude toward evil in two cases: one in which the agent chooses only good, and allows evil to happen as the unintended effect of his or her actions when there are weighty reasons for doing so; and the very different case in which one fixes the heart upon doing or achieving the evil as a means toward some end. Even God, in creating this good world, which is filled with adventures of freedom and responsibility, permitted the free evil deeds of his creatures (which he in no way directly willed to bring about). If there is no difference between permitting evil and setting one's heart on it, God must set his heart on evil. But such a conclusion is not only absurd, it is blasphemous. It is possible for persons to set their hearts only on good. Permitting evil is not choosing it. Choosing evil can never be justified; permitting evil, while obviously not always justified, can sometimes be justified.

Thus, it is not necessarily a violation of the Thomistic principle of completeness to accept bad consequences of actions. This should not be done lightly, and must be avoided whenever possible. But if the alternative to accepting bad consequences is to choose to do an immoral act, one must endure the bad consequences, for to choose to do evil is to set one's heart against what is good, and to determine oneself as a person who rejects what the love of God and neighbor requires.

Catholic teaching has always held that it is a terrible flaw in an action — and a horrible tragedy for the one who does it — to do evil directly for any reason. Even if the most precious and necessary goods could not be achieved except by doing a deed that directly does even a small evil, the good man should not do that deed. He must care to make the world good; but the most important good he is to do, the most pressing service he has, in making the world good, is to make his own heart good, by doing only good actions. If he cannot achieve goods he loves by good actions, he has no morally good way to achieve them. Yet he can rightly hope in God, if, living rightly, he does what good he can do well, and trusts God to realize the goods that he himself cannot achieve in acting well.

*Good Actions and Good Character.* Some protest against the traditional emphasis on freely chosen actions. They argue that actions alone are not the center of moral life. Character, or the basic and enduring moral orientation of the person, has a more profound significance. This has led some moral theologians to locate the basic self-determination of persons not in free choices but in a fundamental or transcendental freedom which cannot be found in any discrete choice but rather in the fundamental orientation of a person's entire life. This fundamental option, and not our free choices, is said to be what determines our basic response to God, our very moral identities, and thus our eternal destiny.[44]

This theory is correct in emphasizing that our lives can and should be organized by a fundamental commitment which shapes and orders all our life in response to God's call. It is mistaken, however, in holding that this basic commitment does not flow from the free, deliberate choices of our ordinary moral life but is rather the fruit of an allegedly profound, somewhat mysterious act at a deeper and ineffable level of freedom.

Choices are spiritual realities and not physical events like the performances that carry them out. As Pope John Paul II has made clear, our free actions have not only a transitive aspect in which an event in the world is caused but also a nontransitive aspect which remains in the human self and determines the kind of person the agent is.[45]

Free choices therefore have enduring effects and in this enduring aspect are the basis for the virtues which form the fabric of a good life. The virtuous person is fundamentally one who has made the right free choices, and has made them in such a way that his or her entire personality, desires, reactions, and beliefs are integrated around these good choices.[46] So Christian morality is not too "act-oriented" but recognizes the importance of a life of integrated and stable commitment to the Lord's work.

Still, the Church also emphasizes that the discrete choices of a person's life are the root of personal self-determination and responsibility. Human action is trivialized if we fancy that a single choice moved by grace cannot be important enough to merit salvation or tragic enough to lose it.[47] Thus, a single free choice can change the fundamental orientation of a person's life, as the Good Thief changed his fundamental option on Good Friday.

The freedom of our choices is that whereby we determine

96

ourselves; it is the locus of the "soul making" which is the center of the moral life. It is the part of our natures which perhaps most fully images the supremely free Creator of all; it is the part of us which allows us to be friends of God, not because we were in any way constrained or forced to be such but because we ourselves choose to be his friends. This freedom, however, has its burdens that make us want to hide from its full reality. We must, as the Church has always taught, use that freedom well; we must make hard choices but only good ones — choices to do actions that intelligently show that we love and cherish all that is good.

# 5

"But every person must follow his own conscience!" Christian faith holds that this statement expresses an important truth about morality.

*Conscience: Its Meaning, Formation, and Relationship to Church Authority*

This statement, unfortunately, is often misunderstood. Many take it to imply that personal conscience is the only thing a responsible person must be concerned with; in other words, that one need not be concerned with the objective principles of morality discussed in the previous chapter.

This implication is entirely unwarranted. The good person will care very much that his or her conscience guides him or her correctly to what is really good to the extent that he or she can discover it. For the upright person is concerned with doing authentically good actions, not only actions that now seem right or appear good. Such a person is concerned with knowing and doing what is truly good.

In this chapter we shall first note certain important distinctions in the uses of the word "conscience." Then we shall consider the duty to follow one's conscience. Finally, we shall treat of the principles for forming a Christian conscience, and of the relationship between the personal conscience of a Catholic and the authoritative teaching of the Church.[1]

## I. Different Meanings of the Term "Conscience"

The word "conscience" has a number of distinct but related meanings. In this section we will first consider conscience in the psychological sense — the conscience described by psychologists as related to parental norms, guilt feelings, and other nonrational factors. Second, we will analyze conscience as the moral evaluation of a particular action. Third, we will consider conscience as a personal grasp of correct moral principles and ways of thinking morally. Finally, we will consider a current account of the relation between moral principles and specific moral judgments — the theory of transcendental conscience.

*Psychological Conscience.* "Psychological conscience" is essentially related to feelings of moral approval or disapproval. Virtually everyone experiences at times — at least with respect to some important actions — either the security of some inner approval of one's decision, or the anxiety of a condemnation within the depths of one's own being. For example, a woman who had been trained from childhood to be submissive might feel that she is being immoral if she does not do just what her husband desires. This emotional self-condemnation might persist even if upon critical reflection she judges it right to behave as she does.

Guilt feelings stirred up by the inner mechanisms of psychological conscience have a great impact on one's life, and they have been widely discussed by psychiatrists. Freud's notion of the superego is one explanation of psychological conscience.[2] Conscience in this sense involves the internalization of parental and social norms and even of traditional taboos. Thus, conscience in this sense is the result of a process of psychological conditioning. The spontaneous reactions, impulses, and feelings associated with psychological conscience may, of course, be more or less healthy and realistic; they may at times be pathological.

Because conscience in this sense is shaped largely by nonrational factors, and is frequently found to condemn what is not wrong or to approve what is wrong, it cannot of itself provide decisive moral guidance. There can be no obligation to obey conscience in this sense. But psychological conscience is one of the factors that a mature and conscientious person will evaluate in the light of moral principles. A person's critical moral judgment must determine the validity of the impulses of psychological conscience.

*Particular Moral Conscience.* Sometimes "conscience" refers to one's considered judgment about the morality of a particular act. This judgment is the result of the attempt to know what is truly right, and it is this judgment that Catholic moral tradition most often calls "conscience." Conscience in this sense does not refer to feelings of approval or disapproval but to reflective moral judgment. Since the judgment of conscience is the result of the thoughtful evaluation a person makes about the moral goodness or badness of a particular action, it can be called "particular moral conscience." The judgment involved can be about an act one is considering doing (technically called *antecedent conscience*) or about an act that one has already done (*consequent conscience*).[3] In each case one is attempting to speak the moral truth about some action of one's own: "Is this particular act really a morally good act or is it an evil act?" The person responds to such questions in judgments of conscience like these: "I should not do this, because it would be wrong" or "What I did was good." It is in this sense — in the sense of a judgment about the rightness or wrongness of particular acts — that St. Thomas Aquinas and much of Catholic tradition after him use the term "conscience."[4] Conscience in this sense can be defined as one's best judgment as to what in the circumstances is the morally right thing to do.

It is important to note that since the judgment of conscience is an act of the intellect, it cannot merely be a feeling or a personal decision to act or live in a certain way. This is not to say that the affective or existential dimension is unimportant in the moral life or that the feelings of an upright and integrated person are irrelevant in making judgments of conscience.[5] The point is simply that living morally requires the conviction that given acts either are or are not truly in accord with correct moral standards. Concern for the truth is essential. Intelligent judgments, not feelings or choices, should direct the lives of mature persons.

It is precisely because the judgment of conscience is one's

100

best judgment about what one should do that a person is morally obliged to act in accord with his or her conscience.[6] We shall consider this matter more fully in our discussion of the duty to follow conscience.

*General Moral Conscience.* A person's awareness of the basic principles for making moral judgments is also often called "conscience." In this sense, conscience is one's personal awareness of the most basic moral truths.[7] It is in this sense of the term that one's conscience can be said to be an awareness of the law of God written in the human heart (Romans 2.14-16), and it is in this sense too that conscience refers to our awareness of ourselves as moral beings, summoned to seek the truth about our lives and to live them in accord with this knowledge. This dynamic thrust of our personality is called "transcendental conscience" and will be discussed below. Vatican II refers to conscience in this general sense when it affirms that conscience is that through which man "sees and recognizes the demands of the divine law" (*Dignitatis Humanae*, no. 3).

Conscience in this sense grasps the norms that will guide one in evaluating particular actions. Thus, it is by this general conscience that a person knows that one should do good and avoid evil; that one should aim at harming no one; that one should love God and neighbor; and that one must never do deeds that are of their nature base, that always attack basic goods in ourselves or other persons.[8] Conscience likewise knows that the Ten Commandments follow from these basic principles and must be understood in the bracing way that faith has understood them.[9] The mature and responsible person grasps also, in intelligent conscientious reflection, more detailed moral precepts that can be seen to be true from a right understanding of basic moral principles and of the Ten Commandments. Thus, typical adult Catholics grasp personally not only the broad truth that killing innocent people is wrong but also the more specific truths that abortion and suicide are always wrong.

In a famous paragraph of the *Pastoral Constitution on the Church in the Modern World*, the Fathers of Vatican II stated the importance of conscience in the sense we are now discussing. They also make reference to the particular judgment of conscience and show its connection with our awareness of the moral law and of ourselves as moral subjects impelled to seek the truth. The Council Fathers say:

> Deep within his conscience man discovers a law which he has not laid upon himself but which he must obey. Its voice [that is, the voice of this law],[10] ever calling him to love and to do what is good and to avoid evil, tells him inwardly at the right moment: do this, shun that. For man has in his heart a law inscribed by God. His dignity lies in observing this law, and by it he will be judged. His conscience is man's most secret core, and his sanctuary. There he is alone with God whose voice echoes in his depths. By conscience, in a wonderful way, that law is made known which is fulfilled in the love of God and of one's neighbor. . . . Hence, the more a correct conscience prevails, the more do persons and groups turn aside from blind choice and try to be guided by the objective standards of moral conduct. Yet it often happens that conscience goes astray through ignorance which it is unable to avoid, without thereby losing its dignity. This cannot be said of the man who takes little trouble to find out what is true and good, or when conscience is by degrees almost blinded through the habit of committing sin.[11]

This statement by the Council sums up many of the points we have been considering. First, conscience involves an awareness of something objective and truly good — a law which man does not give himself but discovers. Second, moral conscience, in the sense of man's best judgment about what he is to do, must be obeyed — even when it is mistaken. Man will be judged according to the law which conscience knows, and the very dignity of man consists in submitting to this law, that is, in doing what he perceives to be good. Third, the invincible ignorance which causes the conscience of an upright person to err is firmly distinguished from the ignorance of one who does not sufficiently care about finding the truth concerning what is right, and from the blindness of one whose conscience is dulled by habitual sin.

Conscience, understood in this sense, presents us with an objective standard of morality. We have a duty to obey this standard precisely because we perceive in the light of faith and of natural intelligence that it is directing us toward what is authentically good. It is, of course, possible for us to be ignorant of at least some part of this standard, or to make use of it in inadequate ways. But we cannot escape responsibility for these shortcomings if we are not serious about discovering what is truly right.

*Transcendental Conscience.* The morally mature person recognizes that feelings and social conventions do not determine what is morally right and morally wrong. We know that our own moral feelings can be misguided and that societies can be more or less corrupt, and at times incline us to approve what no truly good person should approve. The morally serious person is convinced that questions of right and wrong cannot be settled arbitrarily but need to be determined in accordance with the truth. Precisely because of this realization that moral conscience in its authentic sense is concerned with moral truth, some contemporary theologians have developed an account of moral awareness which they call "transcendental conscience." One of the leading proponents of this theological view, Walter E. Conn, has suggested that conscience can best be considered as "the dynamic thrust toward self-transcendence at the core of a person's very subjectivity, revealing itself . . . as a demand for responsible decision in accord with reasonable judgment."[12] Summarizing the work of developmental psychologists such as Erik Erikson, Jean Piaget, and Lawrence Kohlberg, and relying heavily on the philosophical and theological studies of Bernard Lonergan, Conn properly rejects any normative significance to conscience understood in a merely psychological sense. In his opinion, the term "conscience" refers basically to the *whole person* as a moral self, as a being inwardly impelled to act responsibly in accordance with the truth.

Conn and theologians like him are surely correct in emphasizing that conscience, in its moral sense, is intimately linked to our quest for truth. Human persons are unique in that they are question-asking beings, anxious to discover the truth not only about the physical world in which they live but even more the truth about what they are to do if they are to become fully the beings they are meant to be. In her teaching, the Church clearly recognizes this unique characteristic of human existence.

103

More significantly, she explicitly uses the term "conscience" in speaking of the human person's inner drive to discover the truth about human action and being. In a remarkable passage in Vatican Council II's *Declaration on Religious Liberty*, the Council Fathers first note that "the highest norm of human life is the divine law itself — eternal, objective, and universal, by which God orders, directs, and governs the whole world and the ways of the human community." Then they continue by saying:

> God has enabled man to participate in this law of his so that, under the gentle disposition of divine providence, man may be able to arrive at a deeper and deeper knowledge of unchangeable truth. . . . It is through his conscience that man sees and recognizes the demands of the divine law (*Dignitatis Humanae*, no. 3).[13]

Thus, there are grounds for saying that conscience refers to the inner dynamism of the human person impelling the individual to discover the truth about what is to be done and what he or she is to be. Conscience is therefore "a special and very fundamental mode of self-awareness — the awareness of 'how it is with oneself.' "[14] But conscience does more than reveal the gap between what we are and what we ought to become. It is also a summons to realize our full humanity.[15]

The vision supporting this understanding of conscience seems to be behind Pope Pius XII's metaphorical description of conscience as the "inner core and sanctuary of a man, where he is alone with God,"[16] a description which the Second Vatican Council made its own.[17]

The theory of transcendental conscience focuses on several essential aspects of general moral conscience. Despite this, however, the theory of transcendental conscience, as proposed by Conn and others, does not adequately explain the whole of moral awareness. The fundamental weakness in Conn's position is this: it misrepresents the relation between the particular judgment of conscience and the knowledge of basic moral principles. An uncritical acceptance of certain popular philosophical assumptions leads the proponents of this theory to suppose that the natural awareness of morality does not contain any principles having definite implications. Conn argues that the judgment of conscience, while it is not arbitrary, cannot be derived in an objective way from the general principles of conscience.[18] Instead, he argues that authentic moral living "is determined neither by absolute principles nor by arbitrary creativity relative to each situation: authentic living, rather, is defined by a normative structure of consciousness which demands that a person respond to the values in each situation with creativity that is at once sensitive, critical, responsible, and loving."[19]

No one, of course, would advocate responding to moral situations in ways that are insensitive, uncritical, irresponsible, or unloving. But the question concerns the *criteria*, or *norms*, whereby one can know whether one's response is critical, responsible, sensitive, and loving. And Conn's position seems to make conscience itself the norm. It makes conscience altogether autonomous and beyond criticism, because in rejecting the proper role of principles it makes conscience an almost mystical and unanalyzable component of the person. However, one may acknowledge the dynamic thrust of basic moral awareness and yet hold that the basic structures of moral consciousness grasp principles of the sort the Church has held all along to be the basis of moral judgment. Unless there are such principles, it is hard to see how the "dynamic thrust toward self-transcendence" could be determined to be a movement toward authentic self-transcendence, for without critical principles it could become a dynamism toward self-destruction or self-deception.

Moreover, if there is no definite connection between the basic demands of being fully human and particular actions, it is hard to see how one of the basic facts of moral experience can be explained, for the phenomenon of moral evil is essentially one in which one is aware that one is choosing contrary to the concrete implications of the moral law. If the moral law has no definite implications, and all we have to guide our choices is the dynamic thrust of consciousness, it is difficult to grasp any intelligent patterns whatsoever in the workings of conscience.[20]

## II. The Duty to Follow One's Conscience

As we have already seen, a person has the moral duty to act in accordance with his or her own judgment of conscience, precisely because the judgment of conscience is the final judgment that a person makes about the moral goodness or badness of his

105

or her actions. Surely a good person must do what he or she decisively judges he or she truly should do. Nonetheless, since the obligation to follow one's conscience is so frequently misunderstood, it will be of value to extend our discussion of this important topic.

Even if one thinks that one would suffer great losses, or fail to gain important goods if one should follow the demands of conscience, one's duty is to act as one has conscientiously judged one must act. Even if the most august authorities, political or religious, should command one to act in a way that conscience — understood as one's firm and honest moral judgment — forbids, then such authorities should not be obeyed. This evident truth, one clearly affirmed by Catholic theological tradition and by the teaching authority of the Church,[21] must however be clearly distinguished from the question whether one who is *inclined* to make a particular moral judgment of conscience ought not be prepared to change it if any authoritative teaching of Christ or his Church begins to make one aware that one's own former opinion was incorrect.

It is important to recognize that the duty to follow one's conscience is intelligible only when conscience is understood in the sense of a *judgment of conscience* — the best judgment one can make about the truly good thing to do in the circumstances. Merely psychological conscience can generate no such duty.

It is, moreover, important to recognize that a person's judgment of conscience can be more or less mistaken. Any judgment is the result of a person's attempt to discover the truth. Such attempts can fail, especially when one attempts to discover the truth about complex matters. Of course, this is not to say that our attempts to discover the truth about particular moral matters always fail; we are often justifiably certain that we have succeeded.[22]

Our judgments of conscience are not therefore *infallible*.[23] One might perhaps be inclined to think of one's judgment of conscience as infallible if one thought of conscience as a kind of "moral sense" which grasps or intuits the moral qualities of acts, except that this intuitionistic view of conscience is not defensible. It is inconsistent with the common experience of the complexity of the process leading to the judgment of conscience,

106

and with the awareness each of us has of noting and correcting mistakes in the formation of his or her conscience. Clearly, it conflicts with the approach to moral thinking taken by the greatest Catholic teachers and endorsed by the magisterium.[24] Moreover, the moral qualities of acts are not like the observable features of physical things and events: the rightness or wrongness of a particular act is not an observable feature of the act in the way that the size of this page is an observable feature of this page, and cannot be as simply observed as such features can be.

Thus, one's judgment of conscience can be mistaken. However, this does not change the fact that a person is obliged to follow his or her final judgment of conscience, for in such a case one honestly believes that a certain course of action is morally required, and to refuse to act in accord with one's judgment in such a case would be to refuse to act in the way one personally believes to be morally required.[25] The morally upright person will, of course, earnestly seek to see to it that his or her judgments of conscience are true. Such a person will seek to ground his or her judgments of conscience upon a solid basis of moral principles understood in the light of faith. Moreover, such a person will, when unable to reach secure answers personally, seek counsel from those he knows to be trustworthy and wise guides to good moral life.

If a person does not make efforts of this kind, he or she bears the responsibility for his or her mistaken judgments of conscience. The mistake in such a person's judgment is attributable to his or her own neglect. At times this mistake may be attributable to previous bad choices that an individual has made. Such sinful choices, as Vatican Council II reminds us in the passage cited previously, can frequently "blind" conscience, and the blindness in question is voluntary, at least in its cause. Thus, a seriously convinced — even "sincere" — racist is not innocent if his racist sentiments and judgments are the result either of his own negligence in seeking the truth about this matter, or of his deliberate choices not to discover this truth.[26]

Thus, the duty to follow one's conscience means that we have an obligation to act in accordance with our own best judgment of what is right in the circumstances. This obligation also requires that in arriving at this judgment, we have struggled to discover the truth, that we have sought to inform our conscience. As the American bishops put the matter in their pastoral letter on the moral life:

> We must have a rightly informed conscience and follow it.
>
> But our judgments are human and can be mistaken; we may be blinded by the power of sin in our lives or misled by the strength of our desires. "Beloved, do not trust every spirit, but put the spirits to a test to see if they belong to God" [1 John 4.1].
>
> Clearly, then, we must do everything in our power to see to it that our judgments of conscience are informed and in accord with the moral order of which God is creator. Common sense requires that conscientious people be open and humble, ready to learn from the experience and insight of others, willing to acknowledge prejudices and even change their judgments in light of better instruction.[27]

Thus, we shall now turn to consider the question of informing a Catholic conscience.

### III. The Formation of a Catholic Conscience

As noted earlier, the goal of the judgment of conscience is to arrive at a knowledge of what truly is to be done in the concrete. An essential basis for this judgment is each person's awareness of the general principles of the moral law, already discussed above (under the heading of "General Moral Conscience," page 101). These general principles, however, need to be specified and applied to the concrete circumstances of a person's life. While some applications are relatively easy, others are very complex. If one realizes that every direct killing of an innocent person is wrong, and if a given act is readily seen to be an instance of directly killing an innocent person, then it is clear that this act is wrong. But there are cases in which it is very difficult to tell whether the killing is direct or the person innocent in the relevant sense. Moreover, many moral norms are nonabsolute. For example, there are times when the rule that just civil laws are to be obeyed does not apply. Thus, guidance for the concrete choices which make up a person's life does not follow simply from general moral principles.[28]

Forming one's conscience therefore involves two types of

108

activity. First, one must grasp the implications of the basic principles of morality; second, sensitive to all the significant features of one's situation, one must learn how to apply these norms so as to form reasonable judgments of conscience.

Every person must use thoughtful intelligence in making such judgments. The Catholic, knowing that one of the central purposes of revelation is to assist him or her in seeing how to live wisely, will accept what Christ teaches through his Church.

> However, in forming their consciences the faithful must pay careful attention to the sacred and certain teaching of the Church. For the Catholic Church is by the will of Christ the teacher of truth. It is her duty to proclaim and teach with authority the truth which is Christ and, at the same time, to declare and confirm by her authority the principles of the moral order which spring from human nature itself.[29]

Thus, God's revelation in Scripture and Christian tradition as explained and articulated in the teaching of the Church, together with the expression of this teaching in the example of the saints, and the struggles of our ancestors in faith, as well as the Catholic's natural insight into morality — all these together provide the Catholic with reliable guides to form his or her conscience.

Moreover, in making use of these various elements by which God reveals his plan, the Catholic will treat them as forming an integral whole. Such a person will read Scripture *as a Catholic* and will understand the demands of his or her natural insight into moral issues in light of the whole of revelation and the Church's actual living of the faith.

These sources are not regarded by the Catholic as extrinsic sources of information or as external constraints upon his or her conscience. The revelation of Jesus is accepted by an intelligent and mature believer as the fundamental framework in which he or she organizes his or her life and understands his or her existence.

The moral law is not an alien law. For each person, it expresses the demands of his or her own humanity. The divine law is not an extrinsic and foreign ordinance.[30] Rather, it presents the moral requirements of the Gospel to which the believer is freely and gladly committed. In other words, the divine law presents requirements that lie at the heart of a believer's inner life.

Cardinal Newman, in his famous *Letter to the Duke of Norfolk*, points out how precious is the service of the Church in clarifying for us the bracing law of God:

> The sense of right and wrong, which is the first element in religion, is so delicate, so fitful, so easily puzzled, obscured, perverted, so subtle in its argumentative methods, so impressible by education, so biased by pride and passion, so unsteady in its course, that, in the struggle for existence amid the various exercises and triumphs of the human intellect, this sense is at once the highest of all teachers, yet the least luminous; *and the Church, the Pope, the hierarchy are, in the divine purpose, the supply of an urgent demand.*[31] (Emphasis added.)

Thus, the appropriation of these sources by Catholics seeking to form their consciences is a development of their initial Catholic commitment. If one is to be a Catholic, one cannot form one's conscience in any other way. The bishops of Ireland observed: "It is impossible to separate allegiance to Christ from obedience to the teaching Church. One cannot be His disciple while disregarding those to whom He has given a share in proclaiming and teaching His Gospel."[32]

## IV. The Relationship Between Catholic Conscience and Catholic Teaching

The well-formed Catholic conscience, as we have just seen, draws light from the Scriptures and Christian tradition as these are understood and proclaimed by the magisterium and witnessed by the lives of good Christian people. It is thus unlikely that faithful Catholics will discover any serious conflict between the teaching of the Church and their particular judgments of conscience or their general approach toward making such judgments.

Furthermore, if a Catholic finds a measure of conflict between some of his or her convictions and the teaching of the Church, this conflict will be *within* that person's conscience, and not a conflict between the person's conscience and an alien au-

110

thority. This is true because the teachings of the Church — as far as the believing Catholic is concerned — are teachings of a faith he or she has freely accepted and made his or her own. They enter into the formation of the believing Catholic's conscience.

But if this is so, how can we explain why many Catholics today — according to various surveys — have accepted moral views, particularly regarding matters of sexual morality, that contradict Church teaching? Several factors are relevant. The Church's teaching on contraception, for example, has not been effectively presented by many priests and theologians in recent years. Moved by the pressures of the world, it is easy for people to cease believing what is not earnestly preached. Moreover, while many Catholics realize that the Church *officially prohibits* contraception and other disordered sexual activities, still those same Catholics may not perceive that the Church firmly *teaches* in the name of Christ that such conduct is immoral. Some, indeed, may have been induced to think that "official" proscriptions of the magisterium are not Church teachings in the strict sense. They are said to lag behind the "real" mind of the Church, which is allegedly found in the experience of select members of the faithful, especially that of those Catholics who have rejected insistent teachings of the magisterium.[33]

Before examining these confusing situations, it is important to note the essential freedom and autonomy of the mature Catholic. He or she draws light from faith, but this does not mean blind acceptance of the judgments of Church leaders. There are many pronouncements by pastors, theologians, and even by bishops, that are merely private opinions which a conscientious Catholic might, after sufficient reflection, appropriately set aside.

Moreover, the precepts of the moral law taught by faith are always in some measure general precepts which can be applied in the concrete circumstances of life only through the conscientious deliberation of the individual person. Often this deliberation will have a creative element which cannot be anticipated in general precepts. While this personal deliberation is sometimes simple, the necessary reflection is at times much more difficult. For example, most people have a number of positive duties —

to work at one's profession, to say one's prayers, to teach one's children, and so on. In many instances one must judge which duty one is to act on now, if many real duties seem to require attention at the same time. The individual himself or herself must make the judgment in such cases.[34]

In cases such as these the individual's judgment of conscience cannot be deduced from the general norms taught by the Church. One must learn prudence to guide one's life; no simple rules given by authority can substitute for this practical thinking. But there is no genuine *conflict* here between such a person's conscience and the teaching of the Church.

Conflict between personal conscience and Church teaching arises only when a person judges in a way he or she knows to be contrary to the firm teaching of the Church. When conflict arises, the person faces a difficult choice: either follow the Church's teaching, which, when it has been personally appropriated, becomes a living factor within that person's conscience, or reject that teaching — that part of one's own conscience — in favor of the personal judgment that opposes it. In the next section we will consider how it is reasonable for a Catholic to resolve such conflicts.

## V. May Personal Judgment Be Preferred to the Teaching of the Church?

There has been much talk in recent years of the problem of conflicts between personal conscience and the teaching of the Church. Great care must be taken to state this problem precisely. For one who has Catholic faith, who has acquired a happy, personal certainty that the Lord teaches and guides us in the teaching of the Church, the insistent message of Catholic faith is not something alien to conscience. Thus, one does not first form one's conscientious judgment, and then compare that with the teaching of the Church, and finally make another judgment about what to do. Church teaching is there from the beginning in the formation of conscience.

The difficulty arises concretely in something like the following scenario: A couple is faced with a decision about family planning and considers contraception as a possibility. The spouses become aware that the Church teaches that contraception is always gravely wrong, but they also become aware that many people do not believe this — including Catholics. They know that some people argue against the Church's teaching, and make the case that the use of contraception can be responsible, liberating, and even enriching. The question really facing such a couple is a decision about how the two of them should form their consciences: should they form their conscience in accord with insistent Church teaching? Or should they shape it in the light of opinions they might favor, or might find persuasive, even though they contradict the teaching of the Church? The question therefore is not simply whether one may follow conscience when it contradicts Catholic teaching — it is the more fundamental question of how one is to form one's conscience. Should conscience be shaped by Church teaching, or by opinions contrary to this teaching?

Before 1960 there was unanimity among Catholic theologians and pastors on this point. It was common teaching that one who has the gift of faith must form his or her conscience in the light of faith's teachings. Since such faith is known by the believer to be true and to guide us toward what is really good, it would be unreasonable, foolish, and wrong for one to live in ways contrary to the teachings of the Church. It would be contrary to one's deepest interests to do so. Vatican II, expressing the received teaching of the Church on this matter, tells us:

> Bishops who teach in communion with the Roman Pontiff are to be revered by all as witnesses of divine and Catholic truth; the faithful, for their part, are obliged to submit to their bishops' decision, made in the name of Christ, in matters of faith and morals, and to adhere to it with a ready and respectful allegiance of mind. This loyal submission of the will and intellect must be given, in a special way, to the authentic teaching authority of the Roman Pontiff, even when he does not speak *ex cathedra* in such wise, indeed, that his supreme teaching authority be acknowledged with respect, and sincere assent be given to decisions made by him, conformably with his manifest mind and intention (*Lumen Gentium*, no. 25).

Moreover, the Council made it clear by the way it taught that the moral teaching of the Church includes not only very

113

general principles but also specific moral norms. For example, its own teachings on sinful forms of family planning, and on crimes against human life such as abortion, euthanasia, and genocide are stated in specific and categorical terms which are unmistakably intended to guide consciences and are proposed in the name of Christ.[35]

There can be times, of course, when the Catholic is strongly inclined to form his or her conscience in accord with principles which would be much more convenient than the teachings of the Church, or which would accord with philosophies in some way alien to Catholic belief. When tempted to consider whether it might be permissible to commit adultery in some circumstances, one might very much want to use the principle that adultery can be justified when there are good enough reasons, and might be inclined to think that in the situation those reasons were present. The question, however, is not whether such situations arise but whether it can ever be justified to adopt principles of the kind mentioned. The American bishops, following Vatican II, answer this question negatively, and provide the basic reason which faith always has held:

> The Holy Father and the bishops in communion with him have been anointed by the Holy Spirit to be the official and authentic teachers of Christian life. For Jesus "established His holy Church by sending forth the apostles as He Himself had been sent by the Father" (cf. Jn. 20:21). He willed that their successors, namely the bishops, should be shepherds in His Church "even to the consummation of the world" [*Lumen Gentium*, no. 18]. It is their office and duty to express the teaching of Christ on moral questions and matters of belief. This special teaching office within the Catholic Church is a gift of the Lord Jesus for the benefit of all His followers in their efforts to know what He teaches, value as He values, and live as free, responsible, loving, and holy persons. As Christ says, "He who hears you, hears Me" [Luke 10.16]. The authoritative moral teachings of the Church enlighten personal conscience and are to be regarded as certain and binding norms of morality.[36]

In the face of this clear teaching of the Church, a number of contemporary theologians have argued that in the formation of

114

conscience it is permissible to follow personal opinions that contradict the teaching of the Church. Most of these have been developed by theologians who reject the firm teaching of the Church on various questions in sexual ethics.

In support of their position, these revisionist thinkers advance the following arguments. (1) The Church has in fact never infallibly proposed any specific moral norm. (2) It is, in fact, beyond the competency of the Church to teach infallibly on specific moral issues. (3) The authoritative but noninfallible teachings of the Church may be mistaken, and so Catholics have the right to reject them when they are conscientiously convinced that the teachings are wrong.

*Infallible Teaching and Specific Moral Norms.* Those who encourage dissent from the Church's insistent moral teaching ordinarily suppose that they are urging changes in the noninfallible teaching of the Church. In arguing that some acts of contraception or adultery are permissible, they recognize that the Church has taught acts of those kinds to be seriously wrong, but they take it for granted that this teaching is not infallible. Frequently, they point out that it has not been the practice of the Church to make solemn definitions about specific moral points, and it is true that the great body of Catholic moral teaching has not been solemnly defined.[37]

However, as Vatican II has pointed out, there is a form of infallible teaching distinct from proclaiming solemn definitions. The bishops of the Church teach infallibly when they teach authoritatively in matters of faith and morals; "they are in agreement that a particular teaching is to be held definitively and absolutely," even though they are "dispersed throughout the world but preserving . . . amongst themselves and with Peter's successor the bond of communion" (*Lumen Gentium*, no. 25).

Clearly, it is one of the chief duties of the Church to teach the faithful "how they are to live and please God" (1 Thessalonians 4.1). The Church's teaching on basic issues in sexual ethics in her ordinary magisterium has been most firm over the centuries. The Church has regularly insisted that her teaching about divorce, contraception, fornication, and the like is not a mere teaching of men but a teaching of the Lord himself.[38] With virtual unanimity the teachers of the Church have held and handed

115

on the received teachings on sexual morality, and have presented them as unconditional requirements of salvation. When the Church teaches with such firmness and unanimity in the name of the Lord, it seems inescapable that she is exercising the infallibility of the ordinary magisterium as delineated by Vatican II.

For this reason, highly respected theologians have argued at length that the Church's ordinary magisterium concerning contraception meets these conditions for infallible teaching spelled out by Vatican II.[39] Hence, as we shall see more fully in Chapter 7, the Church's teaching on the immorality of contraception is in all likelihood infallible. And the arguments used by these theologians would seem to apply to other teachings of the Church on sexual matters, for the bishops of the Church have taught with equal firmness, with the same kind of unanimity over centuries, and as teachers who hand on what Christ requires for salvation, when they have taught on topics like adultery, masturbation, and so on.

A few theologians respond that the Church is simply not competent to teach infallibly about the morality of specific kinds of action. They would admit that the Church could infallibly teach general principles of morality, such as that people must love one another, or that the faithful must put fidelity to the Gospel before worldly success. But they insist that the Church cannot infallibly teach such specific norms as adultery is always wrong or one must never directly kill the innocent.[40]

The arguments for this position are surprisingly weak. They rely too much on the supposed authority of a relatively small group of dissenting scholars, and on assumptions about moral teaching that presuppose proportionalism. The main argument is that it is impossible for a universally stated Church teaching to take into account all the details needed for a judgment that adultery or contraception is always wrong. If proportionalism were a correct way of understanding moral thinking, then it would be impossible for the Church to absolutely exclude certain kinds of acts as immoral. If a particular act of adultery could be upright when the good effects of doing it in its concrete circumstances outweighed the bad consequences, then the Church would have to look into all the details of every conceivable act of adultery before she could reasonably teach that every act of adultery is seriously wrong. But the Church does not suppose that the mistaken theory of proportionalism is correct, and then proceed to teach only those things which proportionalism can justify. She teaches instead, and has always taught, that there are moral absolutes. Some acts, just by being the human acts they are, are disordered; they cannot be acts of intelligent and faithful love.[41]

Serious reflection on the history of the Church's moral teaching shows that her most firm and insistent moral teachings have been concerned with the specific moral issues about which the dissenting theologians think decisive teaching is impossible. If anything is characteristic of the whole tradition of Catholic moral teaching, it is the constant and insistent proclamation that certain kinds of acts — adultery, contraception, abortion, direct killing of the innocent, and so on — are always seriously wrong. Her teaching on the broad moral principles which justify specific norms has often been less insistent and precise. Scholars have been allowed great discretion in explaining how specific norms follow from the basic principles of love, and why they are always binding. But these variations in theological reasoning have always been carried out within the conviction of the Church that the moral absolutes always proclaimed are true.

If there are more general principles that have been insistently taught by the Church, none has been more firmly taught than this: that one must never do evil that good might come of it (cf. Romans 3.8). This principle is appealed to again and again as part of the defense of moral absolutes. It is the reason why moral absolutes may not be set aside when the consequences of following them are very difficult to accept. In other words, it is the basis for rejecting the proportionalism which denies the competency of the Church to teach infallibly on specific moral questions.

Another reason given to support the claim that the Church cannot teach infallibly on specific moral questions is that such teachings cannot have the clear connection with divine revelation that is required for infallible teaching.[42] But there are two major flaws in this claim. First, this claim supposes that no specific choice can be essential for salvation. However, the Church,

117

reading Scripture in the light of Christian tradition and with the aid of the Holy Spirit, judges that specific choices are essential to Christian life. In particular, the Church holds that some specific choices fail to show the love the Gospel requires in such a way that they exclude from membership in the community of divine love those who make the choices and refuse to repent. Even if there is no independent argument to show how and why such choices must separate one from the love of God, it cannot be denied that the Church has held that they do.

The second flaw in this position is suggested by the first, for the position supposes that unless one can demonstrate how and why a given teaching is related to divine revelation, one is not justified in thinking that it is. The fact that the Church presents it as such is not taken as decisive evidence that a teaching is essentially related to revelation; independent theological explanation of the connection is necessary. This assumption is rationalistic in a way that is contrary to the actual practice of the Church. When there is some dispute about whether something is of revelation — for example, whether Jesus is consubstantial with the Father — the Church does not seek to settle the question by consulting scholarly opinion. In fact, in such disputes there is often a lack of scholarly consensus, and even a body of scholarly opinion favoring the view that the teaching in question is not essentially related to revelation. To settle such questions the Church must rely on the exercise of the teaching office of the pope and bishops. Their determination settles whether or not a point of Christian teaching is essentially connected with revelation. The task of the theologians is to articulate this connection, to help us understand it, and not to determine whether or not it exists.[43]

In short, it would not be responsible to assume that the Church's most firm teaching about specific moral matters is not infallibly proposed by the Church's ordinary magisterium.

*Dissent From Authoritative Teaching.* The focus of theological dissent in the last twenty years has been on the authoritative moral teaching of the Church. In spite of the fact that in recent years competent theologians have made a powerful case that the teachings rejected are for the most part infallibly proposed, most dissenters have not even considered the possibility that what they reject might be infallible. This possibility completely changes the contour of the debate about the status of the Church's received teachings on sexual matters. Clearly, it deserves continuing, careful study. Another question, however, must also be considered, namely whether the dissenters are correct in thinking that dissent from authoritative but noninfallible teaching is justified.

Until the disputes of the last twenty years, all theologians acknowledged that the authoritative judgments of the Holy See in moral matters were practically decisive. Even when its teachings were not infallibly proposed, they were taken to be binding on the consciences of the faithful, who were required to give them internal religious assent. Not surprisingly, such teachings were not lightly made. They were understood as the teachings of Christ, proclaimed by his vicar, the pope, for the sake of guarding the whole Church from serious moral harm.

But in recent decades some theologians have formulated arguments to justify both doctrinal dissent from authoritative teaching and practical dissent which allows formation of conscience in ways contrary to this teaching. We will consider briefly three of the central arguments for the position that such rejection of authoritative Church teaching is justifiable.

The first argument asserts boldly: "It is the common teaching of the Church that Catholics may dissent from authoritative, noninfallible teachings of the magisterium when sufficient reasons for doing so exist."[44] However, this assertion finds no justification within Church teaching or widely accepted theological opinion other than the recent opinions of those very theologians who wish to justify their own dissent from received teaching. Appeal is often made to the teaching of the "approved authors," and, in particular, of the approved authors who wrote on the binding force of authentic teaching in the years prior to Vatican II. During the Council a discussion of the binding character of noninfallibly proposed teachings took place. It was part of the discussion leading to the articulation of *Lumen Gentium*, no. 25. Conciliar officials referred to the teachings of the approved authors as normative in this matter. But when we examine the writings of these approved authors,[45] we find that they do not speak of a *right to dissent*, or of a right to guide con-

119

sciences in ways opposed to authentic teaching. To be sure, they do argue that one might justifiably *withhold assent* provisionally from noninfallibly proposed teaching under certain stringently defined conditions. But withholding a positive act of assent provisionally, while continuing to study the matter with a willingness to accept magisterial teachings on the issues in question, is very different from dissenting actively from these teachings.[46]

The second argument given to justify dissent from authoritative but noninfallible Church teaching was that the "atmosphere," or "spirit," of Vatican II made such great changes in the Church that dissent could now be justified. This claim, however, has proved impossible to sustain in the face of what Vatican II actually says — namely that the faithful are to assent "with a ready and respectful allegiance of the mind" to the authoritative teaching of the Church even when it is not proposed infallibly.[47] Admitting that the explicit teaching of the conciliar documents—in particular, of *Lumen Gentium*, no. 25—forbids dissent, some argue that this conciliar teaching represented "a very dated and very discussable notion of the Church's teaching office."[48] That is, matters have changed since Vatican II spoke. But since the Council, the magisterium has continued to teach that one may not dissent from authentic teaching. Thus, the teaching of the Church on this question remains what was proclaimed at the Council, what has always been held within the Church: the faithful are expected to give internal assent to authoritatively proclaimed teachings in faith and morals.[49]

A third line of reasoning to justify dissent from noninfallible but authoritative Church teaching is that good sense and integrity permit such dissent. This line of reasoning seems to underlie much of the theological dissent of recent years, although explicit arguments for it are not well developed. Noninfallible teachings, it is argued, are fallible — that is, they can be mistaken. Hence, it would be foolish and wrong to demand conformity to them from intelligent people who are reasonably convinced by arguments for contrary positions.

This familiar argument is remarkably weak, if evaluated in the light of faith. In matters which touch salvation it is essential that the faithful be able to walk in secure ways. Faith knows that there is no more secure way of discovering how we are to

120

live and to please God than by attending to what the Church has constantly taught. This is not to say that there are not reasons that many find plausible for accepting opinions contrary to constant and insistent Church teaching. Those who defend the permissibility of some acts of fornication or some homosexual acts can give reasons for these positions that many people find persuasive. But it would surely be an exaggeration to pretend that such arguments give to anyone a real certainty that the enduring teachings of the Church, which also have strong rational defenses, are mistaken.

The conviction that the Church's teachings on moral matters are mistaken is not based on irrefutable rational arguments. This conviction has a number of sources. It can be based on the appeal of persuasive but far from infallible forms of secular thinking, on cultural and social pressures, and on an uncertain hope that life might be happier if Church teaching were set aside. None of these or similar sources provide a reliable basis for rejecting Church teaching. Thus, the requirement that one follow the Church's teaching does not involve a demand that a person violate what his or her own intelligence has discovered. The grounds for rejecting Church teaching are far more fallible than the reasons a believer has for accepting this teaching.

Even if the teaching of the Church on a given point is not infallibly proposed, it is presented in a way that makes it a far more reliable guide than any other a Catholic might have. Moral debates, in areas in which persons have an emotional stake, are notoriously difficult. Where faith does not give guidance, we see astonishing and virtually irreconcilable differences on even the most basic moral issues. Those who believe that Christ the Lord remains always with his Church, teaching and guiding through those he authorizes to speak in his name, have far better reasons for accepting the teaching of the Church than they could ever have for accepting the novel and dubious arguments whose persuasive power is largely based on the insecure prejudices of a secular culture.

We pointed out earlier that a person has an obligation to follow his or her conscience, even though a person's conscience is not infallible. The reason is that a rightly formed conscience provides the best, though still imperfect, guide for action that a person can have. The role of the authoritative but noninfallible teachings of the Church in the formation of conscience is analogous. This teaching is not infallible, but it is the best guidance a person could have. To set it aside in favor of more pleasing but less sure guides is irresponsible; it is a failure to form one's conscience in the way most likely to lead to judgments that are true.

Many fail to formulate the issue this way because they suppose the Church teaching on moral issues is not a matter of Christ's truth but rather of policies, decisions, or rules laid down by ecclesiastical leaders. This misunderstanding of the Church's teaching is a form of legalism. The Church's moral teaching is not simply a set of rules adopted by men. It is teaching based on prayerful and thoughtful reflection of the whole Church on the moral guidance found in divine revelation. It is proclaimed by those who have a duty to hand on and guard what God entrusted to the Church for the salvation of mankind; and it is teaching guided and protected by the Spirit Jesus promised to his Church. Thus, even when the teaching in question is not infallibly proposed, it should be thought of in terms of truth — not simply in terms of decisions which are more or less sensible. In these terms, the authoritative teaching of the Church makes a powerful, rational claim on the loyalty of believers, for this teaching is most likely to be true.

This is so not only with respect to teachings that have been so insistently taught over the centuries that they are probably infallible but also with respect to relatively new Church teaching. For example, the Church's authentic teaching on the matter of test-tube reproduction is that such procedures are prohibited.[50] Although this teaching has not been so clearly proposed by all the bishops of the world that it meets the conditions for infallible teaching by the ordinary magisterium, it is quite possible that it will be so taught in the future.[51] But even now the grounds the believer has for assenting to this teaching are far more secure than any he or she could have for assenting to arguments based on personal longings, cultural pressures, or ethical arguments notably different from those the Church has always held.

*Other Arguments to Justify Rejecting Authentic Church*

*Teaching*. The two general positions just considered — the claim that Church teaching on specific moral questions is never infallible, and that dissent from noninfallible teaching is legitimate — are the basic reasons given for preferring personal judgment to Church teaching. There are, however, other arguments for this conclusion which are often used in conjunction with the two central arguments. We will consider four such arguments briefly.

The first of these is based on the claim that the Church's traditional teaching on questions on sexual ethics is "physicalist" or "biologistic." The objection is that the natural-law theory on which traditional teaching is based left "moral man at the mercy of his biology. He had no choice but to conform to the rhythms of his physical nature and to accept its determinations obediently."[52] That is, the arguments for many of the Church's moral teachings proceed according to the following faulty pattern: since nature tends to act in this way, men have a duty to act in this way (that is, according to the way nature acts). While it can be admitted that some of the theological arguments used in the past to show that certain types of actions were immoral were poor,[53] this does not of itself show that the *conclusions* to which those arguments led were false, for a Catholic is to give assent to Church teachings, not because of the philosophical-theological arguments scholars in any age use to support this teaching but because this teaching is proposed by those who have been divinely appointed as the authentic interpreters of the "Word of God, whether in its written form or in the form of Tradition" (*Dei Verbum*, no. 10).

Moreover, it is by no means the case that all who have developed arguments for the Church's received teaching have employed some form of objectionable physicalism. The writings on sexual morality by the present pope, which are used throughout this book, are clearly not physicalistic; they articulate a form of Christian personalism. The arguments of St. Thomas Aquinas, often strangely taken as the paradigm of physicalism by opponents of traditional teaching, do not follow the flawed logic of physicalism, for the main concern in these arguments is not the physical structure of acts as such but their finality, and the way they relate to the human goods at stake. For example, dis-

123

ordered sexual behavior is called unnatural because one engaging in such acts is unreasonably choosing in a way that harms or ignores the human good of procreation.

The second of the arguments for rejecting Church teaching in the formation of conscience is that the dignity of conscience requires it.[54] Of course, one morally ought to do what one finally judges to be right. It is also true that governments and other institutions having coercive power should not use this power to force people to act in ways opposed to their conscience. It is this obligation to respect individual conscience — especially in religious matters — which the *Declaration on Religious Liberty* of Vatican Council II articulates so forcefully.

Neither of these truths is, however, relevant to the justification of a Catholic's preferring his or her personal judgment to the teaching of the Church, for the liberty of conscience to which the Council document refers is not a liberty of the individual Catholic to set aside the teaching of the Church. As we have seen, the relationship of the teaching of the Church to the individual conscience is in no way analogous to that of the power of public authority and the individual conscience. The teaching of the Church is not a power alien to the conscience of the Catholic; it enters essentially into the formation of a Catholic's conscience. Moreover, there is no question here of coercion; the question is about the legitimacy of the procedure of one who is a Catholic and who nevertheless sets aside the insistent teaching of the Church.

The "dignity" to which the Fathers of Vatican II refer is the dignity of a person who obeys in a Catholic way the law revealed by conscience.[55] One who accepts a moral teaching opposed to the teaching of the Church is not clearly behaving in a Catholic way, unless, of course, one is truly in invincible ignorance. For a Catholic, a primary source in seeking the truth in moral matters *is* the teaching of the Church.

The third line of argumentation for preferring personal judgment is that the "sense" of the faithful, or their practical experience, provides a better source for knowing what faith requires of them in their moral lives than does the "official" teaching of the "hierarchical" magisterium.[56] It is true that the *sensus fidelium* — the lived, experienced consent of the faithful

124

to the truths of Catholic faith — is one source of our knowledge of the faith and its requirements. But the notion of "consent or sense of the faithful" needs careful analysis. It does not mean that any opinion of any believer is to be taken as normative, for members of the Church can be tempted to forsake the teachings of the Church and to conform to the pressures of the world around them, sometimes with excellent intentions. Nor does *"sensus fidelium"* refer to the opinions of some believers when they disagree with others, and especially when they disagree with the multitude of believers who still hold fast to what has been held by the overwhelming number of the faithful to be God's word down through the centuries.[57] To say that the sense of the faithful meant either of these things would be to replace doctrinal faith with some sort of relativism. It would pretend that what the Church over many centuries has taught to be the enduring word of God is in our age unacceptable. The sense of the faithful must reflect what the believers have in common; it is a sense true to the faith that has been authentically proclaimed in the Church. It is not to be confused with transient convictions, rooted in philosophies and visions of life received from sources alien to the Church.

The final argument to support preference for personal judgment to Church teachings is based on an appeal to the "magisterium of theologians." This argument rightly supposes that theologians have a kind of teaching office within the Church based on their scholarly competence. But the argument wrongly proceeds to give the theologians an authority similar in practice to that of the magisterium of pope and bishops. Thus, some insist that the hierarchy must not teach in a binding way if the consensus of theologians is not in agreement with them. Lacking such agreement, the pronouncements of the magisterium are not binding.[58]

Some have suggested that when the hierarchy and the theologians disagree, the faithful may follow a new version of probabilism — that is, when some scholars reject authentic teaching, one may live by their opinions. However, classical probabilism taught that scholarly opinion lost its authority if it was opposed to the teaching of the Holy See.[59]

This argument supposes that the theological community is

in overwhelming agreement in rejecting received teachings of the Church on sexual matters. But this supposition is false. There is nothing like a true consensus of theologians favoring theological dissent. Increasingly, theologians have come to recognize that their mission is to serve the magisterium of the Church, and that this mission cannot be carried out unless they responsibly accept the authentic teaching of the Church.[60]

Theologians do have a special office within the Church, and it is not improper to call this office a *magisterium*.[61] However, positions which contradict the received teachings of the Church simply cannot have normative status within the Church, for while there is an authentic mission for theologians within the Church, and while they can indeed teach us in significant ways, their role within the Church is clearly subordinate to that of those who are divinely appointed teachers of the faith, namely the pope and the bishops in communion with him. The life of faith is not primarily guarded by scholars. It is a gift of God, proclaimed first of all by the authentic witnesses who are successors to his apostles. One of the greatest theologians of all time expressed this point precisely. Addressing the issue of conflict between theological opinions and the teachings of those divinely appointed to express the mind of Christ within the Church, St. Thomas Aquinas unambiguously declared: "We must abide rather by the pope's judgment than by the opinion of any of the theologians, however well versed he may be in divine Scriptures."[62] He speaks here the judgment of the great family of Catholic theologians.

Thus, the effort to justify a Catholic's putting aside the firm teaching of the Church in favor of his or her own judgment does not succeed. The final moral evaluation of an action by a Catholic must be the judgment of his or her Catholic conscience. There is no way to maintain the authenticity of this conscience without holding faithfully to the insistent moral teaching of the Church. In the light of what faith teaches, the mature Catholic freely and intelligently guides his or her conscience toward what is really good — what following Christ requires.

126

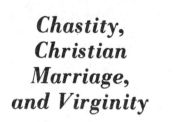

*Chastity, Christian Marriage, and Virginity*

In the first three chapters of this work we considered the teaching of Scripture, of the Catholic moral tradition, and of the Church's teaching office on the questions of sexual morality. The fourth and fifth chapters considered the general moral issues which must be faced by those trying to reach responsible and true judgments about how they should act, not simply in the sexual area but in all the areas of human existence. These teachings of God and his Church, as well as these general moral considerations about moral reasoning and decision making, must be brought to a focus to make clear how they provide the needed guidance for making correct decisions about sexual matters. This application of Catholic teaching to particular questions of sexual ethics will be carried out in some detail in Chapters 7 and 8 of this work.

Before developing this detailed application to specific moral questions, however, it is necessary to consider the virtue of chastity and its relationship to the basic vocations of Christian life. This consideration is necessary because chastity is the virtue by which a person integrates his or her sexuality into his or her overall Christian vocation.[1] One's personal vocation is one's particular way of responding to God's call and of following Christ; it should be the organizing factor in the life of each

127

Christian. One of the dimensions of our lives which must be integrated with our personal vocation is our sexuality, for sexuality is a powerful force within us. It can be used intelligently in the service of Christian love; but it can also be used for self-gratification, and then it becomes a source of personal disintegration, which compromises the organization of life in response to vocation. The virtue of chastity is therefore necessary for mature Christian living.

Of course, the chastity of a consecrated religious is very different than that of a married person. But they are not totally different realities: both require that sexual desire be permeated by love and guarded by self-possession; both involve the appreciation of sexuality as a gift to be used intelligently in the service of what is really good.

This chapter therefore will consider the virtue of chastity in general and its realization in the two most fundamental vocations of Christian life: marriage and virginity. Thus, this chapter will provide the immediate framework for the discussion of the specific questions of sexual morality which will complete this work.

## I. Chastity and Our Sexual Life

It is a commonplace saying that human persons are sexual beings. Human beings are members of a species that is sexual: every human being is either a male or a female. This biological fact about human nature is not, however, simply of biological significance — for sexuality, as Pope John Paul II has noted, is "by no means something purely biological, but concerns the innermost being of the human person as such."[2] In other words, being male or female is not simply an accidental or unimportant aspect of a human person, nor is it something whose significance is simply cultural. The sexuality of men and women affects them not only in obvious physical ways but also psychically, intellectually, and spiritually. Sexual differences make possible the complementarity and special friendship between men and women — relationships that in a host of ways are connected to the economy of salvation: man and woman he made them; in his image he made them.

Human persons are not spirits who happen to have bodies

128

attached. Each one is a living flesh of a kind that is inherently sexual. This is not to deny that the human person has an immortal soul, a spiritual dimension which other animals lack. It is to say, rather, that this soul is a part or dimension of the entire human person — a part that is essentially related to the bodily reality of which it is a principle. The soul of a man is his soul and thus inherently male; the soul of a woman is her soul and thus inherently female. Thus, human sexuality is a modality affecting our entire being as persons.[3]

Human sexuality is not, of course, simply a fact about human nature that must be observed objectively, from the outside, as it were. It is experienced — long before it is analyzed or understood — as a dynamic tendency or urge within us. We experience it as an impulse orienting us toward love and affection with other persons. We experience it too as a dynamic tendency having existential significance, inasmuch as it is bound up with the being or existence of the entire human species, with the generation of new human persons.[4] Obviously, sexuality as experienced in this way has a specifically genital component which is distinct from, although by no means separated from, our generic sexuality.

Because we are sexual, genital beings, it is natural that we respond to the sexual values incarnate in other persons, particularly in those of the opposite sex. It is natural too that there should arise within us sexual desires, accompanied at times by intense feelings of affection. These natural desires are in themselves good, for they are a part of our human nature created by God, and, when properly integrated into the personal vocation to which God calls every person, they play an irreducible role in the self-perfection which is each person's contribution to the kingdom of Christ.

These desires, however, also present a challenge because they are powerful emotions which sometimes resist rational control, and, when they do, they present a serious threat to the very human values they are meant to promote, for these emotions can lead one to sever one's sexual interest in another person from his or her being as a person. In other words, these emotions can lead us to treat persons as objects of sexual gratification, and not as irreplaceable and nonsubstitutable persons with whom we must join in a community that respects the dignity of all.

There is likewise the danger that sentimentality and superficial feelings of affection may blind us to reality and cause us to lose sight of the authentic goods at stake in sexual activity. We may, because of sentimental affection, be prompted to say "I love you," when in reality what we love is the feeling of warmth and affection that we experience in a particular person's presence. There is also the danger that we will become possessed by our sexual desires and inclined to act in accord with them and not in accord with the objective demands of intelligent love. Possession by such desires is incompatible with the self-possession of the mature and integrated person, and makes impossible the use of sexuality as part of a free and intelligent gift of self. What is compelled by passion cannot be a free gift.

Sexual desire and emotional affectivity are part of the raw stuff out of which authentic human love can be shaped, but this material needs to be shaped intelligently if it is to become integrally and fully a component of love.

To achieve this goal the virtue of chastity is necessary. Chastity can be described as a virtue concerned with the intelligent and loving integration of our sexual desires and affections into our being as persons, enabling us to come into possession of ourselves as sexual beings so that we can love well — and so that we can touch others and allow ourselves to be touched in ways that respect fully the goods of human existence, and the irreplaceable persons in whom these goods are meant to flourish. A brief explanation of this description will now be given.

Chastity is a virtue. A virtue is a stable character trait or disposition. Virtues therefore are not actions or feelings, for these are passing and often momentary. Virtues last, and like other traits that are not naturally given they must be acquired over a period of time, and are not readily lost. Virtues are those character traits which enable a person to do well what is morally good. Virtues enable a person to know what is right and to do it without excessive struggle. Thus, virtues are the extension of a person's morally good choices throughout his or her entire personality; they integrate a good person's entire self around what is best and most central in his or her personality.

Our powers of intellect and will must be developed; they must put on muscle if they are to properly guide our lives. The virtues are the developed orientations of the self which enable these powers to do their proper jobs. But virtues are not only traits of the mind and will, they also develop and perfect the other aspects of our personalities so that they are able to respond readily and joyfully to the directions of our intelligence and will.[5]

The mark of a virtuous person is not simply that he or she does the right things. To be virtuous a person must do the just or courageous or temperate thing in the way a just or courageous or temperate person would do it — that is, with the promptitude and joy that mark such a person's good actions.[6] Thus, a virtuous person does not act from fear and out of a merely automatic routine but freely and autonomously.[7] Likewise, the virtuous person does not act from external constraint, or out of a conditioned response, but because the virtuous person wants to do the right thing and delights in doing it well.[8]

This can be illustrated if we consider two employers and the justice each exhibits in dealing with employees. One pays his employees a just wage and provides decent working conditions. So this employer does the just thing. But he does so reluctantly, with no real willingness, perhaps because laws require him to provide decent working conditions, or because economic forces constrain him to pay a just wage. This employer lacks the virtue of justice. The other employer does the same things, but he does so because he wants to; he does so willingly, freely, and with enthusiasm. This employer does the just thing justly, that is, virtuously. For him, justice is not an extrinsic constraint but an orientation of his own personality.

The virtue of chastity is an aspect of the cardinal virtue of temperance, which has as its subject matter the pleasures of eating, drinking, and sex. Chastity is the form of temperance concerned with the pleasures of sex. These pleasures are essentially related to touch — in particular, touches involving the exercise of one's genital sexuality — and secondarily all the pleasures which prepare them by stimulating the desire for them.[9]

These pleasures and the desire for them are, as we have already seen, natural. The clamor to satisfy these desires is often vehement. The point of the virtue of chastity is not to flee from these pleasures or to suppress the desire for them. Thus, those who despise chastity as being a renunciation or denial of sexuality are mistaken. Chastity does not deny the goodness of these pleasures or suppress desire for them because chastity, like all virtue, is reasonable. To be reasonable is to care for the goods of human nature, and sexuality is meant to promote and respect these goods. The reasonable person therefore sees in the desires and feelings of our sentient nature something good that can serve the entire good of the human person if intelligently integrated into a life of commitment to what is really good.[10]

Chastity therefore does not seek to suppress or deny sexuality but rather enables a person to put a loving and intelligent order into his passional life, to take possession of his desires so that the whole self can be integrated and at peace. Thus, in a certain way, the emotions and desires themselves participate actively in the moderation coming from intelligence. This moderation becomes, as it were, a kind of connatural eagerness on their part. Our will and intellect do not dictate from without to restless passion. But our emotions and desires spontaneously, as it were, order themselves to the authentic goods of human persons which the person grasps through intelligence and loves through his will. Thus, it is a mockery of chastity to regard it as a life of constant warfare between unruly passion and imperious reason. Chastity, once achieved, is a basis for inner peace and personal integration.[11]

A virtuous spouse therefore will "feel" differently about the marital act with his or her own spouse and about genital sex with another. He or she will recognize — not only intellectually but with his or her whole being as an emotional, affective, passionate person — that the choice to engage in the marital act is one that is good and that the pleasure and joy associated with it are good and noble too. And he or she will recognize — not only intellectually but with his or her whole being — that whatever delight there might be in genital sex with another person is specious, that it does not crown an act that is beautiful and ennobling but rather one that fails to respect the goods perfective of human persons.

Of course, no one achieves the fullness of chastity swiftly

132

without some struggle and effort. For many people, the effort to be chaste is a long struggle with recalcitrant emotion. For these people, there is not the peace and joy of mature chastity. Even here, however, the effort is not without real rewards, for there is an anticipation of the joy of chaste living, a recognition of the goodness of self-possession, and a nobility in seeking goods one cannot fully experience. Moreover, even here the struggle is not an attempt to overcome or suppress emotion but an effort to integrate one's personality in a way that is really rewarding. Thus, even the efforts of the imperfectly chaste are not to be seen as battles in an endless struggle but as the efforts to begin a life of inner tranquillity and self-possession.

In sum, the virtue of chastity is one that all human beings need if they are to open themselves to integral human fulfillment and to the precious goods that perfect human existence and human persons. And chastity in no way deadens or repudiates sexuality. Rather chastity enlivens it so that being "vitally integrated into the person" it "makes the subject capable, on the plane of his passional life, of the self-determination and self-control which characterizes a mind."[12]

Jesus, the complete human, provides a striking model of chastity. He is a sexual being, a virile yet affectionate male. His life was full of close and affectionate friendships with men and women alike. Yet Jesus was a celibate, a virgin because of the demands of his personal vocation as redeemer of the world. His example teaches us that the chaste person is the one who has his or her priorities right, who intelligently loves the goods of human nature and integrates his or her affective life into the vocation by which each one of us is called by God to pursue these goods.

In subsequent chapters the requirements of chastity both for married persons and for unmarried persons will be set forth in some detail. Here, the general outline of chaste Christian life will be sketched out by considering how the basic vocations of Christian life promote and protect the goods of human sexuality.

## II. Christian Marriage: A Vocation of Chastity

The Christian vocation of marriage provides an important frame of reference for the understanding and development of the virtue of chastity. This vocation is the context within which God calls most men and women to holiness; and even those who are not called to this vocation know from the lives of married friends and relatives that this is a special locus for God's work in saving mankind. Moreover, marriage is the context in which the use of genital sexuality has its proper role in God's plan. So, it is within marriage that the goods to which human sexuality is ordered are properly realized. Since these goods are the basis for chastity, an understanding of marriage is indispensable for understanding chastity.

*The Nature of Marriage.* To understand chastity within marriage, it is necessary to understand the nature of marriage itself, for the nature of marriage is designed by God to enable people to integrate their sexuality into the service of self-giving and new life. Thus, marriage enables what could degenerate into a selfish and enslaving force to become instead a full and integral part of a life in which the greatest goods of human persons are served, and the love which is God himself is revealed.

Marriage is one of the most profound and important aspects of human social existence. Its depths of human meaning and supernatural significance are suggested by the attention it receives in Scripture, by the great theologians, and in the teaching of the Church. The discussions in the first three chapters of this book only begin to explore what faith teaches about this wonderful and mysterious reality. Here, it is possible only to summarize those aspects of Christian reflection on marriage which are necessary for understanding its special role as a vocation of chastity.

All human societies have some institutionalized framework for the begetting and raising of children. Perhaps "marriage" could be used as the name for any of these social arrangements. But the biblical and Christian understanding of marriage does not accept any such arrangements as marriage, for not just any arrangement for having and raising children is conducive to their genuine well-being, or for a promotion of the kind of relationship between men and women that will foster real love and respect between them. The God who reveals himself as our Father, whose love for us is like that of our mother but never failing, will not tolerate just any arrangement for begetting and raising children. So marriage is an institution, but unlike most institutions it does not depend simply on human convention or decision. God himself is the author of marriage. As Pope Pius XI said, reflecting the entire tradition going back to Genesis:

> Let it be repeated as an immutable and inviolable fundamental doctrine that matrimony was not instituted or restored by man but by God: not by man were the laws made to strengthen and confirm and elevate it but by God, the Author of nature and by Christ our Lord by whom nature was redeemed, and hence these laws cannot be subject to any human decrees or to any contrary pact even to the spouses themselves. This is the doctrine of Holy Scripture; this is the constant teaching of the Universal Church; this is the solemn definition of the sacred Council of Trent, which declares and establishes from the words of Holy Writ itself that God is the Author of the perpetual stability of the marriage bond, its unity and stability.[13]

But what is the God-given character of marriage? It is the union of one man and one woman, who mutually give themselves to each other so that they may share an intimate partnership of the whole of their lives until death. Their marital union, which is brought into being by their personal act of irrevocable consent, is of its own inner dynamism and nature ordered to the procreation and education of children and to the fostering of a special and exclusive kind of love — marital or spousal or conjugal love. As spouses, moreover, husband and wife form the single subject of a shared sexual life, and their marital union is fittingly expressed in and by an act proper and specific to them, the marital act. In this act they become "one flesh," and come to "know" one another in a unique and unforgettable way. Through it, spouses symbolize and support all the activities in which they share intimately their lives with each other and communicate the gift of life to new human persons.[14]

This divine plan for marriage was obscured and damaged by the sin described in Genesis 3, with the result that divorce and polygamy disfigured the human reality that God had in mind in bringing marriage into being (cf. *Gaudium et Spes*, no. 47); but this divine plan has been restored in an incomparably marvelous way by our Lord and Savior, Jesus Christ.

135

Although God is the author of marriage and gives to this human reality its defining characteristics and intrinsic conditions of existence, its coming-into-being in a particular instance depends on the free, personal choice of the man and woman who give themselves to each other in marriage. Nothing can take the place of their act of mutual consent. It is this act that brings their marriage into being and makes them husband and wife. In and through this self-determining act they give to themselves a new identity: the man becomes the woman's husband, and she becomes his wife, and together they become spouses.[15] Prior to this act of irrevocable free consent in which they forswear all others to bestow themselves upon each other, the man and the woman live their own independent lives; in and through it they unite their lives, forming a community of sharing that is so intimate and all-encompassing that they can be said to have one common life and to be one flesh.

The paramount significance of this act of marital consent is eloquently expressed in the Yahwist account of the creation of marriage in Genesis 2. There we read that the man, Adam, on seeing the person equal to himself, whom the Lord had fashioned for him, cried out: "Here at last is bone of my bone and flesh of my flesh. . . . For this reason a man shall leave father and mother and cleave to his wife, and the two shall become one flesh" (Genesis 2.23-24).[16] In his perceptive analysis of this passage from Genesis, Pope John Paul II noted:

> The very formation of Gn 2.24 indicates not only that human beings, created as man and woman, were created for unity, but also that precisely this unity, through which they become "one flesh" has right from the beginning a character of union derived from choice. We read, in fact, "a man leaves his father and mother and cleaves to his wife." If the man belongs "by nature" to his father and mother by virtue of procreation, he, on the other hand, "cleaves" by choice to his wife (and she to her husband).[17]

Since marriage is brought into being through an act whereby the spouses give and receive the "word" or person of the other,[18] it is unconditioned, irrevocable, and dependent for continuation in its being only on the continuation in being of the spouses themselves. Thus, both by reason of its God-given nature and the intention of the spouses, marriage is a relationship which lasts until death.

Moreover, in consenting to be spouses, a man and a woman consent to marriage and to all that it entails. Since marriage is an institution for the procreation and education of children, marital consent involves a commitment to this worthy enterprise. Similarly, they commit themselves to fostering the special love of those who would share a common life and hand on that life to their children. Thus, spouses consent to the special expression of marital love — the self-giving of marital intercourse.[19] All of these commitments are expressed in the marriage act whereby spouses take each other for richer or for poorer, in sickness and in health, unto death.

This brief account of the nature of marriage reveals the essential goods to which human sexuality is ordered; these are the three goods of marriage articulated by St. Augustine — (1) the bond of unity between the spouses, (2) children, and (3) marital fidelity. The requirements of faithful service to these goods provide much of the concrete fabric of chastity, but even the most general characteristics of Christian marriage just considered indicate some basic aspects of this virtue. First, they show that sexuality is not created for the sake of the satisfaction of individuals on terms they can themselves arbitrarily set. Rather, it serves great human goods which they can personally appreciate, goods they must share in to fulfill their own lives. Sexuality is for the sake of human relationships — precious relationships whose excellence must enlighten and guide our sexual desires, and which have an objective, God-given character.

Second, the essential role of mutual consent in the actualization of a marriage shows that these relationships are fundamentally a matter of the commitment of the whole person. The implication is that desire, affection, and emotion must serve commitment, and are enriched and made more satisfying by doing so. The reality of marriage is in the selves constituted by the mutual commitment to be spouses. The feelings of the spouses should be integrated into this commitment. They are not themselves constitutive of the fundamental reality of the relationship.

*Chastity and the Goods of Marriage.* As already noted, even

137

the briefest account of the nature of marriage makes clear that marriage is meaningful because it is the context in which very important human relationships can be realized and basic human goods fostered and protected. It is in service to these goods — the goods of marriage first articulated by Augustine[20] — that the fabric of chastity takes shape. A brief review of these goods and their implications for chastity will provide some understanding of that shape.

The good of the sacrament — that is, the indissoluble unity of husband and wife — is the good which constitutes the reality of marriage itself, the bond of union between the spouses. Without this union there is no marriage, no marital giving and receiving, and, so, the tradition regards it as the most essential of the goods of marriage.[21] The centrality of this good is closely tied to its sacramental character.

The feature of this good that is morally most important is the indissolubility of the marriage bond. Indissolubility imposes a moral obligation on spouses not to attempt another marriage as long as their partner is alive. This obligation holds even if it is necessary to separate, even if one is deserted[22] — for marriage, as we saw above, is a total joining of two lives into one; the marital commitment is necessarily for life.

In fact, the indissolubility of marriage not only imposes an obligation not to attempt remarriage, it also makes remarriage in the case of sacramental marriages literally impossible, for the bond of marriage is a reality, not a matter of human convention, and when that bond is created in the life of two Christians, it simply cannot be broken. This bond is intended by God to symbolize the love of Christ for his Church, and as a sacrament of the new covenant it partakes of that divine and human love. And that love cannot be broken by any power in the universe.[23] Thus, as Vatican II teaches, marriage comes to be through the choice of the spouses; but once it has come to be, it does not depend on any choice whatsoever.[24] A spouse can no more become an ex-spouse than a father can become an ex-father, or a mother an ex-mother. They may cease to love each other as spouses should, but they are spouses until death.

In virtue of its being a sacrament of the new covenant, marriage is a special source of grace. A sacrament is a sign which

138

represents a supernatural reality and in some way participates in the reality it signifies. Thus, a sacrament is a means for receiving the grace it signifies.[25] Marriage therefore is a means for the sanctification of the spouses.[26]

The marriage of those who give and receive each other "in the Lord"[27] has present within it not only the power of the spouses themselves but also the power of Christ's love. By virtue of this love their marriage not only can respect the precious goods it is bound to honor, it can also be the bearer of a greater and more healing kind of love. Thus, the marriage of Christians both signifies the love of Christ for his Church, and participates in this love. It draws from this love so that it is capable of revealing it in the lives of the spouses.[28]

Christian marriage is capable of being a sacrament in this sense because the partners are already incorporated in Christ in virtue of their baptism. As Pope John Paul II said:

> Indeed by means of baptism, man and woman are definitively placed within the new and eternal covenant, in the spousal covenant of Christ with the Church. *And it is because of this indestructible insertion* that the intimate community of conjugal life and love, founded by the Creator, is elevated . . . and enriched by his redeeming power.[29] (Emphasis added.)

The act of marrying of baptized persons therefore is an act of the Church and a sacrament of the new covenant to which Christ himself is party. As such, marriage enables the love of the spouses to be caught up "into divine love and is directed and enriched by the redemptive power of Christ and the salvific action of the Church, with the result that the spouses are effectively led to God."[30]

Non-Christian marriages are not sacramental in this full sense; but they are not totally separated from its saving reality, for whenever people seek earnestly the human goods of marriage, there is an openness to supernatural blessings not explicitly recognized. Thus, we can say that even the marriages of non-Christians are touched by grace, for the goods sought in such marriages "come from God the creator and are integrated in an inchoative way into the spousal love of Christ for His Church."[31]

139

The implications for chastity of the indissoluble bond of marriage and its supernatural significance as a sacrament of the new covenant are easy to grasp, for this bond points to the fact that our sexuality is meant to serve a lasting and unbreakable relationship with another person — a relationship that is meant to join the spouses in a common life together. It cannot do this if sexual feelings are not penetrated and guided by intelligent love. Thus, the principle for the use of sexuality is not the exigence of sexual desire or of romantic affection but the demands of lasting commitment. The sacramental character of this bond makes clear that the self-transcendence of marriage is not simply a self-transcendence of each of the spouses for the sake of the common life of their marriage but a contribution to the saving work of Jesus. Thus, their union should be a vocation in which they seek to contribute to the work of Jesus. In particular, their vocation is to signify the great saving union between Christ and the Church. So, chastity is shown to have a vocational, ecclesial dimension.

The procreative good — the good of children — also perfects marriage and generates requirements of chastity but in a way very different from the bond of marriage itself, for the procreative good is one of the goods which fulfills the life of married couples, and toward which marriage is ordered. This good — fulfillment and orientation — is present even when couples are not actually blessed with children. The orientation toward procreation and education of children is implicit in the very fertility of sexuality and in the institutional significance of marriage.[32] Thus, spouses undertake a mission to serve life when they join together in marriage. This service is the natural effect and embodiment of their common life, so perfectly expressed in marital intercourse. Thus, children are "the supreme gift of marriage, and greatly contribute to the good of the parents themselves."[33] Of course, the inherent human significance of procreation is transformed in sacramental marriages, for children are not simply the next generation of the human species, they also are images of God, persons for whom Christ died and rose so that they might become citizens of his kingdom and children of God.[34]

The implications of this good for chastity are perhaps not

140

as easy to see as those of the indissoluble bond of marriage; but they are far-reaching, for the procreative good introduces a new, social dimension to chastity. This good requires a dimension of responsibility for the use of sexuality which goes beyond what is required by the bond of unity alone, for procreation entails responsibility for very dependent persons who made no choice to be a member of a given family. Moreover, this good requires that human sexual activity remain open to new life, and that it be used in such a way as to preserve the delicate balance of community between parents and children.

The third good of marriage is the fidelity of the spouses. This good includes not only the literal fidelity — abstention from adultery — required by the nature of the marital bond and by the procreative good; but it also includes the development of the special love and friendship of the spouses. So, this good is required for the realization of the other goods of marriage but is not simply instrumental to their realization, for the love of spouses is good in itself, a wonderful form of human communion.[35]

Vatican II described marital love as eminently human, inwardly capable of being merged with the divine love of Christ, and utterly distinct from mere erotic attraction. The Council Fathers added that marital love is properly expressed in the chaste union of marital intercourse, that it is faithful and exclusive, and ready for self-sacrifice.[36] In short, this is a love in which all the goods of marriage are realized and celebrated.

The special implications for chastity of the good of fidelity and, in particular, of the love between spouses center on the need for sexuality to serve the needs of others. Genuine love must be ready for self-sacrifice, the antithesis of the self-gratification of sexual indulgence.

The distinctive expression of marital love is the act of marital intercourse. But it would be a mistake to think that marital intercourse is the only expression of marital love. Mutual help, support, and cooperation are also very important. Thus, chastity requires that we order and integrate all of our desires, affections, and aspirations so as to serve the love between spouses that is the foundation of family life. It follows from this, as from the good of procreation, that chastity cannot be limited

141

to the sexual dimension in the narrow sense. All of our familial existence — our entire relationship with our children and our spouses — pertains to chastity. Marital chastity therefore affects in some way the entire existence of husbands and wives, for every part of the life of spouses must be integrated around these basic commitments of married life.

*Conjugal Intercourse.* Conjugal intercourse is the act in which the love of spouses is uniquely expressed.[37] This is so because this act expresses in a special way all the characteristics of marital love and fosters all the goods of marriage.

As a marital act, it is a shared act of the spouses. Thus, it is the action which actualizes their common life — realizes their bond of unity. It is the act whereby they literally become one flesh, and come to know each other in the special way of spouses.[38] Since conjugal intercourse is the common act of persons irrevocably committed to each other, it fosters the love and fidelity of marriage, and signifies in a concrete way the union of Christ and his Church.[39]

Marital intercourse also realizes the goods of fidelity and of children. It can do this only insofar as it is truly conjugal, for only thus will it involve the self-giving needed for the responsibilities of parenthood and the common life of spouses.

This self-giving has several aspects that are essential for chastity. First, there must be an openness to children in sexual activity. Without this openness, the lovemaking of the spouses cannot be the full sharing of a common life, for it rejects the embodiment and responsibility of that life. This aspect of marital chastity will be considered more fully in Chapter 7. Second, self-giving must fully respect the person of the other. It must systematically avoid treating the other as an object for one's sexual gratification. Third, self-giving requires that the spouses have possession of their sexual desires so that they can freely offer themselves in marital intercourse. If their lovemaking is simply a response to sexual desire, if, in other words, it is activity to which they are driven rather than one chosen freely as an act of love, it cannot have the essential features of a gift. Something that must be done to satisfy exigent desire cannot be a gift, for a gift must be freely given and therefore must be within one's power to withhold. Thus, periodic voluntary abstinence from

142

marital intercourse can also be an essential part of the self-giving of marital love. This is especially so when the full realization of the goods of marriage requires that the couple forgo intercourse.[40]

These aspects of the self-giving that should characterize marital intercourse are, of course, normative features which are not always realized. In fact, they are difficult to realize in the lives of many couples; but they are the goal toward which all couples must strive if their sexual relationships are not to degenerate into mere pleasure-seeking or to the pretense of genuine love.

### III. Chastity and the Life of Consecrated Virginity

Marriage is an especially important vocation of Christian life for putting the demands of chastity into perspective. Of course, it is not the only vocation of Christian life, nor is it the only one that helps put chastity into proper perspective. The life of consecrated virginity in which a person completely forgoes marital and familial life for the sake of witness to the kingdom is also important for understanding Christian chastity.

It may seem that the life of consecrated virginity presupposes values quite opposite to those of marriage. In particular, it may seem that this life rejects the values of sexuality for the sake of higher values. These appearances are misleading, for the two vocations are in fact complementary. Pope John Paul II has explained part of this relationship as follows:

> Virginity or celibacy for the sake of the Kingdom of God not only does not contradict the dignity of marriage but presupposes it and confirms it. Marriage and virginity or celibacy are two ways of expressing and living the one mystery of the covenant of God with his people. When marriage is not esteemed, neither can consecrated virginity or celibacy exist; when human sexuality is not regarded as a great value given by the Creator, the renunciation of it for the sake of the Kingdom of Heaven loses its meaning.[41]

Because marriage is so good, its renunciation can reveal how truly wonderful is the life of the kingdom to which the virginal life testifies in a special way; but the relationship works the other way as well. The life of consecrated virginity throws light on the character of Christian marriage, for the life of virginity is a response to the unconditioned demands of Christ's kingdom. This makes clear that marriage as a human reality is subordinate to the demands of Christ's kingdom; the basis for judging marriage, as for judging everything else in this world, is this kingdom.[42] Only as a vocation contributing to his kingdom does marriage have an absolute claim on his followers. The desires for gratification and earthly happiness must give way in the face of these demands, and nowhere are these more clearly manifested than in the response to the call to renounce all for the kingdom, for only in Christ's kingdom can each of us and all of us together realize full human perfection, and full sharing of goods with other human beings and God himself in loving communion.

Thus, the full meaning of Christian marriage requires an appreciation of the life of consecrated virginity. As Edward Schillebeeckx has said:

It is no longer possible within the Christian order of salvation, to define marriage perfectly without at the same time calling upon total abstinence for the sake of the kingdom of God as a correlative possibility. . . . Christianity will never be able to close its ears to the authentic biblical call to total abstinence as a possibility which forms an intrinsic and essential part of Christianity itself.[43]

Those who answer the call to the life of consecrated virginity in no way repudiate the goods of married life. Such goods are perfectly realized in the kingdom of Christ to which their lives attest. Moreover, such persons stand as a constant reminder that we can come into full possession of our sexuality without engaging in genital activity, and that we can reasonably engage in sexual activity only within a vocation in which the precious goods of human sexuality are fostered and respected.

The life of consecrated virginity is an especially important model for those who, although they are not married, are not called to this life of evangelical perfection. For these people, chastity is also essential, and the lives of those who altogether renounce sexual activity provide for them an example that is very powerful.[44]

To sum up this chapter: chastity is an essential virtue of

144

Christian life. It is the virtue by which our sexual dimension is integrated into our lives as followers of Christ. Through this virtue, we are able to reasonably order and direct our sexual desires and emotions so that they serve and do not hinder the vocation to which God calls each of us. Thus, chastity is not a matter of suppressing sexuality but of ordering and integrating so that it can be part of a life of Christian service. In marriage, chastity requires a reasonable use of sexual activity so that the goods toward which it is ordered are intelligently and faithfully loved. In the other vocations of Christian life, genital activity is sacrificed for the sake of the goods which will be harmed and distorted because they cannot truly be realized outside of marriage. In these vocations, a person's sexuality is not denied but lived in different ways. In all the vocations of Christian life, chastity guarantees a life of self-possession in which the demands of following Christ are seen clearly, without the fog of disordered passion. In the subsequent chapters of this book we will see in a more specific way what chastity requires, and why the intelligent love of the followers of Christ makes these seemingly difficult demands.

# 7

God made men and women as sexual beings, and he blessed marriage. Sexual activity in marriage, when it is faithful to the great goods for which marriage was instituted, is very good. It is natural and excellent, and ennobles human

# The Requirements of Chastity Within Marriage

life. Thus, "Married love is uniquely expressed and perfected by the exercise of the acts proper to marriage. Hence the acts in marriage by which the intimate and chaste union of the spouses takes place are noble and honorable; the truly human performance of these acts fosters the self-giving they signify and enriches the spouses in joy and gratitude" (*Gaudium et Spes*, no. 49).

By the choice to marry, a man and a woman commit themselves to participate in the goods for which marriage was instituted. In pursuing faithful love and its extension and embodiment in children, spouses pursue goods naturally desired by human persons; in participating in the sacramental good, they take part in the most sublime ends of marriage and marital union. In Chapter 6 we already described the beauty of married life and of marital acts marked by a commitment to the goods of marriage.

But sex, like every good gift of God to man, can be abused. Married persons can engage in sexual activity in unreasonable and sinful ways; they can fail to respect the values that must be honored in sexual activity. Following the guidance of Scripture and Christian tradition, the Church urges the faithful to avoid kinds of sexual acts that are irresponsible and wrong. It does so not to focus their attention on sin but to hearten them toward a more faithful and human living of their married vocation. In this chapter we consider ways in which spouses can fail to meet the requirements of chastity, the demands of faithful and life-giving love. First we consider adultery, which fails to honor the good of faithful love. Then we treat contraception, which attacks the procreative good. Finally, we treat other violations of marital chastity.

## I. Adultery

Adultery was proscribed in the Decalogue, or Ten Commandments (Exodus 20.14; Deuteronomy 5.18). In a patriarchal society such as existed at the beginning of God's moral revelation there was emphasis on the rights of the husband, and a focus on external deeds.[1] But the Decalogue was concerned with more than the external act and rights externally violated. It explicitly noted the wrongness of *coveting* one's neighbor's wife (Exodus 20.17; Deuteronomy 5.21), an inner act by which the heart of the sinner is harmed.

The malice of adultery was frequently recalled in the Old Testament. As the revelation given to Israel developed, marriage itself came to be seen as a faithful and loving covenant between man and woman, symbolizing the covenant of grace and fidelity between Yahweh and his people.[2] Implicit in this understanding of marriage is the realization that adultery violates far more than the rights of the husband. It attacks the heart of the marriage covenant itself, and strikes at every person guarded by that covenant. Pope John Paul II, commenting on the significance of the story of human origins in Genesis, properly sums up the teaching of the Old Testament: "Adultery . . . means a breach of the unity by means of which man and woman only as husband and wife can unite so closely as to be 'one flesh.' "[3]

Jesus clearly taught that not only the external deed of adultery is sinful but the desire for it as well (Matthew 5.28).[4] Although Jesus forgave the woman caught in adultery, he cautioned her not to sin any more (John 8.11). He likewise made it

147

quite clear that adultery violates the rights of both husband and wife, and that it desecrates the covenant of marriage (Mark 10.11-12; Matthew 19.9).[5] By adultery he clearly meant sexual union with a person other than one's spouse.[6]

Paul saw sexual union between man and woman in marriage as very good. It is a communion in being, a "one-flesh" unity, symbolizing the intensely personal union between Christ and his bride the Church (Ephesians 5.25-33).[7] He taught that a Christian becomes one body with Christ in baptism.[8] And he stressed that the body of the Christian — that is, his whole person[9] — is a temple of the Holy Spirit (1 Corinthians 6.19), a "vessel" to be held in honor as a God-given and sacred reality (1 Thessalonians 4.3-5).[10] Thus, precisely because sexual activity and the body are so meaningful and precious, Paul taught that any act of sexual immorality was an act of desecration, for in such an act the person who had already become one body with Christ, the Holy One of God, was taking something holy — his or her own person now living in Christ — and defiling it. He therefore pleaded with his brothers and sisters in the Lord to "control his own body in holiness and honor" (1 Thessalonians 4.4) and exclaimed: "Do you not know that the unrighteous will not inherit the kingdom of God? Do not be deceived; neither the immoral, nor idolators, nor adulterers, nor homosexuals, nor thieves, nor the greedy, nor drunkards, nor revilers, nor robbers will inherit the kingdom of God" (1 Corinthians 6.9-10). Adultery is wicked not only because it desecrates the living temple of the Holy Spirit but also because it does violence to a unique and exclusive kind of love, a love divinely intended to signify and partake of the love between Christ and his Church.

This brief summary makes it evident that the New Testament considered adultery — that is, sexual union with a person other than one's spouse — an evil, a desecration completely incompatible with the life of a Christian. Its teaching is admirably summed up in the Letter to the Hebrews: "Let marriage be held in honor among all, and let the marriage bed be undefiled; for God will judge the immoral and adulterous" (Hebrews 13.4).

The plain sense of this biblical teaching is faithfully proclaimed by the Church. The Fathers and the great medieval moralists, the approved authors of recent centuries, and the

148

magisterium in all cases speak with one voice condemning adultery. In fact, the wrongness of adultery follows so immediately from what is central to the Christian view of marriage and marital relations that it is commonly taken to be obvious.[11] Adultery is therefore considered by many Christians as a clear example of an inherently wrongful act, and it is used as a reference point to elucidate the malice of other sins.[12]

Given the attack on the Christian doctrine of marriage and sexuality in recent decades, it is not surprising that the magisterium has reaffirmed and proclaimed the traditional teaching on adultery. Thus, Pius XI explicitly condemned adultery in *Casti Connubii*[13]; the Fathers of Vatican II stressed its incompatibility with the fidelity demanded by spousal love (*Gaudium et Spes*, no. 49); the American bishops clearly rejected it as gravely sinful in their pastoral on moral values[14]; and John Paul II has branded it as a terrible breach of covenantal love.[15]

This teaching cannot be set aside as culturally conditioned and therefore no longer normative.[16] The living body of the faithful, guided by the Holy Spirit and aware not only of cultural differences but of the unity through time of the Church, knows that every deliberate act of adultery is seriously wrong.

The grounds for this constant teaching of the Church on adultery are readily discernible. Only a brief account of these grounds is necessary here. Adultery is radically inconsistent with the proper pursuit of the goods of human sexuality and of human persons. Although all the goods honored in marriage — the procreative good, the good of friendship between the spouses, and the good of indissoluble unity — are violated by adultery, it is marital friendship which adultery primarily and immediately harms.

The inconsistency between adultery and marital friendship becomes clear if the special character of this friendship — one described in detail in Chapter 6 — is understood. Like many other friendships, marital friendship is a good thing, valued for its own sake. But this friendship differs from other types of friendship in a number of ways. It is rooted in the covenant of irrevocable personal consent, a consent that establishes the man and the woman as irreplaceable and nonsubstitutable spouses, as husband and wife. It is therefore a friendship that is exclusive

149

of others in the sense that husband and wife pledge to be with and for each other fully until death, and aspire to a unity of personal intimacy, to a communion in being.[17] It is a friendship that involves an intimate sharing of life and love, a sharing so complete that it naturally leads to new life.[18] Marital friendship is essentially related to the most basic and intimate of human communities, the family. This friendship, unique among all kinds of human friendships, is the ground of the family and is nourished and expressed in the life of the family.[19] The intimacy of this friendship, so fittingly expressed in the conjugal act,[20] the unity of spouses in a common life, and the open-ended demands of procreating and raising children require that marital friendship be the permanent and exclusive relationship that Christian teaching holds marriage to be.

Adultery obviously inflicts great harm on spouses and on their children. The deep personal hurt and betrayal experienced by the victims of infidelity, the breaking of the bonds of trust and love, the painful effects of divorce — all these evils and many more are the commonly known effects of adultery. These obvious evils do not arise in each and every case of adultery; but evils of this type are the natural consequences of the harm to marital friendship that is necessarily involved in every act of adultery. The unfaithful spouse is ordinarily deceiving himself or herself when he or she thinks the act of adultery will cause no great harm. These evil effects are therefore useful signs of the inherent evil of this desecrating deed.

The argument is sometimes made that adultery can be consistent with the overall values of marriage and of family life if it is a necessary means to avoid great evils or to achieve great goods. Thus, under some circumstances adultery is said to be justified as therapy for sexual dysfunction, or a necessary way of avoiding loneliness and frustration when the spouses are separated, or as a way of gaining favors or avoiding harms — especially where the favors sought or the harms avoided affect one's family or spouse in a profound way. For example, a woman commits adultery with a concentration camp guard so that she will become pregnant and be returned to the family who desperately needs her.[21] Arguments like these, however, are specious. They are essentially consequentialist and assume that the evil

150

immediately brought about by adultery can be balanced by the good an individual hopes to achieve by it. As we saw in Chapter 4, this assumption is false.[22] In this area, as in all areas of life, one's life is disastrously wounded if one is willing to do evil so that good may come about.

Finally, we must consider the argument that sexual intercourse with a person other than one's spouse, if done with the consent of one's spouse, ought not to be called adultery or at any rate ought not to be considered adultery in a morally pejorative sense.[23] This line of reasoning assumes a subtle form of dualism, for it seems to hold that a man and a woman can continue to give themselves (that is, their conscious minds) to each other uniquely and exclusively even as they give their bodies (now regarded as distinct from their "selves") to another. This fallacious Gnostic assumption forgets the unity of the human person and promotes self-deception.

This argument also involves the false assumption that spouses' rights concerning each other's sexual activities are analogous to property rights or to other rights that can be waived. The mutual rights of spouses with respect to each other's sexual activities are not analogous to property rights or to other transferable rights. Rather, these rights are rooted in the marital covenant and in the marriage itself, in the giving and receiving of the *person* of the other. These realities are not subject to manipulation by the spouses; they come into being in the lives of the spouses from their mutual consent to marriage. But once the marriage comes to exist, it is governed by divinely established norms to which married persons must conform. Consensual adultery therefore *is* adultery, as Pope Innocent XI taught long ago.[24]

## II. Contraception

The sexual revolution is closely related to the development of contraceptives.[25] At the beginning of this century the common moral position — not simply of Catholics but also of other Christians, of Jews, and of other religious groups and even of nonreligious people — was that sexual activity had to be responsibly related to marital promises and to the obvious purposes of sex. Contraception was viewed as an abuse of sexual

151

activity, shameful and wrong. In it spouses abused each other, and they abused a significant kind of human action by failing to respect one of its obvious and humanly very important purposes. For very many, it still seemed highly desirable to have large families. Even in circumstances in which more children were undesirable, the use of contraception to limit families was judged the use of an evil means.

In recent times many elements of modern life seemed to join together to commend having smaller families. Urbanization was one factor. In city life large families were burdensome in ways in which they had not been in rural life. Medical progress made a difference. When almost all children happily survived birth and infancy, there was not so great a desire to give birth to many children. Social fears of overpopulation arose and were intensely stimulated by those who wished to promote new moral visions — visions, in fact, incompatible with Christianity. Limited social resources as well as limited family resources were presented as urgent reasons to control the family and the general population.

Theoretically this control could have been managed by various kinds of self-discipline and sexual abstinence. But development of natural family-planning methods was slower and was not promoted by the media and family-planning advocates in the way contraception was. Many people of high moral standards who instinctively judged that sex was meaningful and sacred did not see clearly the reasons why contraception was not a humanly satisfactory solution to these problems. When the commercial interests favoring contraception and the moral revolutionaries proposing a new secular ethics portrayed in glowing terms the advantages of contraception, many failed to see the moral and social problems that a contraceptive mentality would create.

Certainly contraception was convenient. It enabled people to reach what had clearly become a desirable end by means that were effective and, moreover, required little self-discipline and no sexual abstinence at all. Everyone could have sex whenever it was desired without the inconvenience of unwanted pregnancies. (Many at first naïvely thought only married couples would take advantage of this.) This convenience led to a rapid progress toward broad social acceptance of what had earlier been recognized as immoral. Even various religious groups came to commend the contraception they had once sharply condemned. The desirability of the end pursued by contraceptionists was so clear that many failed to question sufficiently the morality of this precise means toward that end.

Pressure to change the Catholic teaching on contraception became very great. It became especially intense in the 1960s. Nevertheless, Pope Paul VI, emphasizing that he was reaffirming the received teaching of the Christian faith on an important question, refused to alter the Church's stand against contraception. He affirmed in very clear language that contraception is seriously wrong. In doing so he was not denying the importance of family planning and responsible parenthood.[26] His concern was with the moral character of the means used to achieve this end.

Because of the importance of the Church's teaching on contraception and of the difficulties that many experience today in understanding and accepting this teaching, we will treat this matter at some length.

*The Meaning of Contraception.* Contraception, as the word itself suggests, is actively aimed at preventing conception. But it is necessary to begin with a clear definition of "contraception" to make unmistakable the precise nature of the acts to which moral judgments about contraception are intended to apply.

In his encyclical *Humanae Vitae*, Paul VI gave an exact account of the nature of contraceptive actions. A contraceptive act is had in any act of coition which is intended precisely to act against the procreative good, to prevent it from being realized. "Every act that intends to impede procreation must be repudiated ... whether it is done in anticipation of marital intercourse, or during it, or while it is having its natural consequences."[27] Thus, there are various ways in which intercourse can be contraceptive: through the use of mechanical devices (such as condoms or diaphragms), by the use of withdrawal or spermicides, by the use of anovulant pills,[28] by surgical sterilization, and the like. Contraception is always part of a dual act, "contraceptive intercourse." In this dual act of contraceptive intercourse, one chooses to engage in sexual intercourse.

153

While choosing to have intercourse, which is known to be essentially related to the procreation of new human life, and precisely because one does not want the act of intercourse to flower into the fruitfulness which it can have, one performs the contraceptive act. This act is aimed precisely against the procreative good. The coming-to-be of a new human life (which is in itself a great good, though one may perhaps very reasonably desire not to realize it here and now) is treated as an evil, something to be acted against. The precise purpose of the contraceptive act, as we shall more fully show below, is to act directly against the great human good of procreation — to treat it as if here and now it were an evil, not a good.

Contraception or contraceptive intercourse therefore is not identical in meaning with birth control or family planning. Plainly there are other ways to control births and to plan one's family than by engaging in contraceptive intercourse. One can control or prevent births by means far worse than contraception — by abortion, for instance. And one can plan one's family by means that are in themselves thoroughly good — that is, by natural family planning.

With this understanding of the meaning of contraceptive intercourse (or contraception) in mind, we now propose to examine the Church's teaching on this subject and to develop the basic argument to show that this activity is immoral. Yet before presenting the Church's teaching and our argument it will first be helpful to note the objections and difficulties raised against this teaching by some Catholic thinkers in recent years. We shall then, in concluding our discussion of contraception, return to these difficulties and objections in order to answer them more adequately.

*Objections and Difficulties.* A number of recent developments, some sociological and economic, others philosophical and theological, stimulated questioning of the standard Christian teaching on contraception. During the late 1950s and early 1960s, when doubts about the received teaching were raised with increasing force within the Catholic community, a new factor was introduced with the development of oral contraceptives. The pill differed from mechanical contraceptives such as condoms, diaphragms, spermicidal jellies, and so forth in that it did not interfere in any overt way with the sexual act itself. With the pill there seemed to be no behavioral "unnaturalness." Thus, it seemed to some that the pill might prove to be morally acceptable. Possibly the use of the pill as a contraceptive might be accepted without disturbing the fabric of Christian moral life and without having bad effects on the practice of chastity.[29]

These considerations were reinforced by more theoretical criticism of the received teaching. Two such criticisms were especially influential. The first of these claimed that the received teaching was based on an understanding of the natural law that was too physicalistic or legalistic in nature. According to this claim, the natural-law arguments used to support the condemnation of contraception placed excessive emphasis on the biological finality of sexual organs and activity and did not give sufficient attention to the more experiential and psychological dimensions of sexual acts — that is, to their personal significance.[30] The second of these objections was that the Church's received teaching condemning contraception as immoral is derivative and not fundamental, even though it had been constantly taught in the Church. That is to say, the Church was said to have forbidden contraception in the past not because it is in itself wrong but because it was associated with things that really were wrong. In early centuries, it was said, contraception was forbidden because heretics who proposed it believed that life in the flesh is evil. The Church forbade contraception to express her rejection of such outrageous heresy. But, the objection continued, the great values protected then by excluding contraception can now be better protected by other means, without the burdens found in condemning contraception.[31]

*The Church's Teaching.* Fully aware of these doubts, and, in fact, largely to remove them, Paul VI strongly reaffirmed the received teaching of the Church on contraception. In 1968, after painstakingly deliberating over the matter and taking into account the arguments that had been advanced to support the moral permissibility of contraception, he reaffirmed in his encyclical *Humanae Vitae* the constant teaching of the Church that contraception is intrinsically a serious moral disorder. Although this encyclical met with dissent, and even, at times, contempt, the teaching set forth in it has since been firmly pro-

155

claimed by the magisterium. During the spring and summer of 1978 many conferences of bishops used the occasion of the tenth anniversary of *Humanae Vitae's* promulgation as an opportunity to affirm its teaching.[32] In 1976 the American bishops reaffirmed the traditional teaching in their pastoral *To Live in Christ Jesus*, despite pressures to remain silent on this matter.[33] In 1979 John Paul II commended the U.S. bishops for this statement.[34]

At the 1980 Synod of Bishops, representatives of national hierarchies from around the world addressed the question of contraception once again. After careful consideration the bishops stated their agreement with the teaching of *Humanae Vitae* and *Gaudium et Spes* on contraception.[35] John Paul II ratified their statement and reflected on the significance of their consideration of the issue. He said: "Consideration in depth of all the aspects of these problems offers a new and stronger confirmation of the importance of the authentic teaching on birth regulation reproposed in the Second Vatican Council and in the Encyclical *Humanae Vitae*."[36] It is clear therefore that the pope and the representatives of the bishops of the world have considered very carefully the dissent from the teaching on contraception and have rejected this dissent decisively.

The teaching of these recent magisterial statements is always presented as a reaffirmation of the "moral teaching on marriage proposed with constant firmness by the teaching of the Church."[37] And so, indeed, it is. As a leading historian of this question has stated:

> The propositions constituting a condemnation of contraception are, it will be seen, recurrent. Since the first clear mention of contraception by a Christian theologian, when a harsh third-century moralist accused a pope of encouraging it, the articulated judgment has been the same. In the world of the late Empire known to St. Jerome and St. Augustine, in the Ostrogothic Arles of Bishop Caesarius and the Suevian Braga of Bishop Martin, in the Paris of St. Albert and St. Thomas, in the Renaissance Rome of Sixtus V and the Renaissance Milan of St. Charles Borromeo, in the Naples of St. Alphonsus Liguori and the Liege of Charles Billuart, in the Philadelphia of Bishop Kenrick, and in the Bombay of Cardinal Gracias, the teachers of the Church

156

have taught without hestitation or variation that certain acts preventing conception are gravely sinful. No Catholic theologian has ever taught, "contraception is a good act." The teaching on contraception is clear and apparently fixed forever.[38]

This teaching has been proclaimed for centuries by bishops and their representatives in every circumstance. Until 1960 there was clearly moral unanimity in the teaching and believing Church. Even today, despite massive pressures of every kind, the unanimity of the teaching Church remains practically intact.[39] Moreover, the teaching has not been proclaimed as a mere rule or order or disciplinary regulation but as an inherently serious matter, closely related to the essentials of Christian morality as revealed in Scripture and tradition. Contraception has always been regarded as seriously wrong — as constituting objectively grave matter. In other words, the following of this teaching has always been taught to be necessary for salvation.

As the First and Second Vatican Councils clearly taught, the bishops of the Church teach infallibly when they propose matters of faith and morals in ways that reveal that they are acting as decisive witnesses to the teaching of the faith.[40] The Church is infallible in its ordinary magisterium, when that teaching has the characteristics noted in *Lumen Gentium*, no. 25.

Distinguished moralists have pointed out that the Church's teaching on contraception seems clearly to have been proposed by the ordinary magisterium in precisely this way.[41] At the very least, these considerations show that the received teaching must be accepted as a practical norm for preachers, confessors, and married people. Moreover, these considerations show that what is at issue is a teaching of the Church concerning morals and not a mere rule or policy. Thus, to "dissent" from this teaching is not simply to disregard commands of prelates but rather it is to attack what the Church presents as confirmed by divine teaching. Most Catholics are not willing to disregard truths closely related to their faith. The apparent disregard of the Church's teaching on contraception by many Catholics shows that the connection between this teaching and Catholic faith needs to be better understood.

It is true that among the faithful much confusion has been

generated. There is not now evident the clear and morally unanimous support of the received Catholic teaching which is the desired sign of Catholic unity. But the dissent of the last two decades does nothing to cancel out the testimony of the whole Church, teachers and believers alike, over all the centuries. Some dissenters like to argue that the Holy Spirit is guiding their dissent. But, even though they may have noble intentions, their claim of support from the Holy Spirit is very far from proved. There are many other active forces, not identical with the Holy Spirit, that have led the massive social drive toward contraception; and these motives appear to have influenced some Catholic thinkers too.

It has sometimes been the case that positions which had been decisively taught by the Church for a while began to lose their firm hold on many in the Church. Thus, after several centuries of Catholic faith in the divinity of Jesus, and even after the solemn definitions of the Christological councils, worldly influences led to the massive rise of Arianism in the Church. So many began to deny what is the Church's decisive teaching about Christ that St. Jerome did not hestitate to say, "The whole world groaned to find itself Arian." That is, all about them the faithful saw many ceasing to believe that Jesus is literally God. But this failure of some — indeed many — to believe for a while does not erase decisive testimony of the faith over the centuries. Development of doctrine does not mean that the Church could faithfully deny in one age what is affirmed insistently as the word of Christ in another.

Moreover, there is a striking testimony of the faithful in our time in support of the received teaching. Despite the immense propaganda favoring contraception, despite the failure of local teachers of faith to present intelligently and persuasively the position the Catholic faith has always taught, there has been great faithfulness on the part of vast numbers of the faithful. The astonishing growth of the Natural Family Planning (NFP) movement, with its joyful discovery of how valuable the Catholic teaching is, and how it is both livable and able to enrich married life, presages a happy return to a fuller acceptance of Catholic teaching everywhere. The terrible disadvantages of the contraceptive movement are becoming more visible, and it is evident that NFP provides in more human and nobler ways the goods that contraception was seeking to reach.

*Theological Argument.* The Catholic moral tradition contains a number of arguments against contraception. Catholic certainty in matters of morals is, of course, not dependent simply upon such arguments. The testimony of faith is much firmer, but such moral reflection is important for the family of faith.

We wish here to develop an argument that follows the principled pattern of moral reasoning sketched above in Chapter 4. The argument seeks to bring out the anti-life character of contraception, and thereby to show one way in which the Church's teaching on contraception is an authentic application of the sexual morality rooted in the Scriptures. Like that of Scripture itself, the Church's teaching on contraception is integrally pro-life.[42]

In contraceptive intercourse one chooses both to have sexual intercourse and to prevent the act from being procreative. The contraceptive element in the dual act is aimed precisely and directly against the possible coming-to-be of human life. As the American bishops note, such a prevention is a rejection of the "life-giving meaning of intercourse"; and "the wrongness of such an act lies in the rejection of this value."[43]

Three major steps can be noted in the argument to establish this point. First, the procreative good is intrinsically and always good. Second, a contraceptive deed acts directly against this good, and of itself does nothing but assail that good. Third, it is always immoral to so act directly against a basic human good.

Consider the first point: the procreative good is of its very nature always a good. To say this is not, of course, to suggest that in every case it would be wise or right to promote the procreative good. In the concrete conditions of life every kind of real good can be intermingled with serious evils and harms. Truth is a good; but one ought not publish every truth, to the useless harm and embarrassment of others, or in neglect of duties of secrecy. Life itself is good, but one might be wrong to fight simply to sustain another's life (by extraordinary means) when further living cannot be dissociated from excessive pain and humiliation. Similarly, the realization of the procreative good might in a given case involve great dangers to the health of

159

the mother, the stability of the family, or the like. But truth, life, and the procreative good remain in themselves great goods.

The Second Vatican Council and other Church teachings have made clear that Christian teaching honors the procreative good.[44] The teaching of the Church on this matter is clearly based on Scripture, which constantly celebrates the passing on of human life as a great and wonderful thing. To be able to have children is a great good and joy to human persons: a great progeny was among the chief blessings promised to Abraham. Our Lord himself pointed to the great joy that spontaneously follows childbirth; it is good when a child is born into the world.

And what Scripture witnesses is what everyone knows. All who are parents know this quite directly and immediately. Others see it as a desirable possibility — to have a child of one's own would be a good thing. Or if for some special reason they should not have a child, they know that this is not because a child is not a good thing and that having children is not desirable but because in these circumstances such a good would involve also harms that they wish to avoid.

To acknowledge the intrinsic goodness of procreation is to recognize that human life is good and that its transmission is also good. As Christians, we are able to see reproduction as procreation — that is, as cooperation with God in his act of creating another image of himself, another member of the kingdom, another person called to be an adopted child of God.[45]

We shall weave together our treatment of the next two points: a contraceptive act of its very nature always strikes directly against the procreative good, and such an attack on an intrinsic human good is always wrong in every area of life.

Few Christian moralists have doubted that there is "something wrong" with contraception. Even those who favor contraceptive practices in many circumstances have been aware of the overwhelming Christian testimony against it in tradition. Ordinarily they recognize that reverence for the procreative good must be safeguarded; that a "contraceptive mentality" is difficult to reconcile with Christian values. But some have argued that at times and, indeed, frequently in contemporary circumstances, a greater harm could come from not practicing contraception than from using it. But it is fallacious to argue

160

from a claim that great harms come at times from not practicing contraception to the conclusion that contraception is therefore morally permissible. To do so would be to assume that one may do any kind of act whatsoever — even an act that involves a choice against a basic human good — if that would seem to lead to better consequences in the circumstances. One would be justified, for example, in directly and deliberately killing an entirely innocent person if better consequences would seem to come from so acting than not so acting. Against this view that one may do evil that (a greater) good may come of it we have argued at length in Chapter 4. Here, it is important to point out clearly the structure of what happens in contraceptive acts: one *is* deliberately and directly acting against a great human good — that is, one is doing the evil of assailing the procreative good in the hope that good might come of it.

To do a contraceptive deed is to perform an action that in itself and directly has only one objective: to keep an act of intercourse from being fruitful, to see to it that a new human life does not come to be in and through an act of the kind in which new human life can come to be. The contraceptive act is directly aimed against the realization of the procreative good. One is not simply declining to promote that good; one is taking positive steps directly against it. One is choosing precisely to make the sort of act that, of its very nature, is open to the transmission of new life to be closed to this good.

In Christian tradition there has been concern to recognize that some ways of bringing about good and preventing harm are not permissible. There are some kinds of deeds that a good person simply will not do. And parallel patterns can be seen in diverse kinds of bad acts. The logic and pattern of contraceptive acts is like that of perjury committed for "good reasons." In such perjury one attacks truth in an act (an oath) which of its very nature is ordered to the truth, perhaps on the grounds that by doing so one might prevent a "dangerous truth" from doing harm. This is not like seeking to avoid the harm by remaining silent, for in the latter case one honors the truth by refusing to attack it. Again, contraception is like euthanasia (mercy killing) in its logical structure. In mercy killing one chooses to kill, to act directly against innocent life, for the sake of removing the

161

burdens of a painful or debilitated existence. One chooses against life for the sake of what seems to be noble purposes. The withholding of extraordinary treatments, by way of contrast, is not a choice against life. This decision, like the decision to remain silent, refuses to attack the goods at stake while seeking to deal prudently with the evils present in the situation.

In a contraceptive act, one freely and deliberately chooses to attack a great human good. The motive for this act may be upright; one may wish to avoid for oneself and others the harms that would be inseparable from the untimely realization of that good. But there are many ways in which those harms could be avoided, some good and some evil.

Some have sought to avoid the force of this moral principle by saying that in acts like contraception, the evil intended is not the kind of evil one should always avoid but only a premoral or physical evil. The meaning of this objection is that the good of procreation, unlike some other goods, does not include as part of its meaning the morally correct disposition of the human will. Procreation is clearly a good, as are life and knowledge; but these goods can be pursued immorally, and can be realized without any human choice. So, they are not morally defined, and in that sense are "premoral." Such goods can be contrasted with the goods indicated by the virtues; these clearly are morally defined. Justice, for example, is not realized unless the person in question chooses and is disposed to choose justly.

This distinction between kinds of human goods does not, however, provide a way of avoiding the force of the principle that one must not do evil for the sake of good, for while it is the case that life itself or truth or procreation is a premoral good, our free choices bearing on these goods are not simply premoral. And it is precisely these choices that are at issue. In the choice in question, a person chooses against the procreative good, and this choice has a moral deformity, for, as we saw in Chapter 4, one cannot love God and neighbor when one chooses to harm the goods of persons which reflect the infinite goodness of God. Thus, as Paul VI made clear in *Humanae Vitae*, no. 14, the proposal to evaluate actions directed toward premoral goods by the proportionalist principle of the lesser evil does not avoid the inconsistency between proportionalism and

162

the received moral teaching of the Church on the meaning of the principle that the end does not justify the means.

Recall that this same pattern of immoral actions is possible in every aspect of life. One may wish that a truth not be publicized, if that would cause great and unnecessary harm. Hence one legitimately remains silent, or indignantly denies the right of questioners to probe, when one is guarding a legitimate secret. But one must not directly assail the truth, lie, or perjure oneself, or act against one good for the sake of some other good. One may legitimately wish that a life in great pain and near death may come to a peaceful end. One may cease to use extraordinary means to lengthen the life. Fully respecting that life is a good, yet because of the pain and burdens associated with living longer, one might in some circumstances forgo the treatments needed to sustain life. But to treat the good of life, even in its most embattled form, as if it were an evil, and directly to attack it, to kill the dying person — that would be evil.

Similarly with respect to the procreative good, it would sometimes be very unwise for couples to have another child. In some circumstances, the intention not to have a child is appropriate for married couples. But as it is never appropriate or right to do acts that are direct attacks on truth or life or other basic human goods, it is never right to attack directly the procreative good. We are not to do evil so that good may come to be.

In fact, this principle — that one ought not to do evil so that good may come about — is of critical importance in every area of Christian morality. In the early debates over contraception, defenders of received Catholic teaching taught that those who permitted contraception "for good reasons" were adopting a principle that would make any kind of sexual activity (fornication, masturbation, homosexual acts) permissible or good if done for "good reasons." To allow contraception one must deny either that procreation is a good, or assert that it is sometimes permissible to act directly against a basic human good. Either of these is sufficient to justify masturbation, sodomy, and so on. If the procreative good is not a basic good that must always be respected as such, there is no decisive moral barrier to actions like masturbation, sodomy, or adultery. If one can justify acting against a good for overriding reasons, then one can

163

act against the procreative good not only in contraception but in masturbation, sodomy, and so forth.[46]

This argument was denied in the debates of the 1960s by those defending contraception, but the logic of the position they took has now become very clear. Recent history has shown that their original contention was mistaken: contraception could not be accepted while the other prohibitions of Christian sexual morality were maintained. However, many of the revisionists of the 1960s were willing to accept the inherent logic of their position and, in effect, to admit that the original objection to their position was correct. Thus, today the leading moralists who dissented on contraception argue that in given circumstances, when a "greater good" can be served, various sexual acts (such as fornication, adultery, and sodomy) are morally permissible.[47] They concluded that the whole sexual morality of the Church had been based upon mistaken principles.

The development went farther. If the argument for contraception is valid, then in other areas of human existence it will be permissible to do evil so that good may come about; and deeds previously judged intrinsically wrong may be justified morally if there is a sufficiently serious motive. One can kill the innocent or commit perjury for noble reasons. Rather than admit that the pro-contraception argument must be erroneous if it leads to such conclusions, some moralists have simply followed the hypothesis wherever it leads. Instead of seeking to justify contraception in terms of principles compatible with Catholic teaching, they drifted into accepting only those aspects of Catholic teaching that could be reconciled with the proportionalist principles justifying contraception.

But clearly, if a moral principle leads to such perverse conclusions, then it must be an erroneous principle. At the beginning of the debate every Catholic theologian in the debate would have admitted this.[48]

The account given here shows why the approval of contraception contributes to acceptance of abortion. Contraception is an attempt to prevent the handing on of life, and one who is willing to do an act aimed directly against life as it is passed on is likely to remain ready to act directly against life if, contrary to his or her expectations, the unwanted new life begins.[49] Those

164

who act directly against a good to prevent its realization have only too frequently proved ready to take the next step. If the resolve to prevent a child from coming to be is so strong that one is willing to act deliberately and directly against that good, then one will be more disposed to act directly against the acquired life of the child if its conception is not successfully prevented.[50]

*Replies to Objections.* We turn now to a consideration of the factors which have given rise to the doubts and the protests on the part of many. With respect to the special character of oral contraceptives it became clear very quickly that this method did not differ in any essential way from older contraceptive techniques. To think that the use of the pill was different from other contraceptive techniques required a kind of physicalism which is rejected by the Church, and which had been sharply rejected by the dissenters themselves. It is the contraceptive intent of the act itself and not the mere physical form of behavior taken as such that is morally determining.[51] This is confirmed by the fact that the acceptance of the pill has led both in theory and practice to the acceptance of other contraceptives including sterilization,[52] and to the acceptance of other sexual acts which have been prohibited because they are considered unnatural.

The Church's teaching on contraception is not based on a physicalist sort of natural-law theory. It is the anti-life *intent* together with the anti-covenantal and the anti-sacramental effects, and not the mere biology involved, which are held to be morally determinative. Biology is relevant to the person choosing contraception because his or her beliefs about the connection between coitus and conception lead that person to seek to break that connection in some way. But the goodness of human life and the requirement that one not direct one's intention against that good are not truths derived from biology. The morality involved is that of the requirements of intelligent love.

Of course, the objection that the traditional teaching is physicalist often has another sense, namely that the prohibition of contraceptive intercourse gives undue priority to one of the goods of marriage at the expense of the others.[53] However, to state that procreation is *a* basic human good is not to say that it is the *only* good or the chief good. If it is *a* basic good, then one should never act directly against it, as one should not directly act against the unitive good in marriage. It is in this sense only that, like other finite goods, it imposes an absolute obligation.[54]

Of course, there are some who will deny that procreation is an intrinsic basic human good. They hold that when procreation is good, it is so only because it is instrumentally valuable. They hold that it is good only when it is assumed into consciousness and freely chosen. Some argue that no bodily goods — goods such as life, health, and procreation — are intrinsic human goods. They cannot be authentic and full human goods because they, as bodily goods, are on a lower level than the conscious, intelligent sphere of what these critics consider properly personal activity and the level of fully human goods. The goods of the human body — bodily life, health, and procreation — are thus set apart from the mind or consciousness, and the human person is identified with the latter.

To propose this, however, is to advance the doctrine of "dualism," a doctrine that considers a human person as a spiritual reality *in* a body rather than as a unified single reality, this living flesh. Dualism neglects not only the experience of personal unity but also the biblical view of the human person as an integral whole.[55] This dualistic view is also contradicted in the teaching of the Church — for example, in *Gaudium et Spes*:

> Man, though made of body and soul, is a unity. Through
> his very bodily condition he sums up in himself the ele-
> ments of the material world. Through him they are thus
> brought to their highest perfection and can raise their voice
> in praise freely given to the creator. For this reason man
> may not despise his bodily life. Rather he is obliged to re-
> gard his body as good and to hold it in honor since God
> has created it and will raise it up on the last day.[56]

There are also powerful philosophical arguments against dualism — arguments that are well presented by Thomas Aquinas[57] and that are also forcefully presented by contemporary religious and secular philosophers.[58]

It is, in short, necessary to regard procreation as a basic human good. Although it is true that some people at times have children for ulterior purposes, it is also true that for many people these ulterior purposes do not exhaust their reasons for having children. People often have children simply because they see that it is good to bring human beings into existence. Procreation is constantly portrayed in the Scriptures as a blessing and joy, and this proclamation of Scripture is confirmed by common human experience.

The fact that procreation is an intrinsic basic human good is relevant for answering another important objection, namely the contention that the Church's teaching on contraception, though constant, is merely derivative and instrumental to the protection of other Christian values. As noted already, human life and procreation are intrinsic goods of surpassing value in Christian thought. The obligation not to act directly against this good — or any other intrinsic human good — is also an essential part of the Christian moral tradition. The prohibition against contraception is therefore fundamental and not derivative. The prohibition of contraception is not a dispensable instrument for promoting some other position; it is a necessary requirement of Christian respect for the good of human life. This is confirmed by the consensus over the centuries of the approved modern moralists (until the unjustified dissent of the last two decades), all of whom teach that contraceptive intercourse is *intrinsically* wrong. Moreover, this consensus is based on the consensus of the whole tradition: in different contexts by different arguments and with different emphases teachers of the Catholic Church have concurred in condemning contraception as seriously wrong.[59]

## III. Natural Family Planning

We turn now to a consideration of the difference between periodic continence and contraception. The Church has taught that couples may morally regulate the size of their families by methods that do not involve contraceptive acts. These methods have several forms; generically they may be called "natural family planning," or NFP.

Great strides have been made in recent years in perfecting NFP. While earlier forms were less effective, the best contemporary methods are quite reliable, not only for women with regular cycles but for all women. NFP is a genuine, practicable option; it avoids the harmful physical and moral effects of contraception, and it has many important good effects of its own.[60]

167

Despite Church teaching that contraception is intrinsically wrong and NFP is not, some have insisted that NFP does not differ in morally significant ways from contraception. Some claim that NFP is *natural* "contraception," whereas the use of drugs and mechanical devices is *artificial* "contraception."[61]

Some argue that NFP and contraception have precisely the same purpose (that is, the avoidance of conception) and that therefore they must be morally the same. But this contention involves a fallacy of elementary logic.[62] Two acts — or one act and one deliberate omission — each of which has the same purpose need not be morally the same. One can get money to feed one's family by acts of stealing or by honest labor. Though they have exactly the same end, these acts are obviously not morally the same. The purpose of one's acts and policies is not the only factor relevant for determining the morality of these acts and policies. *What one does*, as well as one's reason for doing it, is morally relevant.

It is clear that NFP achieves its purpose in a way that is essentially different from contraceptive intercourse. NFP involves no choice to treat the procreative good as an evil and to act directly against it, whereas contraceptive intercourse does.[63] Reflection on the analogies given earlier in this chapter — the difference between perjury and silence in guarding a perilous truth, or the difference between mercy killing and restrained care for the dying — reveals this.[64]

In practicing NFP a couple adopts a policy to have sexual intercourse at infertile times and to refrain from intercourse at fertile times if they have serious reasons to avoid a pregnancy. Refraining from intercourse is not contraceptive intercourse, since it is not intercourse at all. Moreover, refraining from intercourse has a different intentional relation to the good of procreation than contraceptive intercourse has. In contraceptive intercourse one does what one knows to be a potentially procreative act and one also acts to ensure that the procreative potential of that act is not realized. This is acting against the procreative good. In NFP, however, one's intention to avoid a pregnancy is achieved by forgoing the act that one believes will be procreative; one does not act against a good by altogether refraining from acting.[65]

168

Thus, the refraining from intercourse which is involved in NFP does not involve the anti-procreative intention of contraceptive intercourse. Neither do the acts of intercourse in which a couple engages during infertile periods have this intention. Nothing is done to any of them to render them infertile, since nature itself has made them infertile. The other goods of marriage are quite legitimately pursued in these acts.

Moreover, the whole spirit and style of life promoted by NFP is radically different. As Pope John Paul II has said in *Familiaris Consortio*:

> In the light of the experience of many couples and of the data provided by the different human sciences, theological reflection is able to perceive and is called to study further *the difference, both anthropological and moral*, between contraception and recourse to the rhythm of the cycle: it is a difference which is much wider and deeper than is usually thought, one which involves in the final analysis two irreconcilable concepts of the human person and of human sexuality.[66] (Emphasis added.)

NFP therefore is not contraceptive. Moreover, it not only does not hinder but even promotes the other goods of marriage. The sexual life of the couple using NFP is controlled by chastity. The efforts of self-control must be mutual; thus couples living by NFP are given a motive to unite in a common effort of will. This chaste union obviates the temptation for couples to treat each other as instruments for sexual gratification and allows their sexual expression to be an expression of human communication, of their marital covenant, and of the love of Christ for the Church.[67]

Of course, there will be difficulties in the practice of NFP, just as the Lord has promised us that there would be difficulties of discipleship in other areas of life, for he spoke about carrying the cross daily. Cooperation between spouses in a moderate amount of self-restraint is necessary; but contraception's failure to respect the full meaningfulness of sex, to treat the sexual act as unrelated to the goods that give it its profound meaning, is ultimately destructive. The substitution of easy technological (and immoral) solutions for human ones is a common temptation of our age. But those who persist in finding temperate and human solutions to this problem in NFP testify that this is not only a morally good solution but in many ways enriches the lives of those who follow that path.

## IV. Sterilization

Today, partially because of the dangers of the pill and IUD's (intrauterine devices), more and more people are resorting to sterilization as a means of preventing conception. Those who justify contraception as a way of avoiding pregnancy use the same basic moral justification for sterilization. Since sterilization, however, is for all practical purposes irreversible, some hold that a much more serious "proportionate reason" is necessary to justify the choice to sterilize.[68] Frequently sterilization is advocated as the most appropriate way to cope with the problems faced by a couple who are the bearers of a recessive genetic defect of a serious nature, such as Tay-Sachs disease or sickle-cell anemia. For such couples, there is a twenty-five percent chance that any child they conceive will suffer the crippling disease. Sterilization is also recommended at times for women whose health may be seriously threatened were they to become pregnant.[69] It is frequently urged for couples whose families are now judged to be complete.

The Church has constantly taught that contraceptive or direct sterilization is intrinsically immoral.[70] The Church, along with theologians faithful to her teaching, distinguishes between direct or contraceptive sterilization and "indirect" sterilization. Direct or contraceptive sterilization is an act whose sole and immediate purpose is to destroy the procreativity of the person sterilized, whereas indirect sterilization is a medical procedure whose immediate purpose and direct intent is to remove pathological reproductive organs or to inhibit the natural functioning of such organs when such functioning (for example, abnormal hormonal production) aggravates a pathological condition within the person.

The Church condemns direct or contraceptive sterilization for the same reasons that she condemns contraception. The act in question is one that directly attacks a basic human good. One does evil for the sake of some good to come. Moreover, one could achieve the desired ends reasonably through other means,

170

such as NFP. The Church teaches that indirect sterilization is often justifiable. The principle of totality indicates that a person is permitted to undergo a mutilating operation necessary to protect the life and health of the person, even if sterility resulted as a side effect of the operation.[71]

Some theologians[72] have attempted to claim that the principle of totality can be extended to justify contraceptive sterilization. They have argued that doing so will prevent a future pregnancy that may be hazardous to the life of the mother or that may result in the birth of a child suffering from a genetically induced disability, and in this way contribute to the total well-being of the person thus sterilized and to his or her family.[73] The argument, basically, is that some hoped-for-good-to-come-about can justify the deliberate intention to act directly against a good here and now.

This effort to extend the principle of totality merges, it can be seen, with the attempts of some recent theologians to argue that it is morally permissible to intend to do what they call premoral or nonmoral or ontic evil for the sake of a proportionately greater premoral or nonmoral or ontic good.[74]

Many theologians, as well as decisive Church statements, have vigorously rejected this attempt to justify contraceptive sterilization.[75] The revisionary effort is ultimately based on the belief that we may willingly and directly do evil for the sake of a good-to-come, so long as the good-to-come is "greater" than the good we deliberately and directly repudiate in doing the evil. But, as we have seen, such a position strikes at the heart of Christian morality.

Moreover, the threat of great social evils implicit in such an expanded principle of totality is obvious.[76] There are many who argue that for the good of society as a whole — and indeed for the good of the persons immediately affected — it is right to sterilize the mentally retarded, the indigent, and all those who fail to exercise "responsibility" in begetting.

The temptation to sterilize is perhaps understandable in a technological culture because sterilization appears to be an efficient way of realizing some worthwhile goals. Yet a technically efficient means may not be the morally right means. A sterilizing act performed precisely to remove a pathology or prevent

171

the spread of disease can be morally justifiable; sterilization, substituted for personal control and reasonable self-discipline, cannot be. We are just beginning to recognize the terrible harm that the pill, once hailed as a panacea for the problem of regulating conception,[77] does to women. There are many known serious side effects of sterilization, both for women and for men, and we do not as yet even know the full extent of these side effects. NFP offers realistic and morally good means for avoiding pregnancies when this is necessary. Contraceptive intercourse and contraceptive sterilization seek to provide merely technical solutions to deep human problems; but the solutions they offer also entail morally wrongful choices, the choice to set oneself against a basic human good. As such they are not humanly good solutions.

### V. Other Violations of Marital Chastity

The Church's teaching on contraceptive intercourse and contraceptive sterilization applies not only to the use of contraceptive devices but also to any acts done with the intention of preventing a complete genital act between spouses from being a potentially life-giving act. Thus, mutual masturbation, oral and anal sex, and similar acts in which orgasms are sought apart from natural intercourse, are gravely wrong. The argument developed in the section against contraception applies very closely to these acts when done with contraceptive intent, as well as to acts of contraceptive intercourse in the sense we have defined it.[78]

Moreover, such acts between spouses are not properly ordered to the goods of married life even if they are not done with contraceptive intent. The discussion of masturbation and sodomy, which will be given in the following chapter, will make it clear that the goods of marriage cannot be properly pursued in masturbatory, oral, and anal sexual activity on the part of married couples.[79]

The Church's teaching that natural intercourse open to procreation is the only legitimate form of complete sexual expression, even between spouses, does not imply that mutual genital stimulation other than intercourse is forbidden for spouses as part of the preliminaries to marital intercourse.

172

Marriage is a mutual commitment in which each side ceases to be autonomous, in various ways and also sexually: the sexual liberty in agreement together is great; here, so long as they are not immoderate so as to become slaves of sensuality, nothing is shameful, if the complete acts — the ones involving ejaculation of the man's seed — that they engage in are true and real marriage acts.[80]

But the qualification in this statement is important. The activities of spouses must be moderate, and the danger of becoming "slaves of sensuality" is real. Pope Pius XII warned against this danger by criticizing an anti-Christian hedonism that encourages "the pursuit of the intensest possible enjoyment" in the preliminaries to marital intercourse and in its consummation, as though in this sphere the moral law enjoined nothing more than that the act itself be accomplished normally, and as though the rest, in whatever manner done, could be justified as being an expression of mutual love which is sanctified by the sacrament of matrimony and deserves praise and reward in the eyes of God and conscience. Unfortunately, the dignity of the human being, the dignity of the Christian, which sets a check on sexual excess, can be left out of account.[81]

Spouses are required to seek the moderation and self-restraint necessary to preserve their lovemaking from becoming the pursuit of the shallow and apparent good of isolated sexual pleasure, rather than the authentic good of human love, sexually expressed in shared joy. There are no hard and fast rules for avoiding the immoderate pursuit of sexual pleasure, given that the life-giving and person-uniting goods of marriage are respected. Nevertheless, there are certain marks of immoderation and certain broad guidelines for marital chastity that spouses and confessors may refer to: a preoccupation with sexual pleasure, succumbing to desire in circumstances in which it would be wise to refrain, and insisting against serious reluctance of one's spouse. One has hardly acquired sufficient self-possession if one could not accept peacefully a few weeks or a few months of abstinence in case of real need.[82]

Spouses should avoid also the danger of insensibility and unjustified abstention. These also can be sins against moderation and can violate the reasonable expectations of the other

173

spouse.[83] Marital intercourse should be a gladly agreed-upon activity, but under certain circumstances one is obliged to accede to the reasonable desires of one's spouse. Unreasonable refusal to have sexual intercourse can harm the person-uniting aim of marriage, and such refusal is often inconsistent with the demands of conjugal justice and charity.

### VI. Artificial Insemination and "In Vitro" Fertilization

A basic principle of Christian sexual ethics, as we have seen, is that the goods toward which sexuality is ordered must not be separated from unitive and life-giving acts. There is an "inseparable connection established by God" between the unitive meaning and the procreative meaning of the conjugal act.[84]

This intrinsic connection between the goods of marriage is relevant for understanding many of the contemporary challenges to the Christian ideal of family life. Two such challenges extensively discussed at the present time illustrate the far-reaching character of the Church's teaching on marriage.

Artificial insemination and *in vitro* fertilization (test-tube reproduction) are now very real options made available by modern technology. The Church holds that to bring about human life in these ways is to abuse technology. These are wrong ways of responding to the praiseworthy desire for children.[85] This is not the place to develop fully an argument against these activities. Much has already been done along these lines[86] and more theological reflection on them is in order. Here, we state only the basic principle. These activities are inconsistent with the intimate connection between the procreative and the unitive goods of marriage and of human sexuality. Just as contraception separates sexual activity from procreation, these techniques involve a separation of procreation from sexual intercourse. This separation involves a disregard for the connection between the goods of marriage which harms both of these goods.[87] The procreative good is pursued, but it is pursued in a way that disregards its connection with the unitive good as realized in the conjugal act itself. It is in this act above all that the spouses are "one flesh," and if children are brought into existence otherwise than as the fulfillment of this common life, they will not be given life in an act of marital and procreative love. Rather, they will be the products of technological art; they will be "made," not "begotten." And this is a dehumanization of the engendering of human persons.

Thus, artificial insemination and *in vitro* fertilization cannot be proper parts of sacramental marriage nor can they be proper parts of marriage as a natural institution because they leave out the marriage act itself — the act in which the goods of marriage are pursued in their inseparable unity. Human life should come to be, only in an act of human love, associated with God's creative act of love. This brief discussion is meant to show that the Church's teaching on marriage is a unified doctrine that directs not only the sexual conduct of individuals and spouses but also the most basic institutions and interpersonal relations of mankind. It is the wisdom of a God who loves us and who wills that we be members of his own Trinitarian family that directs us to be at the same time chaste, loving, and open to new life in our use of the sexual nature the Lord has given us.

CHAPTER

# The Requirements of Chastity Outside the Covenant of Married Love

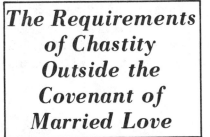

Chastity is not a virtue for married persons alone, for the goods at stake in human sexuality need to be cherished and reverenced in every person's life. The self-possession of a chaste person is necessary not only within marriage but also within every Christian vocation and, indeed, within every humanly satisfactory life. A proper regard for the human body, a wholesome respect for the handing on of the great good of human life, respect for the real integrity of intimate human relationships — all these are necessary not only for the married but for those who plan marriage, for all who choose the splendor of committed virginity for the sake of the kingdom, and for all whose lives should, however indirectly, support or image marriage and its goods. This includes every person.

Everyone is called to a love that binds persons together in ways that reflect the personal communion of divine love. Single persons exhibit chastity when in the service of human friendship they do not merely behave impulsively; when they do not permit unworthy pursuit of passing gratification to lead them to act in ways that fail to honor goods far more precious than simple pleasure. They pursue chastity when they refuse to depersonalize the human body by using it as though it were but an instrument for gratification. Of course, the lure of pleasure is great and the instincts of selfishness are strong so that the demands of chastity for the unmarried can at times be difficult. But the difficulty is none other than that of truly reverencing persons and the goods of persons in the actual conditions of our life. Like the other difficulties in living well, it can be made light by the grace of Christ.

In the preceding chapter we presented the most central requirements of married love and marital chastity. Here, we present a similar moral analysis of the general requirements of chastity for those who are unmarried. Our special focus will be on those choices and acts which the Church has always taught to be unchaste kinds of acts, for these are acts which must be avoided if the personal and interpersonal fabric of the most basic of human relationships is to be protected from the ravages of lust and selfishness. We will first analyze premarital sex or fornication, then masturbation, followed by homosexual activity. We will conclude this chapter by briefly considering bestiality, rape, incest, and sins of thought. In treating these issues, we draw upon the relevant teaching of Scripture, Christian tradition, and magisterial doctrine. We will note also some of the currently popular objections to, or difficulties with, received Catholic teaching.

## I. Premarital Sexual Relations

Christian tradition, as we have seen above in Chapters 2 and 3, has always regarded sexual intercourse between unmarried persons to be seriously wrong. The Church sees this prohibition as part of the natural law. This does not mean that in the turmoil of our sinful world everyone "naturally" grasps the truth of this norm. Nor does it mean that there will not be some who will even regard nonmarital sexual activity as being a good thing, for such actions can be very attractive and even seem to be good. What the Church means in saying that sexual intercourse between unmarried persons violates the natural law is (1) that the malice of this kind of activity follows necessarily from a reflective understanding of the human goods at stake in sexual activity and the requirements of intelligent concern for these goods; and (2) that, as in other areas of human life, persons who fail to observe the requirements of intelligent concern

177

for what truly perfects their human nature, harm themselves and others.

The Church's teaching on the immorality of extramarital intercourse is also based on the conviction that God's revelation, as expressed in Scripture and tradition, unequivocally condemns it. For those who have faith, the word of God is an even surer guide to good living than arguments from the natural law. In making use of Scripture and tradition in this chapter as throughout this entire book, we are avoiding what is called a proof-text approach — that is, using isolated biblical texts as simple proof for a moral or theological belief, doctrine, or principle. Catholic doctrine on matters so long reflected upon and so constantly taught as these is not built upon superficial appeals to isolated fragments of Scripture. Rather, the basis for the Catholic conviction on specific moral questions is the integral vision of human persons and of human sexuality which, with the guidance of the Holy Spirit, is drawn from the word of God as understood, believed, and taught within the family of faith over the centuries. Thus, citation of a given scriptural text or magisterial teaching is meant to highlight statements in which the convictions of the faith are succinctly and powerfully brought to a focus.

*Scripture.* The Old Testament contains the roots of the Christian prohibition of extramarital intercourse, for within the Old Testament the values protected by this prohibition begin to be articulated. This is clearest in the Old Testament insistence on the virginity of women before marriage.[1] This insistence is not equally clear in the case of men — perhaps the patriarchial structure of Israelite society played a part here.[2] Despite this limitation, the Old Testament kept constantly before the eyes of the Chosen People the beauty of monogamous marriage as willed by Yahweh. The Wisdom literature is filled with warnings against sins of lust. Fornication, or *porneia*, is portrayed there as an apostasy from God and a devising of idols.[3]

By the first century A.D., the reflective faith of the Jewish community, instructed by the prophets and the authors of the Wisdom books, came to a remarkably full understanding of the significance of Old Testament teaching on extramarital intercourse. They understood the biblical injunction "Thou shalt

178

not commit adultery" broadly to "prohibit various immoral sexual activities,"[4] and they valued chastity highly. The words of Philo Judaeus, a faithful Jew who lived in apostolic times, are typical of the attitude of first-century Judaism:

> We, the descendants of the Hebrews, have excellent customs and laws. Other nations allow their young men of fourteen years of age to go to prostitutes and to other women who sell their bodies. But according to our laws, all *hetairas* [kept women] are condemned to die. Until there can be legitimate relations, we do not have intercourse with a woman. Both parties enter marriage as virgins.[5]

What is only pointed to in the Old Testament is clearly affirmed in the New Testament — namely that all sexual intercourse outside of marriage, all fornication, is seriously wrong. This teaching is expressed in the numerous condemnations of *porneia*. This word is usually translated into English as "fornication." Not all of the uses of *porneia* and its cognates in these passages, however, refer directly and clearly to premarital sex. This is not surprising, since "*porneia*" (like the word "fornication" in English) did not refer merely to premarital sex.[6] However, this term does not simply mean uncleanness but refers to certain kinds of sexual activity which, like fornication in the narrow sense, fail to honor the goods that sexual activity should always respect.

Matthew and Mark report that Jesus includes *porneia* in a list of evil activities which make a person unclean (Matthew 15.19; Mark 7.21).[7]

These brief indications of the mind of the Lord on this matter were greatly elaborated on in the evangelization and catechesis of pagans by the early Church. The Gentiles did not share the Jewish conviction about the importance of chastity, and so clear teaching was especially needed. Thus, pagan converts were told bluntly that they must abstain from fornication (Acts 15.20, 29; 21.25). The Pauline literature, in particular, not only contains repeated references to fornication as a serious sin but also an explanation of why it is incompatible with Christian life.

The First Letter to the Corinthians contains much of what Paul says about fornication. Paul lists fornicators among those who will not inherit the kingdom of God (1 Corinthians 6.9).

The body, he reminds the Corinthians, is not for fornication but for the Lord (1 Corinthians 6.13, 14). He then explains why sexual intercourse with prostitutes is wrong for Christians. The bodies of Christians are members of the body of Christ. The Christian who has intercourse with a prostitute joins his body to hers and becomes one flesh with her (1 Corinthians 6.15-17).

St. Paul goes on to say: "Keep away from fornication. All the other sins are committed outside the body; but to fornicate is to sin against your own body. Your body, you know, is the temple of the Holy Spirit who is in you since you received him from God" (1 Corinthians 6.18-19).

After proposing virginity as an ideal expression of Christian love, Paul notes that, because of the danger of fornication, in the ordinary case it is good for each man to have his own wife and each woman her own husband (1 Corinthians 7.2). He goes on to add a comment specifically directed at widows and the unmarried: "It is good for them to stay as they are, like me, but if they cannot control the sexual urges, they should get married, since it is better to be married than to be tortured (1 Cor. 7.8, 9)."[8]

Thus, the Church has always understood extramarital sex to be gravely wrong — not only because specific scriptural texts teach this but also because of her understanding of the overall thrust of God's revelation concerning the meaning of love and sex, and of how the goods of sexuality should be honored. Scripture and tradition, as understood and interpreted by the Church, are at one in holding that premarital intercourse is seriously wrong.[9]

*Why Extramarital Intercourse Is Immoral.* The reasons why the Church condemns extramarital intercourse as seriously immoral are clearly set forth by Pope John Paul II in *Familiaris Consortio.* There, referring to "God's plan" for marriage and the family, John Paul II emphasizes that the human meaning of sexual activity is not merely biological, nor is it aimed at mere pursuit of pleasure. It "concerns the innermost being of the human person as such." Sexual intercourse is realized in a truly human way "only if it is an integral part of the love by which a man and a woman commit themselves totally to one another until death." When spouses give themselves humanly and gener-

180

ously to one another in marital intercourse, they signify a will to honor each other and to respect the goods each needs to fulfill his or her life. The self-giving in sexual intercourse is a lie if it fails to be "the sign and fruit" of this total and generous self-giving.

The Holy Father goes on to explain that this total self-giving is possible only within marriage, for marriage is the covenant of conjugal love by which man and woman freely unite their lives into an "intimate community of life and love willed by God himself." Outside of this covenant something is withheld. Instead, one reserves for oneself the possibility that in the future one might decide otherwise than to maintain the community of life and love. Thus, outside of marriage the self-giving is by definition not total. The pope concludes from this analysis that the limitation of sexual activity to marriage is not an unreasonable or arbitrary imposition on people's freedom but an "interior requirement of the covenant of conjugal love."[10]

Pope John Paul's statement draws out the point of the Church's teaching on extramarital intercourse. The Church believes that her absolute prohibition of this kind of activity is reasonable, that it is not simply an inexplicable taboo or ritual requirement for Catholics. The reasons presented by the Church are all related to the fact that extramarital intercourse bruises human persons, their intimate relationships, and their personal integrity. Moreover, since Christians are united with Christ in baptism, the relationships and integrity harmed are not just those of the parties involved but include the body of Christ, which is defiled by such actions.

The failure to respect these goods becomes clear if one carefully considers the different types of extramarital intercourse. Acts of fornication done solely for sexual pleasure obviously trivialize the act of sexual intercourse. In such acts the partners simply use each other and their sexual powers to grasp pleasure for themselves or to give each other pleasure. Such a use of a human person, even if there is mutual consent, is a violation of human dignity,[11] for human love is more meaningful than this. This kind of sexual intercourse totally fails to serve the genuine goods of human sexuality. The procreative good is ignored and the harm to children who might come into being

181

through such relationships is overlooked. Indeed, today many children conceived in extramarital relations are killed within the womb, and many others are raised under deplorable conditions. The good of marital friendship and fidelity is set aside in favor of satisfying a craving for pleasure or to express a much less committed affection. The sacramental significance of sexual activity is ignored or scorned.

When fornication is chosen to promote and to express romantic affection or "love," the trivialization of human sexuality and its goods is not so apparent — but it is present nonetheless. The partners are not, of course, treating each other *merely* as sources of gratification. Still, substantial and necessary goods of human sexuality are ignored and undercut, and this kind of sexual activity abounds in self-deception and mutual exploitation. This becomes clear if one inquires as to the nature of the "love" expressed in "romantic" fornication, for clearly this is not the strong, genuine love of marriage in which spouses decisively commit themselves to each other without reservation. The human disappointment and suffering that flow from sexual activity without love as complete and lasting as marital love is only too evident in our time.

The affection between fornicators can, no doubt, be deeply felt; but it is deeply flawed. It cannot be the love of Christian marriage. Marital love is in part constituted by an unconditional pledge of fidelity. Those who are not married have not made this commitment. Consequently, their love simply cannot be the intimate love of those who have joined their lives into one life together, who have made themselves "the single subject, as it were, of sexual life."[12] They have not given themselves to each other by an act of irrevocable, unconditional consent. It is profound self-deception for affectionate fornicators to think that their love is like that of married persons for each other.

Thus, the "love" of fornicators just cannot be the love of spouses. Then what sort of love is it? If it is not mere sentiment and affection ungrounded on a real union of lives, it must be some sort of sharing of life; but since it is not marital, it can be no more than a conditional or partial sharing of life. Their act of intercourse does not unite two persons who have made themselves irreplaceable in each other's life, and united in a common

182

life in the pursuit of all the goods of marriage. Yet this union, this common life, this complete love, is what sexual intercourse is meant to symbolize; it is also what many romantic fornicators wish it to symbolize, even though they know at some level that their refusal to make the commitment of marriage makes this impossible. Thus, the self-deception — the "lie" of which John Paul II spoke.

The love of fornicators is therefore suspect. Authentic human love is a love grounded in full respect for the being of human persons and for the goods needed to fulfill human persons. And where sex is involved, such love demands respect for the good of procreation and for the irreplaceable value of the person to whom one chooses to disclose one's intimate self in coition. But the "love" of fornicators spurns these real goods of human persons and of human existence. Their union is not intended to be fruitful, since no care is taken for possible children — unless it is care not to have them. The conditions for responsible and fruitful love are not met; the commitment necessary for the sharing of a common life is deliberately not made. If the love which was expressed and promoted in such acts were the love it claimed to be, one could pledge oneself with the full love of marital commitment. Willingness to choose the appearances of marital love — the friendship, sexual intimacy, and sharing of life — while rejecting the substance of common commitment to common goals clearly indicates an unwillingness to make serious commitments to human goods. This unwillingness, in turn, is incompatible with the character traits needed to be a faithful partner, responsible parent, and follower of Christ. Thus, the truth as well as deep insight of the Church's teaching that sexual intercourse is a moral and human good only within marriage is based on a realistic appreciation of the meaning of sexual union and the irreplaceable value of human persons.

*Objections.* There are many today, both in the general culture and within the Christian community, who question this teaching. Many popular objections are based on the conviction that the total prohibition of extramarital intercourse is simply unrealistic. We admit, of course, that morality sometimes requires very difficult things, and that many will choose not to live wisely and well. But, as the discussion of free choice in Chapter

183

4 makes clear, it is possible for people to choose to do difficult things if they can see the real good to be achieved by the difficult choice. And God is ready to give his saving grace.

A slightly different popular objection is based on a denial that there is any great good at stake in the prohibition of extramarital intercourse. This objection leans toward the view that sexual activity is really trivial, and that recreational sex is not in need of any special justification. Of course, this view is totally at odds with common human experience. It has been one of the main purposes of this book to articulate and focus this experience.

There are, however, more serious objections which have been articulated in the writings of theologians. Three of these are worth discussing in some detail: (1) that sexual intercourse should always be in the context of an interpersonal relationship that involves some affection and commitment but that it need not be limited to the relationship of marriage; (2) that extramarital intercourse always has some ontic deformity but can be morally justified for serious reasons; and (3) that sometimes intercourse between the unmarried really is marital; it is not really premarital but only preceremonial. We will consider these objections in the remainder of this section.

The first objection is that sexual coition does demand a measure of concern and care for the other but does not require the marital covenant.[13] There is, of course, a difference between really exploitative, promiscuous, and commercial sex on the one hand, and, on the other hand, intercourse between unmarried persons who have some feeling and concern for each other. Still, those who make this objection fail to note that extramarital intercourse is always seriously flawed. It always includes some lack of love, some inability or unwillingness to give oneself away in love, some refusal to commit oneself irrevocably to another. This lack of love makes it impossible for their genital embrace to have the meaning that it is meant to have. By enjoying the expression of full love without giving full love itself, they wound each other as well as any child who might come into being as a result of their act. To say that uncommitted love can rightly be expressed by sexual intercourse is to fail to take sexual responsibility seriously enough.[14]

184

The second objection is that the requirement that sexual activity be limited to marriage is only an ideal which can be set aside if there are sufficiently serious reasons.[15] There are many kinds of sufficient reason according to the objection: for example, the socioeconomic structures of our society are said to impose terrible burdens upon young people today. Many individuals who are deeply committed to each other are, as it were, prevented from marrying. Such unmarried couples may at times rightfully choose to have intercourse: "In this case the union of the partners has much of the personal and human reality of marriage. Often the partners in such intercourse *intend* to marry and will do so if and when their circumstances permit."[16] (Emphasis added.)

This argument is not sound. First, this position clearly contradicts the teaching of the Church which has been outlined above. Recognition that the Church's position has considerable merit, and that it protects, for the most part, the human values involved is not acceptance of that teaching. Second, it is clear that this objection is based on the theory of proportionalism; the ontic evil of premarital intercourse is supposedly offset by the other advantages in the forced and unnatural circumstances described. We saw in Chapter 4 that proportionalism is a way of moral thinking that is incoherent on its own terms, inconsistent with the Catholic tradition of moral reasoning, and incompatible with both precepts and basic principles taught insistently by the Church. In the case at hand, we have a variation of the proportionalist claim that one may do evil that good may come about. The necessities of uncontrollable external factors do not provide grounds for abandoning Christian principles; if they did, the law of the cross would be nonsense. Remaining faithful to what love requires is essential for guarding human values and the very prospect of true happiness.

The third objection is based on a distinction between *premarital* and *preceremonial* sexual intercourse. This is a distinction between those who are not married — though perhaps they intend to be married — and those who are really married (that is, those who have committed themselves irrevocably to each other as spouses but have not yet gone through the formal exchange of vows). The former — so the argument goes — may

185

not morally have intercourse; the latter, however, since they are — for all intents and purposes — married, may licitly conduct themselves as spouses.[17]

Obviously, this distinction can be easily abused. For example, Anthony Kosnik and his associates call sexual relations between those who have a firm intention to marry but have not committed themselves in the marital covenant, preceremonial and not premarital relations.[18]

The precise question, however, is this: Could two persons who have already exchanged vows of marriage privately, under limited circumstances, licitly engage in the *marital act* and do so precisely because they are *already* married?

In very rare cases, an affirmative answer is appropriate. It has always been the teaching of the Church that it is the consent between the man and the woman that brings marriage into being.[19] Moreover, during much of the Middle Ages the Church recognized the validity of clandestine or secret marriages; but at the Council of Trent she decreed that from that time forward, *for Roman Catholics*, valid matrimonial consent could *not* be given unless this consent were given in the presence of the parish priest (or his duly appointed representative) and two witnesses.[20]

The decision was based on the fact that very great evils occurred because of clandestine or secret marriages, and there is no reason to think that such evils will not occur today if such unions are recognized as marriages. Marriage deserves protection by public safeguards. It is not a private affair between two isolated individuals but a public act of two persons in a society. The family is indeed the most basic and important community within society. The stability and legitimate constitution of the family are obviously important — for spouses, children, and society at large. Thus, the act which constitutes a family is a public act in which all society has a stake. Consequently, the Church may rightly insist, as the state ordinarily does, that the act in which one person marries another be public.[21]

Of course, there could be instances in which two Catholics could validly and rightly exchange vows and make themselves thereby to be married persons without the witness of the priest and two witnesses. For example, if the persons involved lived in an area where no priest could reasonably be expected to be pres-

186

ent for a long time, or if the persons were in a concentration camp. But this is not what some contemporary writers are ordinarily talking about when they distinguish between "pre-ceremonial" and "premarital" unions. They tend to blur the central difference between an *intent to marry* (which is revocable and is proper to engaged persons) and the *actual consent to marriage*. Only the latter creates the reality of marriage; this alone makes man and woman to be husband and wife, and for Catholics it can be done validly only in the presence of the parish priest (or his deputy) and two witnesses, with certain quite rare cases recognized as exceptions by the Church herself.

In conclusion, we have seen here that the logic of love implicit in Scripture and in the teaching of the Church provides substantive reasons to support the Church's centuries-old teaching that extramarital intercourse is an act that simply fails to respect either the reality of sexual intercourse as a life-uniting and life-giving act, or the preciousness of the persons involved in it. When faith insists that every act of fornication is immoral, it is not speaking the language of legalistic restraint. Rather, it is teaching the requirements of authentic love.

## II. Masturbation

Masturbation is the deliberate stimulation of the genital organs to the point of orgasm which is not a part of sexual intercourse.[22] Thus understood, masturbation can be done either by a person acting on himself or herself (thus, its frequent description as "self-abuse"), or by one person acting on another. Throughout her history the Church has consistently held that masturbation, when it is a freely chosen act, is seriously wrong, for it always involves a failure to respect the human goods which all sexual activity should take into account. The Fathers of the Church,[23] the medieval Scholastics, and all moral theologians[24] until most recent times have been unanimous in condemning every deliberate act of masturbation as a serious violation of the virtue of chastity.[25] This same teaching has been proposed by the magisterium of the Church from the time when it was discussed by Pope Leo IX in 1054 to the present.[26]

In 1975, responding to the questions that had been raised by some contemporary theologians regarding the malice of masturbation, the Sacred Congregation for the Doctrine of the Faith firmly reasserted this teaching of the Church:

> ... both the Magisterium of the Church — in the course of a constant tradition — and the moral sense of the faithful have declared without hesitation that masturbation is an intrinsically and seriously disordered act. The main reason is that, whatever the motive for acting in this way, the deliberate use of the sexual faculty outside normal conjugal relations essentially contradicts the finality of the faculty. For it lacks the sexual relationship called for by the moral order, namely the relationship which realizes "the full sense of mutual self-giving and human procreation in the context of true love." All deliberate exercise of sexuality must be reserved to this regular relationship.[27]

The Church's certainty that of its very nature masturbation is gravely wrong is first of all rooted in divine revelation. Theologians have frequently cited certain key texts as witnesses to the scriptural condemnation of masturbation — for example, the Onan text in Genesis 38.8-10, or 1 Corinthians 6.9, where St. Paul lists among those who are excluded from the kingdom the *malakoi* or the "soft," or Romans 1.24, where he points out that those who reject God come to dishonor their own bodies.[28]

Contemporary scholarship points out that these texts do not *unambiguously* refer specifically to masturbation.[29] But in condemning irresponsible uses of sex generally, Scripture certainly does include a condemnation of masturbation. As the 1975 *Declaration on Certain Questions Concerning Sexual Ethics* states: "Even if it cannot be proved that Scripture condemns this sin by name [masturbation], the tradition of the Church has rightly understood it to be condemned in the New Testament when the latter speaks of 'impurity,' 'unchasteness,' and other vices contrary to chastity and continence."[30]

The Church has rightly understood Scripture to teach that genital activity should take place only within marriage in ways that rightly express marital love. From St. Paul (1 Thessalonians 4.1-5, 1 Corinthians 6.15-20) Christians have learned that their bodies are the temples of the Holy Spirit, that their flesh has become one with the flesh of Christ. Our genital organs, Christians have thus rightly concluded, are not playthings or

188

tools that we are to employ simply for pleasure. Rather, they are integral to our persons, and our free choice to exercise our genital powers is thus to be in service of human persons and of the goods perfective of human persons. The goods to which sexual activity is ordered, as we have seen throughout this work, include procreation, marital friendship, and chaste self-possession. By respecting these goods when we use our genital powers, we honor the body that has, through baptism, become one body with Christ and a temple of his Spirit. When we do not respect these goods in our genital activity we act immorally, and we desecrate the temple of the Holy Spirit and abuse the body-person who has been purchased at such great price. It is this deeply biblical vision of human sexuality and of the human person that is at the heart of the Church's teaching on the immorality of masturbation.

This vision does not exclude a more purely ethical analysis of the immorality of masturbation, for one who chooses to masturbate exercises his or her genital powers of sexuality in a way that does not take into account the precious human goods that these powers are meant to serve. These are life-uniting and life-giving powers. And in choosing to masturbate we use these meaningful powers in ways which ignore or disdain their life-uniting or life-giving meaning. Psychologists note that there is a sort of narcissism involved in such acts, a turning in on oneself, in the use of powers which should serve one to go beyond oneself. This reason takes on added significance for the Christian, who is to regard him- or herself as a "vessel" consecrated to the Lord and a temple of his Spirit.

*Objections.* Despite the overwhelming weight of a tradition rooted in the scriptural view of sexuality, and the seriousness of the reasons presented in the tradition, some recent moralists have rejected the Church's teaching on masturbation. Three distinct lines of argument have been made: (1) some have argued that the constant teaching of the Church that divine revelation condemns masturbation as seriously wrong is simply mistaken; (2) others have argued that the Church is mistaken in teaching that all acts of masturbation are wrong, for only some masturbatory acts are really lustful; and (3) others actually hold that masturbation is of itself morally neutral and not in fact a bad kind of act. We will consider these objections in order.

The first objection is that the weight of traditional teachings on masturbation is not a reliable indication of God's revelation because this tradition is based upon a misunderstanding of Scripture. According to this view the true bases of the traditional condemnation of masturbation are found in Stoicism with its view that procreation alone is the purpose of sex, and in Manicheanism with its dualism and consequent denial that bodily life is good.[31]

This objection includes several unacceptable claims. The first is that Scripture does not condemn masturbation. This is altogether unacceptable, for it goes far beyond the denial that some specific texts unequivocally condemn masturbation, and proposes instead that the scriptural vision of man does not exclude masturbation. The Church, the authentic interpreter of Scripture, draws a contrary conclusion; and, as we have seen, her judgment is entirely sound.

The second unacceptable component of this objection is that the Church is radically mistaken in her most firm and insistent interpretations of Scripture. This overlooks the fact that the Church is guided by the Holy Spirit in proposing moral truths as part of what is necessary for salvation. A teaching so seriously proposed over so many centuries is certainly authoritative for believers. In fact, it would not be implausible to count her teaching on masturbation as part of the infallible exercise of the ordinary magisterium of the Church.[32]

The third disputable component in this first objection is that the Church's teaching on masturbation is based on Stoicism and a version of Manichean mind-body dualism. This is far from true. In fact, dualism of a pernicious sort seems to underlie the arguments which revisionists use to justify masturbation and other sexual activity that the received tradition has rejected.[33]

Those who accept masturbation cannot consistently regard their bodies and sexual activities as integral parts of their own selves and their personal lives, for such persons cannot regard their bodies as governed by the concerns central to their being, as sharing fully in the pursuit of intelligible goods. Their sexual organs and activities are taken, rather, as instruments for plea-

190

sure. The Church is not dualistic; permissive sexual morality is.

Nor is the Church's position based on a Stoic view that procreation is the only legitimate purpose of sexual activity. We have seen how the Church has grown in her explicit appreciation of the fact that sexual activity serves other human goods as well. The development of this appreciation has in no way been accompanied by any tendency to abandon her absolute prohibitions of masturbation, for masturbation serves none of the great goods to which human sexuality is ordered, and fails, in its pursuit of pleasure, to respect any of them adequately.

Obviously, the person-uniting and procreative aspects of sexual activity are ignored and undercut in solitary masturbation. These values are trivialized in homosexual masturbation, and, less clearly, though nevertheless really, in masturbation even between spouses. One reason for this inadequacy is found in the fact that normally the immediate purpose of masturbation is the pleasure associated with orgasm. It is this pleasure alone that is sought in such acts and not the pleasure in doing substantially good acts. Seeking pleasure in this way — as part of a kind of unsatisfactory self-integration — is necessarily incompatible with concern and respect for all the human goods.[34]

The second objection to the Church's teaching on masturbation is that it is not a grave moral disorder in some circumstances. Some who make this objection distinguish various kinds of masturbation: adolescent, compensatory, of "necessity," pathological, medically indicated, and hedonistic. Masturbation in most of these categories is held, contrary to the teaching of the Church, not to be seriously wrong.[35]

Now the Church has always acknowledged that circumstances alter cases. To perform an act of masturbation in some circumstances may be far more reprehensible than in others. Moreover, the Church recognizes that not all acts of masturbation are done with the full consent and knowledge necessary for grave personal guilt. Nevertheless, the Church has consistently maintained that objectively every act of masturbation is seriously wrong. To distinguish several different kinds of masturbation is not to provide any reasonable ground for thinking that some forms of masturbation are not gravely wrong. But reflection on some of these kinds, such as pathological masturbation, does correctly suggest that masturbation is at times not a fully voluntary human action.

"Medically indicated masturbation" may appear to be a genuine exception to the Church's general condemnation of masturbation. (This would mean, for example, procuring a solitary orgasm solely to obtain a specimen of semen for medical examination.) This type of activity could seem to be directed toward a morally upright and nonlustful purpose. It should be noted, first of all, that if this type of act were morally permissible it would be so not because there is an act of masturbation essentially like other acts of masturbation but one which can be morally justified because of its motive. Rather, it would be permissible because the act would be morally speaking a different kind of act — a medical act. Hence, there is in no case any reason for concluding that there are exceptions to the Church's firm judgment that all acts of masturbation are wrong. Still, it is by no means clear that medical masturbation is not in fact an act condemned by the Church's teaching on masturbation, or that, if it is in fact a different kind of act, it is an act which is not also morally wrong.

The designation of medically indicated masturbation as a medical act appears to be a rhetorical redefinition of the act based on the purpose of the masturbation. The inducing of orgasm seems to be of the essence of the act as a moral act — it is by inducing the orgasm that the sperm is procured. Thus, we have, in fact, a disordered sexual act — one directed toward orgasm outside of marital intercourse. The fact that there is a good purpose for such an act does not remove its disorder.[36] Moreover, even if medically indicated masturbation could be shown to be a different sort of act than lustful masturbation — that it is simply an act of obtaining semen for medical purposes and not the performance of a distinctively sexual act — it still does not follow that acts of this type would be permissible. There are, after all, other effective and practical ways to procure sperm. This activity, even if not essentially directed toward sexual pleasure outside of marriage, ordinarily so stimulates such pleasure, and so inclines the agent to delight in sexual pleasure unrelated to the real goods of sexuality, that it may be an unreasonable way to pursue the medical end. Thus, Pope Pius

XII's authoritative condemnation of medically indicated masturbation is realistic and well founded.[37]

We turn to the third objection to the Church's teaching on masturbation: that masturbation is objectively a neutral act which *by itself* lacks any moral disorder. There are several versions of this thesis. One is that no *single* act of masturbation can be seriously wrong; if masturbation is wrong it is only because of the larger lifestyle in which it occurs.[38] Another version is that masturbation cannot be seriously wrong because masturbation is natural or normal, an inevitable phase in personal growth.[39]

The first version of this position — that a single act of masturbation cannot be gravely wrong, that only a sustained practice of masturbation as an essential part of one's life could have such gravity — is based on a view of human action we have shown in Chapter 4 to be mistaken, for the primary locus of moral responsibility is in freely chosen actions, not in patterns of behavior. One's freely chosen acts are what establish one's moral personality; one's character is established by these acts and can be radically changed by one of them.[40]

Of course, one can hold that a single act of masturbation cannot be seriously sinful because masturbation is just not the sort of thing that can be seriously sinful — that is, masturbation is not concerned with "grave matter." This is the second version of the view that masturbation is objectively neutral from the moral perspective. Although it is not surprising that many secular writers on sex regard masturbation as innocent or even good, and hold that the only evil associated with it is the mistaken guilt feeling induced by allegedly wrong moral teaching,[41] it is surprising that some Catholic moralists approximate this view. The reason why some Catholic moralists deny that masturbation is concerned with grave matter appears to be their conviction that something so statistically common cannot be seriously wrong.[42]

Now it appears to be the case that masturbation is very common, especially among adolescent males.[43] The moral significance of the statistics in this matter, however, is anything but clear. They report that many people have engaged in this behavior, but they do not indicate the nature of the individual's responsibility for such acts. Nor do they indicate the extent to which those who have masturbated do so frequently, or do so with or without judging their actions to be immoral or shameful, and so on.

Surely, these statistics do not contradict the experience of many confessors over the centuries which shows that those who earnestly desire to turn away from such practices find the resources to do so. It must be remembered that true moral norms state what ought to be the case, not what statistically is the case. A moral norm is not therefore a statistical generalization and cannot be refuted by information about what is statistically common. Thus, it does not follow from the fact that because the normal attitudes of a certain population are racist, the racism of the population is not objectively immoral. Nor would it follow from the fact that because most believers denied their faith during a certain persecution, it is not seriously wrong to deny one's faith. This argument therefore does nothing to undercut the common teaching of the Church that deliberate masturbation, like other sexual sins, is *seriously* wrong. The received teaching of the Church is only too clear. From the perspective of faith, there is no ground to doubt that masturbating is gravely wrong. Christian tradition has taught this constantly,[44] and the reasons for this teaching are integral to the Church's understanding of sexuality, chastity, and human life.

But the statistical information on which this invalid argument is based may suggest that masturbation is often not a fully human act.[45] As we have already indicated, the Church recognizes that even when a person does what is seriously wrong, the agent is not always fully responsible for the act. The act may be compulsive behavior for which the agent bears only indirect responsibility; moreover, an act can be in some measure deliberate and still not be fully free if it proceeds from weakness of the will. Whether or not a given act is truly a human act is determined by an empirical consideration of the circumstances of the act and the agent's state of mind and heart at the time. Nevertheless, the results of behavioral sciences can be very helpful in making these often difficult determinations. Moreover, the knowledge gained from behavioral sciences can be very useful in helping people to deal with compulsive behavior or morally bad habits. It would be a mistake, however, to assume that, in gener-

194

al, individuals or certain types of individuals are not responsible for their sexual behavior: "This would be to misunderstand people's moral capacity."[46]

To sum up: the Church has always taught that masturbation is seriously wrong. Even though the Church recognizes that sins of this type are sometimes not fully imputable, and pastors have shown great gentleness and understanding in helping those who wish to overcome sins of this type, the Church has never qualified her authoritative teaching on the serious wrongness of masturbation. Moreover, the objections to this teaching are based on poor arguments or perspectives contrary to the received teachings of the faith. There is no doubt therefore that the Christian ideal of chastity excludes masturbation, and that it is possible for Christians to acquire the ability to live in accord with this teaching.

### III. Incomplete Acts of Lust

The Church has regularly taught in her ordinary teaching that all lustful acts (though not all acts of immodesty) are objectively gravely sinful. This is true not only of complete acts, acts which aim to complete sexual satisfaction through orgasm, but of all direct and deliberate acts of lust. Thus, solitary acts that would stir up sexual pleasure but not proceed toward complete sexual satisfaction, and acts of fondling or kissing aimed precisely at stirring up sexual arousal in oneself or one's partner — even if one does not intend this to lead toward complete external sins — are objectively gravely sinful.[47]

There is always some difficulty in teaching these matters in balanced ways to young people. The sexual practices common even among admired people in our media age and the forms of kissing and fondling that are seen in entertainment by persons presented even as role models may make it seem strange and excessively prudish to suggest that there could be grave immorality in conduct which seems so common. Yet there is a profound inner consistency to the truth the Church teaches in her sexual ethics. Young people conditioned to believe that kisses and caresses of a kind that are intentionally lustful (though they may not fully realize this, and may not be fully culpable if they engage in these), will find it unreasonable to believe that mas-

195

turbation or premarital sex can really be wrong in somewhat later years.

Care, imagination, intelligence, and sensitivity are always necessary in teaching sexual ethics to the young. They need to realize that excluding deliberately lustful dimensions from the acts in which they show affection in no way means that they cannot be spontaneous and joyful in their expression of real affection. Intelligent teaching of all that the Church has learned of chaste and self-possessed love is liberating and bracing; it does not impoverish human life.

### IV. Homosexual Acts

Homosexual acts are genital acts performed between persons of the same sex. The acts referred to as homosexual acts are usually acts of sodomy (that is, acts of anal or oral intercourse); but other acts are also included — for example, acts of mutual masturbation. The focus of this section is on the moral character of such acts, and of the lifestyle constituted on the basis of such acts. Thus, our focus is not on the homosexual condition. This condition is not defined by the performance of homosexual acts. Those who are homosexual in personality are oriented toward homosexual acts — some of them almost exclusively so. Unlike most who are not homosexual in temperament, homosexuals are frequently tempted to perform such acts.

A homosexual person may be described as an individual who (1) is attracted physically and erotically by persons of his or her own sex; (2) usually has no similar attraction to the opposite sex; and (3) in many instances has a positive revulsion for sexual actions with a member of the opposite sex.[48] The only attribute common to all homosexuals is the erotic attraction to persons of the homosexual's sex.[49]

Several consequences of this description of the homosexual condition should be noted. First, one may be a homosexual and not engage in homosexual acts, and one may not be a homosexual and nevertheless engage in homosexual acts. Thus, the prisoner or adolescent who engages in homosexual acts is not necessarily a homosexual; and a homosexual may live a life of perfect chastity. Second, this description allows for a spectrum of personality types going from a completely heterosexual orientation

196

to a completely homosexual orientation. Empirical studies show that there are some people in all of the divisions along this spectrum.[50]

*Stress on Homosexual Acts.* The moral judgment of the Church is directed toward homosexual acts and not toward the homosexual condition. To a large extent this condition is not voluntarily established and is thus outside of direct rational control.[51] The reason for this emphasis on homosexual acts is that morality is concerned with how a person should live one's life, to the extent that living one's life is within one's control, and one's freely chosen acts are the part of one's life that is most fully within one's control. The homosexual condition may make certain acts appear to be attractive options, but this condition is not itself freely chosen — it is not an act. Nor for many homosexuals is the condition something that can be readily or even significantly altered. Homosexual acts, however, can be freely chosen and even when done without entirely free choice are frequently in some measure voluntary. These acts therefore are proper objects for moral evaluation; and the homosexual condition is morally relevant as part of the determination of the imputability of homosexual acts.

*Immorality of Homosexual Acts.* The Church's constant teaching on the morality of homosexual acts is unequivocal: such acts are of their very nature seriously wrong. This teaching is clearly based on Scripture and is rooted in the biblical understanding of sexuality. The Bible teaches that the sexual differentiation of the human race into male and female is divinely willed, that male and female complement each other and that marriage, rooted in the irrevocable consent of man and woman to be "one flesh" for life, alone respects the goods of human sexuality. Thus, Scripture teaches that marriage provides the normative condition for genital sexual expression; all other expressions of this kind, whether between man and woman or between members of the same sex, are to be evaluated in the light of this norm.[52]

In addition to this general scriptural account of human sexuality, there are specific biblical passages referring to homosexual acts, and in each of these passages such acts are unambiguously condemned. There are five clear references to male homosexual acts and one to female.[53] The reference in Romans 1.26-27 is in some ways the most telling since homosexual behavior is regarded as a punishment for disbelief: "For this reason God gave them up to dishonorable passions. Their women exchanged natural relations for unnatural, and the men likewise gave up natural relations with women and were consumed with passion for one another, men committing shameless acts with men and receiving in their own persons the due penalty for their error."

Thus, the Church's constant and firm teaching that homosexual acts are seriously wrong is clearly rooted in Scripture. There is no doubt that the Church has taught and believed homosexual acts to be wrong. This is reflected in the writings of the classical theologians and in the approved authors of recent centuries.[54] This teaching has been authoritatively reaffirmed by the Holy See as recently as 1975:

> For, according to the objective moral order, homosexual relations are acts which lack an essential and indispensable finality. In Sacred Scripture they are condemned as a serious depravity and even presented as the sad consequence of rejecting God. This judgment of Scripture does not of course permit us to conclude that all those who suffer from this anomaly are personally responsible for it, but it does attest to the fact that homosexual acts are intrinsically disordered and can in no case be approved.[55]

Finally, it is perhaps worth pointing out that the enemies of Christianity have noted the essential connection between Christian ethics and the condemnation of homosexual activity. As James Hitchcock has pointed out:

> Beginning at least as early as Victorian and Edwardian litterateurs like John Addington Symonds and E.M. Forster, intellectualized homosexuality in the modern West has consciously repudiated Christianity as a distorted, inhumane religion which snuffed out the joyous, guilt-free paganism of ancient times. The intent of this homophilia has been to re-create as far as possible the conditions of that ancient paganism, for which the destruction of Christianity as a cultural influence has been seen as an essential prerequisite. Such a view of history, which from the

198

homosexual viewpoint is to a great extent correct, is continued into the present by, among others, Gore Vidal, the admirer of Julian the Apostate, who manifests both the obsessive anti-Christian sentiment and the contempt and hostility toward heterosexual values which seems characteristic of much of the homosexual subculture.[56]

*Contemporary Objections to Catholic Teaching.* Despite the long-standing teaching of the Church on the objective immorality of homosexual activity, some recent Catholic writers have denied that homosexual activity is always wrong.

These writers argue that (1) the biblical evidence is inconclusive and (2) homosexual activity between homosexually oriented persons (which, they maintain, was not envisioned by the biblical writers) — when this occurs within a relatively stable relationship — is either essentially good and natural, or is at least morally acceptable as the best that can be expected of persons with a homosexual orientation.[57] These writers argue, with respect to the biblical foundation for the teaching, that the story of Sodom and Gomorrah does not involve a condemnation of the homosexual practices of those cities but rather of their inhospitality.[58] Likewise, they claim that the condemnations of homosexual activity in the New Testament are condemnations of idolatrous homosexual acts or of homosexual acts chosen by heterosexuals.[59]

These objections based on the interpretation of Scripture are not well founded. They generally presuppose that the received position on homosexual acts is entirely dependent upon a few isolated proof texts. In fact, however, the Catholic teaching follows necessarily from the whole scriptural vision of what man and woman are, of what sexuality means, and of the nature of morality. If the classical texts on homosexual acts were to be removed altogether from Scripture, the immorality of such acts would still be an obvious implication of the biblical view of sexuality. It should be noted, however, that recent attempts to destroy the force of the classical texts have been shown to be seriously flawed.[60]

*Theological Reasons.* The 1975 *Declaration on Certain Questions Concerning Sexual Ethics* summarizes the reasons why homosexual actions are always wrong. Such acts are "intrinsically disordered" and "lack an essential finality."[61] That is, they are genital acts, acts of profound meaning and importance to the person who performs them and to human society. But they fail to show responsible concern for the precious human goods (that is, those of marital friendship and of procreation) toward which genital activity must be directed to be true to its own nature and meaning.

We have seen that Scripture celebrates sex as life-giving of its very nature. True, not every upright genital act will originate a new life; neither need one intend that it will. There are other worthy goals of sexual activity also. But the life-giving aspect of sexual activity must always be guarded and respected, or sex is trivialized and made inhuman. Genital activity must always be of a kind that does not assail or scorn the procreative good; it must not be structured in ways that rob it of its life-giving thrust. The life-giving meaning of human sexuality is always good and worthy of respect. An awe for this power and a love for the life it can give are essential for the human development of sexuality. But homosexual activity must leave altogether out of consideration this aspect of human sexuality which transcends the activity itself and is essential for its human significance.

Genital activity, moreover, has a life-uniting or person-uniting dimension or meaning. Genital acts serve to join two persons, two lives, by a special kind of love. This is marital love — a love that has an exclusive and enduring quality about it, precisely because it has reference to the life-giving end or meaning of genital sexuality.[62] This is a love which opens those whom it unites to what is other than themselves, to a transcendent goal or good toward which they can commit themselves and their shared lives. But this sort of love is simply incapable of being expressed in homosexual activity. In the homosexual union "the authentic human sense of the other, as nourished by the enriching and complementary otherness of the other sex, is conspicuously absent."[63]

There is, in short, a frustrating sterility in homosexual liaisons, an absence of any reference to the procreative good of human genital sexuality and a very impoverished and truncated mimicking of its unitive good.

Many forms of homosexual life clearly seek the pleasure of

orgasm isolated from any genuinely and authentically satisfying human good.[64] To seek pleasure in good acts, acts that retain their ties to and further real human goods, is not morally wrong. But to organize one's life around the pleasure of orgasms in acts which separate sexual activity from its precious human goods is unreasonable and immoral. Homosexual life is a bitter form of life, for it is founded on actions which pursue not the real goods of human persons but only the mere appearances of these goods. The unhappiness of many homosexuals is a sign that their lives are not properly oriented toward what is truly good.[65]

Many object that not all homosexuality is of this kind. Some homosexual relationships are relatively stable, and at times, perhaps, are as stable as the relationships between some faithful spouses. Homosexuals can love each other, and wish to share and unite their lives.[66]

But even these homosexual relationships, if they involve homosexual actions, are deeply flawed. They do not and cannot have the inner dynamism toward permanence and fidelity which the marriage relationship can have. Homosexual activity is essentially disordered because it cannot be directed toward nor have a proper respect for the goods of human sexuality. Recall that the lovemaking of spouses is directed either toward having children, or is expressive of a love that essentially includes an orientation toward the fruitfulness of procreation. The love of spouses can and must be enduring because it is essentially related to enduring goods; but homosexual love simply is not ordered to any transcendent good that essentially requires of the partners utter self-giving and faithfulness until death. A marital kind of friendship cannot obtain among homosexuals; their sexual act cannot express a marital kind of love, for they cannot be what spouses are. Their sexual acts cannot be procreative and cannot express a love that is inherently fruitful and procreative.[67]

There are many things homosexual lovers may share and which may form a basis for their life together. However, it is hard to see how their *sexual acts* could express or promote these common goods. To use genital activity, which is essentially ordered to indispensable and distinctive human goods, to serve an affection that cannot minister to such goods — to do these things is to distort radically the finality and sense of these important human acts. That is to say, homosexual acts are of their nature seriously immoral.

Some argue today that true homosexuals can find satisfaction only in homosexual acts, and that there is no reason to believe that all homosexuals are called to the exceptional gift of perfect chastity for the kingdom. Hence, homosexual acts must in some way be permissible for them. But this argument is mistaken, for many people not called to virginal lives (freely undertaken to serve God) find themselves in circumstances in which no sexual activity is licit for them. An example would be a young married person deserted by his or her spouse. Such persons may not have the special graces related to the life of consecrated virginity, but Catholic teaching insists that God makes it possible for them to live as they are required, and that they may not excuse themselves from grave responsibilities because fidelity is, under the circumstances, extremely difficult.

What is the person who finds himself with a homosexual orientation to do? This personal and pastoral question goes far beyond the scope of this study. Nevertheless, homosexual persons can have happy and holy lives, rich in meaning. The fact that they are deeply inclined toward acts of a kind that faith and intelligent reflection show to be immoral is no indication that it might be permissible or even good for them to engage in such acts. There are many persons besides homosexuals who must refrain from the sexual acts toward which they are intensely inclined. Consider the case of spouses whose partners are ill for very long periods, or who are long separated from their partners for any reason. Consider too the case of the heterosexually person who deeply yearns for marriage but never finds someone willing to marry him or her. Such lives, into which the cross of sexual deprivation enters, can still be richly fulfilled lives.

Persons of a homosexual orienation deserve the love and support of the Christian community. They are called to friendship with God and to holiness of life, as are all human persons; and they have distinctive heavy burdens to bear. If, as many homosexuals do, they carry their burdens with generous and chaste fidelity, they support and strengthen all Christians. They

202

become witnesses to the nobility of making great personal sacrifices to guard the great human goods sexuality is ordered to. Should they fall in their human weakness, they should still receive the compassionate concern that all persons long for.

The judgment that homosexual acts are wrong does not suggest how one should react to the homosexual-rights movement. Certainly the rights of all persons must be supported. This does not mean that any group has the right to demand that society count as innocent those acts or forms of life that are intrinsically immoral. What it does mean is that the difference in personality structure innocently incurred by some may not be treated as excuses for despising or treating unfairly brothers and sisters in Christ.

## V. Bestiality

Bestial acts are those in which a human being copulates with a nonrational animal.[68] Such acts are repulsive to most people and are fairly uncommon.[69] Most people regard bestiality as seriously perverse, and this common opinion is confirmed by Scripture and Church teaching. In the Old Testament, bestiality is condemned as seriously wrong; its punishment was either death or exile.[70] Bestiality is universally condemned by the approved authors as the worst of the unnatural sins against chastity.[71]

The reasons for this severe judgment are readily seen. In bestiality, sex is used in a way that totally thwarts its interpersonal dimensions. Moreover, there is a complete perversion of the order between man and nature intended by God. Sexual activity should express a sublime love for another person and respect for great human goods. To use sexuality to gratify oneself in ways that make personal relationships and shared care for great goods impossible is a gross abuse of one's sexuality.

One might expect that even those moralists who deny that there are absolutes in most areas of sexual morality would clearly acknowledge that bestial behavior is, objectively, always gravely wrong.

But some revisionary Catholic authors cannot bring themselves to condemn even bestiality unequivocally, perhaps because the principles needed to do this would require acknowledging moral absolutes elsewhere as well. It is not enough to acknowledge that "this practice renders impossible the realization of the personal meaning of human sexuality." Concern for the personal growth of those sadly involved in such conduct is good: "Persons so involved need to be gently led to a deeper understanding and appreciation of the full meaning and significance of human sexuality,"[72] for bestial behavior can surely indicate a pathological condition. But moralists should not avoid the duty of providing a moral evaluation of such acts. Bestial acts can be freely chosen; and, if freely chosen, they are always seriously wrong.

## VI. Rape

The grave immorality of rape seems to be admitted by all.[73] Certainly it is condemned by the Church as a form of lustful behavior that is especially wicked because of the forced and unjust violation of the intimacy of another person.[74]

Rape is the extreme case — perhaps the paradigm case — of treating the person assailed, usually a woman, as a sex object. One of the least controversial objectives of the women's liberation movement has been the protesting of the treatment of women as sex objects, whether in the extreme form of rape, or in pornography, or in the attitude of those who regard women as little more than sources of amusement. The bodies of men and women are not things to be used; men and women are personal in all of their reality. The sexual dimension of a person is properly respected only if it is used in a personal way, in pursuit of a free and personal union.

Rape has become much more frequent in recent years.[75] Many moral factors may be related to this fact. Many in our time consider masturbation morally harmless, and masturbation involves treating one's own body as a "sex object." Pornography is epidemic and recreational sex is widely approved. Both of these phenomena degrade women and treat them not as persons but as objects. Moreover, self-possession in chastity is widely mocked as prudery or as unhealthy repression. Our culture tends to forget that chastity is a necessary requirement for making sexual activity a personal relationship concerned with

204

authentic human goods, and for guarding the world from the barbarism of crimes like rape.

The horror of rape and the trauma it frequently induces in its victims point to the personal and especially intimate depths of human sexuality. Rape is not only an unjust invasion of the person, it is an especially abhorrent invasion. It is altogether more offensive than other violent assaults. Why should this be, if our sexuality were simply another biological function, without inherent ordering to precious values, to be used as people like? The natural abhorrence of rape — even on the part of those who insist that there are no special moral norms in the area of human sexuality — makes clear that sexual activity has a special significance. It is not a routine human activity like taking a walk or eating a snack.[76]

The victim of rape is a victim, not an offender, and deserves sensitive care. Those threatened with rape are not required to offer resistance that is foreseen to be useless or perilous to their lives; but they have the right to resist violently, even if the life of the assailant is endangered. Their own dignity requires that they not cooperate willingly in this assault on their persons. Society has a grave duty to help establish conditions that minimize the occurrence of this crime.

The efforts of a woman to prevent the sperm of her assailant from fertilizing her ovum is not a contraceptive act. To say that it is legitimate for her to seek to prevent conception in this way is not an exception to the universal prohibition of contraception. Contraception occurs only when one who chooses to have sexual intercourse seeks to prevent the act from having its fruitful outcome.[77] But abortifacient procedures after a rape are morally of a very different nature; they are not defenses against an unjust invasion but attacks on an innocent person — that is, they are acts of abortion[78] and therefore are not permissible.

## VII. Incest

Incest is a sin of lust between two persons closely related by blood or affinity. Sexual intercourse or lustful fondling between parent and child or stepchild, or between siblings, would exemplify this sin. We are not here concerned to treat the reasons why marriage between close relatives is forbidden by divine and

205

positive law. What we want to point out here is that there is a twofold malice in incest. It is a sin of lust, an act in which pleasure is irrationally pursued, with gross disregard for the values toward which of its nature and of divine will human sexuality is essentially ordered. But it is also ordinarily seen as sin against piety, a failure to give the special honor and love due to those bound together in the close ties of the family.[79]

Sins of incest seem to have become much more common than they once were. At one time the instinctive revulsion against this sin was strong and an effective repressant. But an age that has liberated lust and tended to enslave human persons more deeply to passion has blinded many to the cruelty of this deed, and the grave harm that it so regularly causes. The reasons *why* incest is wrong are parallel to those that explain the malice of other lustful acts, and a culture that fails to recognize the depth and value-relatedness of sexual activity generally needs great help to escape falling into the most inhuman excesses.

### VIII. Purity in Thought and Modesty

Realistic moral thinking has always been concerned with purity of heart as well as of external action. The ninth precept of the Decalogue, "You shall not covet your neighbor's wife" (Exodus 20.17) is illuminated by the saying of Jesus: "Everyone who looks at a woman lustfully has already committed adultery with her in his heart" (Matthew 5.28). The inner life of a person — that is, the desires and inclinations freely cultivated in the mind and imagination — is also important in the moral life as it is taught by Catholic faith. Catholic morality is not concerned only with achieving good effects in this world but in guiding men and women toward excellent lives through the free actions of their lives — internal actions as well as external ones.[80]

Obviously self-possession in thought, imagination, and desire has considerable instrumental value for leading a chaste life. One who so controls the inner life will find it much easier to avoid the evils we have been discussing in this chapter and the last. However, the value of internal chastity is not merely instrumental. To have a pure heart and mind is itself an excellent and irreducibly important thing. Without inner self-possession,

206

not only will a person's whole life be in moral disarray but the person's very self is fatally compromised.

Here, we note briefly basic guidelines that illumine the morality of thoughts and desires concerning sexual activity.[81]

1. Simply thinking about sexual matters is obviously not of itself sinful. To think about sexual activity even of the most sinful kind may be done innocently, even virtuously, when it is done for reasonable motives and with intelligent respect for all the values concerned, including the values of one's own self-possession and integrity. Theologians, moral educators, artists, and many others often have important reasons to reflect on matters that could easily stir up sexual passions. A morally mature person knows ways to make the dangers of falling into sin remote when responsibly reflecting on such matters.

2. One may, however, entertain sexual thoughts in thoroughly lustful ways as well. This is not a matter simply of "thinking about" such matters but of choosing deliberately to direct the affections in seriously disordered ways, irresponsibly disregarding the goods the heart should cherish. Thus, a certain kind of evil desire is really lustful and seriously wrong — namely the choice or resolve to do deeds that are gravely wrong. Such an inner act is of the kind condemned by the Lord in the Gospel (Matthew 5.28). Another kind of inner act is also lustful — namely what might be called "deliberate complacency" in unchaste thoughts. In choosing to take delight in inner representations of things that are lustful, one is choosing in a disordered way, making oneself an unchaste person. Thus, if done with full deliberation, such choices are gravely sinful; when such delight is accepted with less freedom or deliberateness, the measure of guilt will be less, and when the delight is completely nonvoluntary there is no guilt at all.

3. Those who entertain thoughts of a sexual nature that are likely to stir the passions and perhaps lead them to fall into external or internal sins of lust without the good reasons and care suggested in number 1 (above) — but also without the lustful choice noted in number 2 — may be said to be behaving in an *immodest* rather than in a strictly lustful way.

Modesty is a virtue that guards chastity. There are many kinds of actions that can be good or bad: kisses, embraces, forms of dressing and dancing, thoughts of sexual matters and the reading, conversations, forms of entertainment, and the like that stimulate such thoughts. Such actions can be virtuous; kisses and embraces, for example, can be excellent expressions of a right affection, or they can be strictly lustful. For example, when one engages in any of these activities as a prelude to lustful acts, or if they are now engaged in with lustful desires or complacencies.

One behaves immodestly when one's internal or external acts in matters that could lead toward sins of lust are not reasonable. Such acts can be objectively either grave or venial. If one engages in immodest thoughts or behaviors out of curiosity or playfulness — in circumstances in which there is no serious danger of falling into sins of lust, but some risk is present (and there is no reasonable ground for creating that danger) — one's sin is ordinarily venial. Behavior of a kind that ordinarily stimulates sexual passions vehemently, and is a proximate occasion of serious sin, is gravely wrong.

Since in questions of modesty we are not speaking of acts that are intrinsically wrong but of inner and outer acts whose morality is derived from their relationships to other factors, the concrete morality of immodest acts is derived from the circumstances of each case. Obviously what constitutes modesty in dress, language, and the like is highly relative to time and circumstances. But this does not suggest that modesty is merely a matter of opinion; intelligent rules of thumb can be formulated which hold for most cases. It can be clear and certain that, in these given circumstances, to attend a certain obscene motion picture or to read a particular obscene book would be a grave offense against modesty, or even a direct offense against chastity itself.

Parents, confessors, catechists, and other moral teachers need an intelligent grasp of the basic principles of Christian modesty such as they have been given in the ordinary teaching of the Church. Their own education in modesty is not derived merely from study but from the experience of acquiring self-possession and chastity, and from learning the need to guard chastity with intelligently lived modesty. We live in times in which it is difficult to give materially specific directives with

208

clarity. Still, moral teachers must seek to give concrete guidance in these matters with sensitive and intelligent care, for a contempt for modesty is evident in much modern entertainment, literature, and advertising. The minds and imaginations of people can be corrupted, and their efforts to achieve self-possession in sexual matters can be undermined, if moral education does not include a bracing education in Christian modesty.

Sexual morality must be taught in the Church in the spirit in which Jesus taught.[1] In the preceding chapters we have spoken of "the biblical foundations, the ethical grounds, and the personalistic reasons" that underline Catholic teaching in sexual ethics.[2]

# Pastoral Conclusion

But this splendid and saving teaching must be proclaimed in a very flawed world, in which cultural conditions can make it very difficult to follow even necessary precepts. It must be presented to people who are very weak. It must be spoken to contemporary men and women who frequently find acceptance of Catholic doctrine in this area difficult because of the pervasive pressures of the world, and even because of the halfhearted support of — or, in some cases, dissent from — this teaching on the part of many in the Church herself.

Pastoral wisdom requires great faith and profound concern for what is true and truly good. It must be compassionate. To be credible, it needs to be active and earnest in assisting the faithful to overcome those grave obstacles which make it difficult to accept and live what faith teaches in the area of human sexuality,[3] for the goal of pastoral theology is to help the faithful actually live their lives in accordance with the teachings of faith. By no means is pastoral theology concerned with replacing the excellent and necessary precepts of the Gospel with more lenient maxims which undermine essential respect for human values and faithfulness to the requirements of love.

In this concluding part of the book, we can only sketch the most basic elements of a pastoral stance that flows from Catholic teaching. First, we shall speak of the importance of teaching truthfully, courageously, and compassionately the Catholic vision of marriage and of sexual morality. Second, we shall speak of the care that must be taken to assess rightly the culpability and personal responsibility of those who act in ways objectively opposed to the Church's sexual teachings. Third, we shall note how important it is that those who teach the precepts of the Gospel should also labor to assist people, and to help transform the conditions of the world, in ways that make adherence to those norms seem more possible and attractive. Finally, we shall note why love and concern for persons — even in the most difficult cases — require faithfulness to the bracing principles of Catholic moral life.

## I. Teaching the Truth Courageously and Compassionately

Jesus strengthened and heartened the people to whom he preached by speaking with authority (Matthew 7.29). He spoke as one who knew with certainty what is true and truly good. And he spoke out of a life of such excellence that his hearers realized that he was in fact teaching the truth their hearts longed for and needed.[4] Even when he taught difficult precepts, he enabled his hearers to realize that he spoke in defense of their lives and of their greatest good.

Over the centuries the Church has spoken with authority in the name of Jesus on questions of sexual morality, as she has in all essential areas of moral life. The Church has spoken with a bracing authority, because in a bewildered and suffering world, she has known with certainty important and saving truths, and has recognized that forceful teaching is necessary to support persons in their weakness.

Even in the midst of the spiritual confusion of our time the pastoral leader must teach the sexual ethics of the Church with the merciful firmness of Christ. The duty to teach the doctrine of the Church in this area is certain,[5] and the harm done to the

211

faithful when this doctrine is not courageously proclaimed is all too clear. Public-opinion surveys reveal that many Catholics do not accept the sure teachings of the Church in this area. As a result, many tend to live in ways that assail the most precious values, goods that are indispensable for a full and happy life on earth, and necessary for love of Christ and the secure hope for eternal life.

Though the life of self-possession and of disciplined love is ultimately far happier than the life wounded by lust, the young and the weak do not know this through their own experience. In many ways the world around them tends to deceive them, by telling them that the excellent ways of Christ are too difficult, or that what seems so attractive to the flesh must be right for them. Consequently, if pastoral leaders within the Church seem uncertain whether the sexual morality always proclaimed by the Church is true, they undermine whatever resolve the weak and the young can muster.

Recent popes have regularly reminded scholars and pastoral leaders of their duty to teach with one voice the truth about marriage and sexual morality which has constantly been taught in the family of faith.[6] The fact that there has been an unprecedented outburst of illegitimate dissent from this teaching in our time, the fact that the modern media induce many of the faithful to accept the unhappy ethics of shallow hedonism, the fact that those who proclaim the teaching of the Church on these matters are subject to ridicule and loss of popularity — all these things do not remove the duty to proclaim faithfully the teaching of the Church on sexual morality,[7] for the faithful have a right to receive all the authentic teaching of the Church.[8]

The faithful are not receiving the teaching of the Church about sexual morality unless they are given that teaching in a fully Catholic way. Thus, they must not simply be told that the Church "officially" teaches this or that, for this does not help them to realize that the Church teaching is true and good, that it proposes the way the Lord wills us to live, and that, consequently, they have a grave duty to believe it and live by it. Only the conviction that the Church's teachings are true — and that they can be lived with the help of God's grace — will provide the strength needed by one who is tempted to commit fornication or

212

to enter an invalid marriage. Those who speak for the Lord must do all they can to provide this strength, and to do this they must speak his truth as what it is — the way to live.

## II. Subjective Innocence and Guilt

Pastoral care must seek to be honest and charitable in its assessment of the measure of subjective guilt incurred by those who lapse into behavior that objectively is mortally sinful. Catholic faith teaches that sins of lust are so gravely disordered that those who perform them freely and with a sufficient understanding of their malice separate themselves from the love of God and endanger their eternal salvation. Moreover, the Church teaches that, while passion and ignorance frequently lessen or take away the personal guilt of sexual sinners, people can and do commit mortal sin by lustful thoughts and actions. It is useful to list here some of the considerations essential for a balanced pastoral approach to this question.

1. To say that lustful actions, such as acts of fornication or masturbation, are objectively gravely sinful is certainly not to say that every person who engages in behavior of these kinds necessarily incurs personally the guilt of grave sin.[9] Ignorance and antecedent passion can lessen or remove such guilt. The lives of many are lived in such difficult conditions, in utter poverty, experiencing grave injustices and in the midst of gravely scandalous provocations, that it can be very difficult for them to grasp the serious nature of sins of lust. Psychological impediments (for example, in the case of compulsive actions) may remove responsibility considerably — or, in some cases, entirely — from lustful behavior. Those who are told by trusted teachers and advisers that it is permissible to do kinds of actions that faith has always condemned as gravely wrong can at times follow this bad advice with some real measure of good faith. Those who are deeply troubled by bad actions they have performed — while influenced by scandals, injustices, false teaching, or compulsions of which they were the victims — deserve gentle, strong, and competent pastoral care.

2. In individual cases a spiritual guide may have specific reasons for judging that a particular person has not sinned gravely by indulging in objectively grave immoralities — for ex-

213

ample, if the action in question is compulsive to the point that it is not within the person's control. But there is no reason whatever for assuming that virtually all who commit objectively grave acts of this kind escape the guilt of personal mortal sin. People can and do commit mortal sins by lustful deeds and by deliberately indulging in lustful desire.[10] Nor is it right to suggest that a person who wishes to live his or her life generally in ways pleasing to God but engages occasionally in lustful deeds of a kind common enough in worldly society retains a fundamental stance of faithfulness to God, and does not lose grace or endanger eternal salvation by such acts. Single gravely wrong acts (normally preceded by less grave sins) can be formal mortal sins, for if one is perpared to do, and chooses to do, an action that is gravely evil and known to be opposed to the demanding will of God (or does not know this precisely because of a gravely culpable unwillingness to learn the truth), then one does not maintain one's devotion to God but rather expresses the spirit of one who does not in fact love him in even the minimum measure required to live in his grace (cf. John 14.15).[11]

3. The fact that one does not know or believe that it is mortally sinful to engage deliberately in a particular lustful act is very relevant; but it does not always indicate that one has not incurred personally the guilt of formal mortal sin,[12] for ignorance in this matter can itself be gravely sinful. Self-deception is only too easy for human beings. One who culpably maintains ignorance of truths that God has made very accessible by gifts of public revelation and the graces that make the assent of faith possible can sin mortally without personally acknowledging any responsibility. In fact, those who commit mortal sins in any area are only too ready to seek to persuade themselves that what they choose to do is reasonable and right for them. Thus, they add to their sin by acting against the truth accessible to them.

4. Antecedent passion and the reality of human weakness are important considerations in assessing subjective guilt. But the fact that an objectively grave act was done out of weakness and with some influence of passion is no certain sign that mortal sin was not committed. As long as the person maintains substantial personal freedom, knows that a proposed action is gravely wrong (or is gravely culpable in his ignorance of that

214

fact), and in choosing to act or not act retains essential self-mastery, one is capable of grave sin, and of meritorious fidelity to God.[13] Christians are bound to be faithful to God even when it is very difficult to do so.

5. In evaluating subjective guilt, the role of those who have any kind of teaching or advising role is very different from that of casual acquaintances and friends. Ordinarily, it is quite proper to have a generous interpretation of other people's conduct. It is inappropriate to judge that our friends and acquaintances have in fact formally sinned, even if it is manifest that some of their conduct exhibits behavior of a kind that the Church teaches to be gravely wrong. But teachers and advisers have special duties; frequently, they have the duty to help others escape self-deceit. Thus, any general presumption that those who are doing things which the Catholic faith teaches to be gravely wrong should be assured that they are in "good faith" is a serious mistake. False assurances of this kind can be extremely harmful. They can support forms of malice that directly imperil the salvation of the one advised, and they can imperil also the salvation of the adviser. In giving spiritual direction, an adviser must have profound concern for the truth. When one is morally certain that grave sin has been committed, or that it has not, his advice should follow his considered judgment. When it is far from clear whether or not mortal sin has been committed (in forming judgments in these matters, the guidance of those moralists and spiritual authors whose work has faithfully mirrored received Catholic positions is to be followed), advice must reflect the uncertainty of the situation. Grace is a most precious gift; mortal sin is a terrible evil. One who may have committed a mortal sin, or may yet be entangled in a practice of actions that are objectively mortally sinful, needs the earnest help of his advisers to find his way toward a better state.

6. In certain rare cases and for special reasons it may be right to be silent about the objective immorality of actions that another appears likely to engage in. Divine revelation, however, was given to the Church concerning moral matters because it is good for men to know the truth about how they should live to gain eternal life; and Catholic pastoral leaders would fail gravely in their duties if they did not make publicly known the full

215

malice of sexual sins. When, moved by grace, a person asks about the morality of sinful behavior that he or she has engaged in or proposes to engage in, that person is to be answered truthfully; and one must not routinely suppose that even habitual sinners or very weak persons will be unable or unwilling to respond to the calls of grace. Human lives are made far better when the light of truth and the many supports of faith are made richly accessible. To be quiet about Catholic teachings concerning sexual morality in order to escape conflicts with those who brazenly deny these teachings, or out of a fear of mockery from worldly forces, or because of a mistaken judgment that the less the faithful know about the truth God has revealed the less likely they are to commit sins — this is not the stance of pastoral love. Rather, "to diminish in no way the saving teaching of Christ constitutes an eminent form of charity for souls."[14]

7. Pastoral care is, of course, concerned with more than subjective guilt or innocence in this matter. Catholic moral teaching about sex speaks the truth about basic human goods and is concerned about what really is good for human persons. Lustful actions are really bad for human beings, and harm them, even if they are not known to be bad, even when they are not morally imputable to the one performing the action. Hence, the pastoral teacher and adviser must be concerned to help people know what is good in these matters, and assist them to walk in ways that really serve their fulfillment and their salvation.

8. The remembrance that human beings can and do commit mortal sins should not lead to despair or excessive sadness. All teaching and guidance in sexual ethics is to be carried out in a spirit of faith and of trust in divine mercy. Difficult and excellent things are commanded in the new law. Human weakness could be inclined to fear that what faith teaches is too difficult; but it is a commonplace in Catholic teaching that the entire fulfillment of the moral law would be impossible for fallen humankind without the assistance of the grace and mercy of God. His grace and mercy, fortunately, are accessible. Advisers who have experienced how true it is that God enables very weak persons to do what he has required of them can speak with realistic encouragement to even the weakest sinners.

### III. Teaching With Practical Assistance

The Christian teacher must not only teach the excellence of the ways in which the Lord would have his people walk, he is also called upon to give the many forms of practical assistance which they need to live as they are called to live.

*Instilling a Desire for Holiness and a Love of Chastity.* The Second Vatican Council stressed at length the essential need in the Church for stirring up a hunger for holiness, for a growth in faith, hope, and love, and for living with entire faithfulness to the demands of love. Thus, pastoral leaders must stimulate the faithful to live in exemplary ways which make this life happy in the midst of trials, and which make the people of God worthy of eternal life. Holiness of life is not the special goal of a certain elite within the Church: each one of God's people is called to holiness and can fulfill his or her vocation only by pursuing holiness faithfully. Education in chastity must be carried on in the context of this duty to pursue holiness. Thus, chastity is not to be sought in abstraction from other virtues. It is to be sought as a necessary ingredient in a holy, free, and good life.

In the confusion of our time, pastoral leaders must see to it that the faithful are taught well the meaning of chastity. It is not an irrational form of repression. It is an essential part of temperance and self-possession, for it gives to the emotions, affections, and passions themselves an orderly direction so that the human desire for sexual pleasure is itself wisely directed only toward pleasures which are properly related to the splendid human goods realized by the proper use of human sexuality. Thus, the chaste person finds it easy to forgo pleasures which it would not be wise or good to pursue. The full realization of chastity is different, therefore, from that type of continence in which many people must struggle more or less constantly against serious sexual temptation because, although they genuinely want to be chaste, they have not succeeded in fully integrating their personalities and sexual desires around their morally good choices. This struggle is necessary for most people; but it is not the goal of chastity, for chastity itself involves peace and self-possession, not constant struggle with temptation.

It is true that chastity is far from the greatest of the virtues.

217

As St. Thomas Aquinas — along with much of Catholic tradition — holds, chastity is a form of temperance, which is the least of the cardinal virtues.[15] Nevertheless, Catholic tradition has also emphasized the indispensable importance of this lowly virtue, for the self-control and tranquillity it provides are necessary conditions for the full development of the more exalted virtues. The offspring of lust, so often listed in the moral tradition, make this clear: "blindness of mind, lack of balanced consideration, inconstancy, precipitation, love of self, hatred of God, excessive clinging to the present world, and horror or despair of the world to come" are all characteristics of those who cannot live lives integrated by the moral and theological virtues.[16]

Pastoral leaders must see to it that those who educate the young in chastity have themselves learned the ways of Christ not merely theoretically but are themselves pursuing holiness of life. They must have tasted for themselves how true it is that temperance and chastity can be achieved even in a sinful world. They must be persons who firmly and fully believe the truth of Catholic teaching about marriage and sexual morality, and who have tasted in their lives the joy and freedom of living chastely. Those who have experienced the ways in which self-possession is happily achieved can give heart and encouragement to beginners in the school of Christ.

Central to their efforts, as Pope John Paul II has pointed out, must be education in the true sense of freedom. True sexual liberation is not achieved by pretending that each person may without fear do any kind of act toward which he or she is intensely inclined, whether it serves real human goods and the authentic fulfillment of life or not. It is not achieved in the life of one driven by one's passions, without faith-enlightened concern for what is required by love of oneself and others. It is achieved when one's passions are mastered, when one can freely choose to live as one needs to live to acquire in joy what a person needs and wishes for his or her entire fulfillment, and for serving the common good of one's friends in the family of God.[17]

Pastoral care must not only make clear the excellence of chastity but also assist in removing the impediments to chaste living and in providing the natural and supernatural supports needed to make chastity flourish in the Christian community.

*Social Conditions and Chastity.* Many people in the world "lack both the means necessary for survival, such as food, work, housing, and medicine, and the most elementary freedoms." In wealthier countries "excessive prosperity and the consumer mentality, paradoxically joined to a certain anguish and uncertainty about the future," deprive the faithful of the courage and generosity needed to pursue holiness and self-possession.[18] People everywhere are wounded by the invasions of the mass media, which bring into every home solicitations to live lives patterned on philosophies entirely alien to the Gospel. Realistic education in chastity cannot be carried on without awareness of these evils, and without serious efforts to overcome them as far as possible.

It is not necessary, however, to overcome every social evil before inviting the faithful to holiness of life. Still, the faithful are heartened when they see that their leaders are aware of the burdens under which they labor to serve Christ, and when they can see that pastoral leaders are earnestly helping them in visible and realistic ways.

Strong Christian community life must be built up to assist the faithful in countering social pressures toward accepting the many forms of lust that appeal to fallen man. It is essential to avoid that despair which judges that in the circumstances of our time young people will fall into fixed practices of masturbation or fornication, that the married will adopt a contraceptive mentality and practice, that adultery will be commonplace, for this kind of despair leads to a compromise of pastoral practice and even Catholic teaching. Since on this view pastoral practice can really do nothing to prevent these evils, there is a temptation to downplay their importance and to seek a Christianity that accepts these practices as a normal part of a good Christian life. Christian experience from the time of its birth knows that these counsels of despair are entirely wrong. The fire of the early Christians' love, their pursuit of perfection despite their weaknesses and the corruptive influences of the life of the Roman Empire, enabled them to build communities in which chastity flourished. Certainly grave sin did not leave these communities entirely, as they will not leave ours; but Christian communities whose members cherish and nourish chastity make it possible

219

for all those willing to respond to God's grace to grow in the freedom and strength of virtue.

*Specific Alternatives to Sinful Practices.* Many Catholic people today engage in behavior that is objectively mortally sinful because they have difficult problems and are not aware of realistic and not excessively burdensome ways of resolving them. Many Catholic spouses practice contraception, even in ways that are in fact abortifacient,[19] or mutilate themselves by various forms of sterilization, because they do not know any effective and morally acceptable ways of limiting family size. Often this decision leads them to resentment of the Church or to a kind of despair.

But much of this sorry condition could be removed if pastoral leaders carried out their duties in the way John Paul II has pointed out. A virtuous decision concerning a difficult problem can be made much easier if pastoral leaders see to it that contemporary forms of natural-family planning — which are secure and safe, and which are stronger supports for marital love — were made really accessible to all Catholic people in every place, and if courageous preaching were to make clear why the use of natural-family planning and the use of contraception manifest radically different philosophies of life, and involve "in the final analysis two irreconcilable concepts of the human person and of human sexuality."[20] In this matter the Church *must*, the pope points out, offer "practical help," and "this implies a broader, more decisive and more systematic effort to make the natural methods of regulating [family] fertility known, respected, and applied."[21]

*The Assistance of Supernatural Helps.* The commendable ways of love in which faith calls us to live are difficult — although it is necessary to walk in these ways, for life to become human and happy. Divorce is bitterly painful to both spouses and children; yet to live in faithful love of one partner until death, in shared love of the goods that make life together happy, requires serious efforts not likely to be sustained without the assistance of grace. The distinctive gift of Christ, our teacher, is that he gives those who believe in him not only knowledge of what is good but also "power to become children of God" (John 1.12). Things that would be beyond human power are possible to those who seek assistance from the Lord in confident prayer and in devout use of the sacraments, especially the sacrament of reconciliation and the Eucharist. These sacraments need to be received in the spirit in which the Church has always urged that they be received. Those turning aside from bad habits, or seeking in young years to acquire temperance, benefit greatly by finding a confessor whose spiritual assistance will give them light and encouragement, and who can strengthen their resolve to acquire that purity of heart which supports faithful and generous love.

*Pastoral Care for the Family.* The family itself is the "little church," the first school of virtue for the young, the community in which love and the requirements of love must first be learned. But the Christian family is assaulted in many ways by the alien forces that are so powerful in our culture, and so pervasive in their influence through the mass media. The many forms of care which the Church owes to the family were pointed out by the Synod of Bishops in 1980, and summarized by John Paul II in his apostolic exhortation *Familiaris Consortio.* All these need to be put into effect to help the family of our time to be the school of human values. Unless chastity flourishes within families, the larger society will not be able to recover a love of chastity and the values that it protects.

*Pastoral Care for Young People.* The education in chastity given to the young must be intelligently and faithfully shaped. From earliest years children must be educated in the demands of love, in the self-giving it requires, in the self-possession necessary for love. They must be helped to experience the joy of overcoming that selfishness which is the enemy of true love of self and of others, and to feel the freedom of being liberated from overwhelming needs to act as immediate pleasure suggests.[22]

Other realistic helps must be given to the young if the Christian community seriously wishes to make chastity a reality for many of them. Not only must they be educated in ways of critically evaluating what the mass media and modern forms of entertainment make popular so that they may love and enjoy those aspects of popular culture that are suitable and learn not to be harmed by those elements that are harmful, but the community must also assist them to find forms of creative play and

221

experiences of beauty that are in full harmony with their Christian vision of life.

Sex education for the young is basically the responsibility of parents. When others in the Church assist them in this, sex education must still be carried out under the attentive guidance of parents.[23] Many secular forms of sex education assume that most young people will adopt the lustful practices so common in our society — masturbation, fornication, and the like; and they seek not so much to guide people away from immoral activity and the great harm that does to their inner lives, as to protect them from the most visible effects of immoral activity: venereal diseases and unwanted pregnancies. Often these programs assume the hedonistic attitudes of our time, and consequently set up sexual-education programs so as to help people realize for themselves and others as much pleasure as possible, in ways that do not "hurt" others. But the harm that is done by separating sexual activity from the indispensable human goods toward which it is essentially ordered tends to be entirely neglected. Pastoral leaders have the duty to see that no such sexual education is tolerated in Catholic contexts, and that those who direct Catholic programs sincerely believe Catholic teaching in the whole area of sexuality so that they may genuinely help the young to grow in the love of chastity.

*Chastity, Justice, and Peace.* Christian life cannot be taught in segments; it is a living whole, and neglect of any essential element redounds to the harm of every part. In recent years some groups of Catholics have stressed the importance of the social teaching of the Church, the questions of justice and of peace, and others have stressed the importance of personal holiness or guarding life, of purity of mind and body. Different stresses can, of course, be acceptable, for it is not possible for everyone to focus energies on all things. But there must be real respect on everyone's part for all the essential goods which fulfill human life.

It would be fatal to a Catholic pursuit of justice and peace to count it unimportant if the faithful should fall into grave sins of lust, for the fruits of lust — as we have seen above — lead to a contempt for that love and concern for others' rights that may interfere with the satisfaction of one's own undisciplined desires. Chastity is far from the greatest virtue, but the greatest ones are not possible without it. Nor may those who struggle to support personal holiness of life minimize the importance of caring for a just social order, for one who promotes chastity — but not the social conditions that favor it and flow from it — fails to appreciate the essentially social character of the entire fabric of Christian life. Self-possession without love for others is not the Christian virtue of chastity.

## IV. Making the Burdens of Chastity Light

In the preceding segment of this final section, the practical assistance required of the Christian teacher of chastity was discussed. This is a requirement of love, for the Christian teacher is one who wants to share the good news with those for whom Christ died. Nowhere is this requirement more exigent than in the case of those who find the ways of chastity too difficult to follow. The leaders of the Church have shown great concern and compassion for these people. The bishops taking part in the 1980 synod on marriage took great care to make clear that they understood well how the circumstances of life today make faithfulness to the teachings of faith on contraception, divorce and remarriage, and fidelity within marriage so difficult for many people. And in his apostolic exhortation on the family, summing up the work of the synod, Pope John Paul II spoke with great gentleness on the pastoral care of the family in very difficult cases.[24]

The Church's sensitivity to these difficulties should not be understood as an acceptance of what are in fact counsels of despair. One must compassionately understand what leads many into invalid marriages, into habitual fornication, toward practices of contraception or to sterilization. But proper compassion for persons should not lead to an approval of sin, however reluctant, for when men and women — pressed by hard circumstances — solve their problems in ways that are objectively gravely evil, they are doing deeds that deepen the wounds and sorrows of their lives. They are creating disorder and pain in the world in which they live, for such sins are not simply violations of arbitrary precepts; they are attacks on basic human values that are indispensable for authentically human lives. Deeds that are in fact base and sinful are never reasonable solutions even to tragic problems.

That is why the Church has always rejected "pastoral solutions" which in fact involve approval of kinds of actions that the Church knows to be immoral. When John Paul II presented the received Catholic teaching for pastoral practice for persons who are living as spouses in invalid marriages, contracted after civil divorces, he revealed a sensitive understanding of the difficulty of their position. But he did not pretend for a moment that it could be good to tell them that if they "really think" that it is good for them to perform actions within invalid marriages that are in fact adulterous, then these are good acts for them. He insisted (as the received teaching of the Church always has) that persons who are living in unions that are in fact adulterous may not be told that it is permissible for them to receive the Eucharist.

He readily understands (as every compassionate person would) how extremely difficult it is to be faithful to Catholic teaching at times. Consider the case of a woman who has been abandoned by her husband and who has several children. She is suffering from loneliness and poverty, and has the opportunity to marry an attractive man who is deeply devoted to her and her children. But the Church teaches that by the will of Christ she may not do so, that to marry anew while the one to whom she is yet bound in marriage remains alive is in itself a bad kind of action. The prohibition may seem brutal legalism. Some may be tempted to find a "pastoral solution," that is, to tell her that in this case to enter into a union which the Church knows to be in fact adulterous would be permissible. The Holy Father presents a much different answer. There is a pastoral duty to help the woman understand that it is not shallow legalism but concern for faithful love and for spouses and children everywhere that requires faithfulness to the teaching of Christ. She must be helped to see that her pain is not meaningless and cruel, that she is able to transform the loneliness and suffering into a generous witnessing of the importance of faithful love — a reminder to everyone of the duty to make every sacrifice to make marriages endure. Meanwhile the community has great duties to her, to assist her in bearing the burdens she carries for the sake of all.

Pastoral love does not propose solutions that are opposed to the true and healing teachings of faith, for when one commends evil kinds of deeds in the hope of achieving a better life, one enters into a hopeless path. If the revelation of God together with the faith of the Catholic Church is true, objectively evil deeds wound both the world and the inner lives of those who perform them. It is often only by very difficult ways that one can save one's life, maintain its integrity, and ultimately its blessedness.

Christ never hid from his disciples the excellence and the difficulty of his teaching concerning marriage and sexual morality. The Gospels portray him as not at all surprised when the apostles themselves found his teaching on divorce difficult to believe (Matthew 19.10). He assured them, however, that this excellent but sometimes seemingly harsh teaching (in fact indispensable for guarding faithful love and the procreative good in this broken world) would indeed be made bearable by the gift of God. Even more, Christ insisted that the whole burden of his teaching was an easy burden, that the yoke he imposes on his own (for their sake) would be a light one (cf. Matthew 11.30).

There are many paradoxes in Christian morality. By dying we come to life. By the cross we come to joy. The hard way is easy; but walking the easy path leads to unbearable sorrow. To come to the viewpoint of faith is not an easy task; but the conversion of heart this requires is indispensable for the saving of both human and divine goods in our lives.

Those who wish to live chaste lives, faithfully respecting every human value in their choices, will experience trials and stress but also great comfort and consolation. Contemporary literature and experience reveal that those who deliberately perform lustful deeds in the hope of escaping pain and stress tend to fall into even greater anxieties and strains; and they have sadly forfeited realistic expectation of more deeply needed supports.

St. Thomas Aquinas asks pointedly whether the new law, with its sublime moral teaching, is more burdensome than the old law. He responds, with the traditional voice and experience of Christianity, that it is not.[25] He acknowledges that in one sense it is more difficult. It requires a form of life that is intrinsically more demanding because it is more excellent. Yet it is made easy in a number of ways. Those who with devoted hearts accept the graces that invite them to life in Christ receive from the Holy Spirit gifts that make bearable, even light and pleasant, what otherwise would certainly have been too difficult and even unsupportable. It is the experience of divine mercy — as well as the confidence in divine mercy — that supports the pastoral wisdom which is never willing to do evil that good may come of it. Those who take their stand there are not lonely; they stand with the apostles, the Fathers, and the saints of all the ages: their faithfulness to principle is love and compassion, not legalism.

## INTRODUCTION

1. Perry London, "Sexual Behavior," in *Encyclopedia of Bioethics*, vol. 4, ed. Warren Reich (New York: Macmillan, 1978), p. 1567.
2. *Ibid.*
3. *Ibid.*, p. 1569.
4. See Louis Janssens, "Considerations on *Humanae Vitae*," *Louvain Studies*, 2 (1969), 249. Janssens is a prominent Catholic moralist.
5. See Ashley Montagu, *Sex, Man, and Society* (New York: Putnam's, 1969), pp. 22-23.
6. See Philip S. Keane, S.S., *Sexual Morality: A Catholic Perspective* (New York: Paulist Press, 1977), pp. 100-110; Anthony Kosnik et al., *Human Sexuality: New Directions in American Catholic Thought* (New York: Paulist Press, 1977), pp. 148-149, 152-169.
7. See Daniel C. Maguire, "The Freedom to Die," in *The New Theology, No. 10*, ed. Martin E. Marty (New York: Macmillan, 1973), p. 189. See also Keane, *Sexual Morality*, pp. 109-110, for a justification of the use of contraceptives by nonmarried persons.
8. See Charles E. Curran, "Dialogue with the Homophile Movement," in his *Catholic Moral Theology in Dialogue* (Notre Dame, Ind.: Fides, 1972), pp. 184-219. See also John McNeill, S.J., *The Church and the Homosexual* (Kansas City, Mo.: Andrews and McMeel, 1976).
9. Herant A. Katchadourian and Donald T. Lunde, *Fundamentals of Human Sexuality*, 3rd ed. (New York: Holt, Rinehart, and Winston, 1980), pp. 489-490.
10. John Paul II, *Familiaris Consortio*, no. 31. [*NOTE:* Besides *Vatican Council II: The Conciliar and Post Conciliar Documents* and *Vatican Council II: More Post Conciliar Documents*, ed. Austin Flannery, O.P., excerpts from

227

the conciliar and post-conciliar documents (such as *Familiaris Consortio*) can be found in a number of other sources, including *The Pope Speaks* and *NC Documentary Service*.]

### CHAPTER 1

1. See John L. McKenzie, *The Two-Edged Sword: An Interpretation of the Old Testament* (New York: Doubleday, 1966). See also Raymond Collins, "The Bible and Sexuality I," *Biblical Theology Bulletin*, 7 (1977), 149-167, at 152.
2. An excellent account of the Baal myth and its attendant fertility cult is in McKenzie, *Two-Edged Sword*, ch. 3: "The Gods of the Semites"; see, in particular, pp. 76-77 where McKenzie translates the myth into the modern context: "Many modern Europeans and Americans, if transported into the Babylon of the second millennium, after an initial adjustment to the inconveniences of such things as language, travel, and plumbing, would find themselves spiritually at home. They would never feel at ease with the ancient Hebrews" (p. 77).
3. On this, see (in addition to McKenzie) Joseph Blenkinsopp, *Sexuality and the Christian Tradition* (Dayton: Pflaum, 1969), ch. 1; Stephen Sapp, *Sexuality, the Bible, and Science* (Philadelphia: Westminster, 1977), ch. 1.
4. See the entry "Man" in *The Dictionary of the Bible*, John L. McKenzie, (Milwaukee: Bruce, 1965).
5. This is stressed by many current Scripture scholars. See, for example, McKenzie, *Two-Edged Sword*, ch. 4; James Plastaras, *Creation and Covenant* (Milwaukee: Bruce, 1967), ch. 1; Pierre Grelot, *Man and Wife in Scripture* (New York: Herder and Herder, 1965). See also Edward Schillebeeckx, *Marriage: Human Reality and Saving Mystery* (New York: Sheed and Ward, 1965), ch. 1.
6. While the woman is the man's equal as a human person, she is portrayed in Genesis 2.18-25 and in Genesis 3 as subordinate to the male. The subordination in question in Genesis 2.18-25 — and later in the New Testament (in Ephesians 5.22-23; Colossians 3.18-19; 1 Peter 3.1-7; and elsewhere) — does not mean that woman is inferior to man in dignity and personal value. Rather, it is a kind of subordination required for allowing the community of husband and wife to function in unity. For a careful discussion of this matter, see Stephen B. Clark, *Man and Woman in Christ: An Examination of the Roles of Men and Women in the Light of Scripture and the Social Sciences* (Ann Arbor: Servant Books, 1980). His critical discussion of Genesis 2.18-25 is on pp. 23-28; this book is valuable for its extensive documentation and critical analysis of the current literature which disputes the biblical account of subordination.
7. For a good analysis of this text, see Walter Brueggemann, "Of the Same Flesh and Bone (Gn 2.23a)," *Catholic Biblical Quarterly*, 32 (1970), 532-542. Brueggemann shows that the formula used in Genesis is a com-

mon covenantal formula in the Old Testament. It is thus rich with the overtones of covenantal fidelity.

8. Collins, "The Bible and Sexuality I," 153-154. See also the Wednesday addresses of John Paul II from September 19, 1979 to May 6, 1981. These have been collected into two volumes: *The Original Unity of Man and Woman: Catechesis on the Book of Genesis* (Boston: St. Paul Editions, 1981) and *Blessed Are the Pure of Heart: Catechesis on the Sermon of the Mount and the Writings of St. Paul* (Boston: St. Paul Editions, 1983). For a very helpful summary of these and some more recent papal addresses, see Richard M. Hogan, "A Theology of the Body: A Commentary on the Audiences of Pope John Paul II from September 5, 1979 to May 6, 1981," *Fidelity*, 1.1 (December, 1981), 10-15, 24-27.

9. Schillebeeckx, *Marriage*, p. 16.

10. *Ibid.,* pp. 20-21.

11. See Eugene Maly, "Genesis," in *The Jerome Biblical Commentary*, ed. Raymond Brown, S.S., Joseph A. Fitzmyer, S.J., and Roland E. Murphy, O. Carm. (Englewood Cliffs, N.J.: Prentice-Hall, 1968), p. 12, par. 25.

12. Clark, *Man and Woman in Christ*, p. 22; see also Grelot, *Man and Wife*, pp. 37-38.

13. See Gerhard von Rad, *Genesis* (Philadelphia: Westminster, 1967), p. 53.

14. Collins, "The Bible and Sexuality I," 156.

15. For an analysis of the meaning of the shame experienced by the first humans after their sin, see John Paul II, "Meaning of Original Human Experiences," December 12, 1979, in *Original Unity of Man and Woman*, pp. 85-96.

16. See Clark, *Man and Woman in Christ*, pp. 31-36. Clark notes that there are three major views concerning the way the primordial sin affects the male-female relationship. The first view, favored by feminist writers, is that the subordination is a direct consequence of the first sin and the consequent curse. According to this view, any kind of subordination of woman to man is evil. But this view overlooks the fact that there is subordination in Genesis 2, prior to the fall. The second view holds that the oppressive character of the subordination is a result of sin. This view is favored by Scripture scholars. The third view is that the subordination of the wife to her husband is a blessing and not a curse. This view has some plausibility but little textual support. It is not incompatible with the second view.

17. For commentaries on Genesis 3, see McKenzie, *Two-Edged Sword*, ch. 4; Schillebeeckx, *Marriage*, ch. 1.

18. See Schillebeeckx, *Marriage*, pp. 27-30.

19. Collins, "The Bible and Sexuality I," 158.

20. See Schillebeeckx, *Marriage*, pp. 32-33.

21. See Collins, "The Bible and Sexuality I," 161.

22. This conclusion is drawn by Anthony Kosnik et al., *Human Sexuality: New Directions in American Catholic Thought* (New York: Paulist Press, 1977), p. 30.

23. See Joseph Jensen, O.S.B., "The Relevance of the Old Testament," in *Di-*

*mensions of Human Sexuality*, ed. Dennis Doherty (New York: Doubleday, 1979), pp. 1-8, at 6-7.

24. See Collins, "The Bible and Sexuality I," 160.
25. See Schillebeeckx, *Marriage*, pp. 83-84; Grelot, *Man and Wife*, pp. 32-33.
26. Collins, "The Bible and Sexuality I," 163. See also Carroll Stuhlmueller, "The Relevance of the Old Testament: Prophetic Ideals and Sexual Morality," in *Dimensions of Human Sexuality*, pp. 8-16.
27. See Collins, "The Bible and Sexuality I," 164-165.
28. Jensen, "The Relevance of the Old Testament," p. 8. See also Manuel Miguens, O.F.M., "Biblical Thoughts on 'Human Sexuality,' " in *Human Sexuality in Our Time: What The Church Teaches*, ed. George A. Kelly, (Boston: Daughters of St. Paul, 1979), pp. 102-118.
29. For a fuller development of these points, see Schillebeeckx, *Marriage*, pp. 108-109, 125-140, 155-176.
30. This is a Mishnaic text quoted by Raymond Collins, "The Bible and Sexuality II," *Biblical Theology Bulletin*, 8 (1978), 3-4.
31. Some contemporary writers, including Tom Driver, claim that Jesus was married because marriage was expected of all males. Such arguments not only ignore the evidence of the texts but also underestimate the freedom both of God and of man.
32. 1 Corinthians 7. For commentaries see Schillebeeckx, *Marriage*, pp. 124-136; Lucien Legrande, *Virginity in the New Testament* (New York: Herder and Herder, 1966).
33. See Kosnik et al., *Human Sexuality*, p. 26.
34. Schillebeeckx, *Marriage*, pp. 127, 131.
35. See George T. Montague, S.M., *Maturing in Christ: St. Paul's Program for Christian Growth* (Milwaukee: Bruce, 1966).
36. For an analysis of these divorce texts, see Schillebeeckx, *Marriage*, pp. 141-154; on the "exceptive clause" in Matthew, see Joseph Fitzmyer, S.J., "The Matthean Divorce Texts and Some New Palestinian Evidence," *Theological Studies*, 37 (1976), 197-226.
37. See Schillebeeckx, *Marriage*, p. 154ff; Grelot, *Man and Wife*, pp. 86-90.
38. See Schillebeeckx, *Marriage*, p. 154: "Christ not only expressly condemned divorce (showing, in other words, that the indissolubility of marriage is a *moral* obligation); he also said that any divorce that might possibly take place had no effect whatsoever on the bond of marriage itself (pointing out, in other words, that the indissolubility of marriage is an *objective* bond)."
39. See John J. O'Rourke, "Divorce in the New Testament," *Dimension: Journal of Pastoral Concern*, 1 (1969), 138-146.
40. See Rudolf Schnackenburg, *The Moral Teaching of the New Testament* (New York: Herder and Herder, 1964), p. 133.
41. See, for example, Collins, "The Bible and Sexuality II," 8-9.
42. See Joseph Jensen, O.S.B., "Does *Porneia* Mean Fornication? A Critique of Bruce Malina," *Novum Testamentum*, 20 (1978), 161-184.
43. See John J. O'Rourke, "Commentary on 1 Corinthians," in *A New Catho-*

*lic Commentary on Holy Scripture*, ed. R.C. Fuller (Nashville, Tenn.: Nelson, 1969), pp. 1143-1154, for an account of Gnostic attitudes toward sexuality.

44. See Collins, "The Bible and Sexuality II," 11-12.
45. See John A. Robinson, *The Body: A Study in Pauline Theology* (Naperville, Ill.: A.J. Allen, 1962), for an account of St. Paul's teaching on the body.
46. See Collins, "The Bible and Sexuality II," 12. See also Barnabas Ahern, C.P., "Christian Holiness and Chastity," in *Declaration on Sexual Ethics*, Part 2, *Commentaries* (Washington, D.C.: U.S. Catholic Conference, 1977), pp. 111-120.
47. See Schillebeeckx, *Marriage*, pp. 114-117. Of course, most scholars today hold that Ephesians was not written by Paul. Nevertheless, it clearly develops Pauline ideas and is part of the canonical New Testament.
48. See John Mahoney, S.J., "The Church and the Homosexual," *The Month* (May, 1977), 166-169.
49. See John J. O'Rourke, "Does the New Testament Condemn Sexual Intercourse Outside of Marriage?" *Theological Studies*, 37 (1976), 478-479. See also Schillebeeckx, *Marriage*, pp. 154-155.
50. See Stanislaus Lyonnet, "Sin," in *Dictionary of Biblical Theology*, ed. Xavier Léon-Dufour (New York: Desclée, 1967), pp. 480-487, especially 480-481.
51. *Ibid.*, p. 486.

## CHAPTER 2

1. Several works can be noted here, but none can be recommended without qualification, and none, of course, is an attempt at a systematic history of the Catholic theological treatment of human sexuality or sexual morality: see Derrick S. Bailey, *The Male-Female Relationship in Christian Thought* (New York: Harper and Row, 1968); John T. Noonan, Jr., *Contraception: A History of Its Treatment by Catholic Theologians and Canonists* (Cambridge, Mass.: Harvard University Press, 1965); Joseph Kern, *The Theology of Marriage: The Historical Development of Christian Attitudes Toward Sex and Sanctity in Marriage* (New York: Sheed and Ward, 1964). In addition to these works there are a number of works on the theological study of sexuality by various saints and doctors of the Church. Some of these will be cited in this chapter. There is a wealth of useful material in the relevant articles in the *Dictionnaire de Théologie Catholique*, ed. A. Vacant, E. Manganot, and A. Amann (Paris: Librairie Letouzey et Ane, 1902-1950), 15 vols.
2. See Noonan, *Contraception*, pp. 56-106; Arno Karlen, *Sexuality and Homosexuality* (New York: Morrow, 1972); F. Van der Meer, *Augustine the Bishop: The Life and Work of a Father of the Church* (New York: Sheed and Ward, 1962), ch. 1.

231

3. See Noonan, *Contraception*, pp. 57-70, for an account of Gnosticism.
4. Irenaeus, *Adversus Haereses*, I.28 (PG 7.690). [*NOTE:* In referring to the writings of the Fathers of the Church, the title of work will first be given, followed by book and chapter number (in this instance, I.28), or book, chapter, and section number (for some Fathers). Reference will then be given to the pertinent volume and column in the famous collection of patristic sources provided by J.P. Migne. Migne collected the works of the Greek-writing Fathers into 161 volumes, published in a town near Paris between 1857-1866. In this collection he provided the Greek text with a Latin translation in parallel columns. The reference is to the volume of this collection and to the column containing the Greek text. Thus the text of Irenaeus to which reference is made is found in Migne's *Patrologiae Cursus Completus: Series Graeca* (hereafter PG), vol. 7, col. 690. Migne likewise collected the writings of the Fathers who wrote in Latin into 221 volumes, which he published originally between 1844-1855. These volumes, called *Patrologiae Cursus Completus: Series Latina* (hereafter PL), provide the Latin texts of the Fathers in pages made up of two columns, and the reference is to the volume of this collection and the column or columns concerned. Thus a reference such as PL 34.394 in Note 10 below means vol. 34 of Migne's collection of Latin texts, col. 394.]
5. Justin Martyr, *Apologia*, 1.29 (PG 6.373).
6. Athenagoras of Athens, *Legatio*, 33 (PG 6.965, 968).
7. See Noonan, *Contraception*, p. 75; here, the appeals to nature by these Fathers are said to be a way of reinforcing positions held on other grounds.
8. See Clement of Alexandria, *Stromata*, 3.12.84 (PG 8.1177, on procreation and marriage); 7.12.70 (PG 9.497, on marital virtue).
9. See L. Godefroy, "Le Marriage au Temps des Peres," *Dictionnaire de Théologie Catholique*, 9.2, cols. 2077-2123.
10. See Theodoret, *Quaestiones in Genesi*, c. 3, q. 37 (PG 80.136); Augustine, *De Genesi ad Litteram*, 9.3 (PL 34.394); John Damascene, *De Fide Orthodoxa*, 2.30 (PG 94.976).
11. See Kern, *Theology of Marriage*, pp. 41-60.
12. Gregory of Nyssa, *De Opificio Hominis*, 17 (PG 44.187); John Chrysostom, *De Virginitate*, 17 (PG 48.546); *Homilia in Genesi*, 18 (PG 53.153); Theodoret, *Quaestiones in Genesi*, c. 3, q. 37 (PG 80.136); Damascene, *De Fide Orthodoxa*, 2.30 (PG 94.976).
13. Clement of Alexandria, *Stromata*, 3.7 (PG 8.1162).
14. Lactantius, *Divinarum Institutionum*, 6.23 (PL 6.715f): "Whoever cannot control his affections, let them keep within the confines of the marriage bed." Chrysostom, *De Verbis Illis Apostoli, "Propter Fornicationem"* (PG 51.210): "There are two reasons why marriage was instituted, that we may live chastely and that we may become parents."
15. Developing Catholic doctrine has made it clear that the procreative good is not the only good at stake in marriage; but this development has in no way suggested that this good is not essential. See *Gaudium et Spes*, pars. 48, 50.

16. Among Augustine's explicit treatments of marriage are *De Bono Conjugale* (PL 40.373-394), *De Nuptiis et Concupiscentia* (PL 44.413-474), and *De Conjugiis Adulterinis* (PL 40.451-486).
17. For criticisms of these misrepresentations of Augustine, see John Hugo, *St. Augustine on Nature, Sex, and Marriage* (Chicago: Scepter Press, 1969). See also Eugene Portalié, *A Guide to the Thought of St. Augustine* (Chicago: Henry Regnery, 1960).
18. *Opus Imperfectum Contra Julianum*, 6.30 (PL 45.1582).
19. See, for example, Louis Dupré, *Contraception and Catholics* (Baltimore: Helicon, 1964), pp. 26-27.
20. See Portalié, *A Guide to the Thought of St. Augustine*, pp. 297-313; Hugo, *St. Augustine on Nature, Sex, and Marriage*, pp. 52-67.
21. See *ibid.*
22. *Contra Julianum*, 6.15.47 (PL 44.849).
23. *De Nuptiis et Concupiscentia*, 1.25 (PL 44.429-430).
24. For Augustine, sin as such is only in the will; see *Confessions*, 8, chs. 5, 9-10; *The City of God*, 22, ch. 24.
25. See Hugo, *St. Augustine on Nature, Sex, and Marriage*, pp. 52-63.
26. See *De Natura et Gratia*, 43.50 (PL 44.271): "God does not command the impossible, but by commanding He admonishes you that you should do what you can and beg Him for what you cannot." This text is quoted in the Decree on Justification of the Council of Trent — see *Enchiridion Symbolorum Definitionum et Declarationum de Rebus Fidei et Morum*, ed. Henricus Denzinger and Adolphus Schönmetzer, 32nd ed. (Freiburg: Herder, 1963), no. 1536. [*NOTE:* Hereafter this volume will be referred to as DS followed by the paragraph number or numbers — in this case, for example, DS 1536.]
27. For the Augustinian distinction between use and enjoyment and its application in articulating the proper attitude toward God and earthly things, see *De Vera Religione*, 24.45 (PL 34.165-166) and *De Doctrina Christiana*, I.35.39 (PL 34.42). See also Vernon J. Bourke, *Joy in Augustine's Ethics* (Villanova, Pa.: Villanova University Press, 1979).
28. See *De Bono Conjugali, De Nuptiis et Concupiscentia*, passim.
29. *De Bono Conjugali*, 16.18 (PL 40.385-386).
30. *Contra Julianum*, 5.9 (PL 44.806).
31. *De Genesi ad Litteram*, 9.7 (PL 34.397).
32. *De Bono Conjugali*, 6 (PL 40.377-378).
33. *De Conjugiis Adulterinis*, 1.12 (PL 40.459); *De Nuptiis et Concupiscentia*, 1.17 (PL 44.424-425); *De Bono Conjugali*, 6 (PL 40.377-378).
34. *Enarratio in Psalmos*, 50.7 (PL 36.591-592). The complete text says: "It is not therefore because it is sin to have to do with wives that men are conceived in iniquity. . . . This chaste operation *(opus hoc castum)* in a married person hath not sin, but the origin of sin draweth with it condign punishment."
35. *De Gratia Christi et Peccato Originali*, 2.43 (PL 44.407-408); see *De Nuptiis et Concupiscentia*, 1.16 (PL 44.424).

233

36. *De Bono Conjugali*, 6 (PL 40.377-378).
37. *Ibid.*, 9 (PL 40.380). Augustine follows this point by noting the connection between marital friendship and procreation: "For from these come the propagation of the human race in which friendly association is a great good."
38. *In Johannis Evangelium*, 9.2 (PL 31.1458-1459).
39. *De Bono Conjugali*, 24.32 (PL 40.394-395).
40. *Ibid.*
41. See Edward Schillebeeckx, *Marriage: Human Reality and Saving Mystery* (New York: Sheed and Ward, 1965), p. 286.
42. *Ibid.*, p. 283.
43. Vatican Council II, for example, makes use of Augustine's teaching on the three goods of marriage; see *Gaudium et Spes*, par. 48, n. 1.
44. See John T. NcNeill and Helena Gamer, "Records of Civilization," in *Medieval Handbooks of Penance: A Translation of the Principal Libri Poenitentiales*, vol. 29 (New York: Columbia University Press, 1938). See also John T. McNeill, *The Celtic Penitentials and Their Influence on Continental Christianity* (Paris: 1938). Noonan, *Contraception*, pp. 152-170, provides an account of the penitential materials relevant to sexual morality.
45. These proscriptions were rooted in the belief that the corruption of the sexual appetites by original sin required abstinence from sexual activity to show the proper respect for God within the worship of the Church. Thus, it is unlikely that these proscriptions are the result of Stoic or Manichean influences on the authors of the penitentials, but rather arise from their reading of Scripture.
46. See Noonan, *Contraception*, pp. 179-193, for an account of medieval Gnosticism, the ideal of romantic love, and their connection.
47. Peter Lombard, *Libri IV Sententiarum*, III, d. 37, c. iv: "Non moechaberis, 'id est, ne cuilibet miscearis, excepto foedere matrimonii. A parte enim totum intelligitur. Nomine igitur *moechiae* omnis concubitus illicitus illorumque membrorum non legitimus usus prohibitus debet intelligi.' " The internal quote is from Augustine, *Quaestiones in Exodi*, q. 71, no. 4, PL 31.622.
48. Peter Lombard, *ibid.*, IV, d. 28, c. ii.
49. See, for example, Bonaventure, *In IV Sententiarum*, d. 33, a. 1, qq. 1, 2; *Summa Fratris Alexandri*, P. III, q. 35, m. 4; P. II, q. 147, m. 2; Albert the Great, *In IV Sententiarium*, d. 33, a. 5; Thomas Aquinas, *In IV Sententiarum*, d. 33, q. 1, aa. 1-3 (=*Summa Theologiae*, Supplement, q. 65, aa. 1-5).
50. It was the unanimous opinion of the medieval theologians that the distinction of humankind into man and woman was for the sake of procreation. This point was made by Peter Lombard, *Liber Sententiarum*, II, d. 18, c. 1; the commentaries on this text reinforce the point. See, for example, Aquinas, *In II Sententiarum*, d. 20, q. 1, a. 1; *Summa Theologiae*, I, q. 98, a. 2, sed contra.

51. *De Malo*, q. 15, a. 1: "Finis autem usus genitalium membrorum est generatio et educatio prolis; et ideo omnis usus praedictorum membrorum qui non est proportionatus generationi prolis et debitae ejus educationi, est secundum se inordinatus." See also *Summa Theologiae*, II-II, q. 153, a. 2; *Summa Contra Gentiles*, bk. III, ch. 122.

52. Bonaventure, *In IV Sententiarum*, d. 33, a. 1: "In matrimonio est quidam amor singularis, in quo non communicet alienus: unde naturaliter omnis vir zelet uxorem quantum ad hoc, ut nullum alium diligat, ut diligat ipsum in actu illo: et omnis uxor similiter zelet virum ad hoc. . . . Caritate adveniente, quae facit omnia communia, numquam facit uxorem communem propter privatum amorem qui debet esse in matrimonio."

53. See Note 73 below on the authorship of this work.

54. See Lombard, *Liber Sententiarum*, II, d. 31, c. 2, and the commentaries on this text. See also Aquinas, *Summa Theologiae*, I-II, q. 83, a. 4; *De Veritate*, q. 25, a. 6.

55. Lombard, *Libri IV Sententiarum*, II, d. 31, c. 4; IV, d. 26, cc. 2-4; Bonaventure, *In II Sententiarum*, d. 31, a. 1, q. 3.

56. See *ibid.*

57. The medieval theologians often spoke of the goods of marriage as "excusing" marital intercourse, but they regarded these goods as intrinsic perfections of marriage. Aquinas, for example, says the following: "Ista bona, quae matrimonium honestant, sunt de ratione matrimonii; et ideo non indiget eis quasi exterioribus quibusdam ad honestandum, sed quasi causantibus in ipso honestatem, quae ei secundum se competit." *In IV Sententiarum*, d. 31, q. 1, a. 2, ad 2 (=*Summa Theologiae*, Supplement, q. 49, a. 1, ad 2).

58. See Bonaventure, *In IV Sententiarum*, d. 31, a. 2, ad 1, 2, 3.

59. See Hugh of St. Victor, *De Sacramentis*, II, P. XI (PL 176.479-520). See Schillebeeckx, *Marriage*, pp. 320-324, for a summary.

60. Hugh of St. Victor, *Summa Sententiarum*, tr. 7, c. 2, PL 176.155. This is cited by Lombard, *Libri IV Sententiarum*, IV, d. 26, c. 5.

61. See Fabian Parmisano, O.P., "Love and Marriage in the Middle Ages I," *New Blackfriars*, 50 (1969), 604. For an analysis of Thomas Aquinas's discussion of this matter, see Germain Grisez, "Marriage: Reflections Based on St. Thomas and Vatican II," *Catholic Mind*, 64 (1966), 4-19.

62. The doctrine that marriage was one of the seven sacraments developed during the Middle Ages; Aquinas, following Lombard, held that it was one of the sacraments; see *Summa Theologiae*, Supplement, q. 42, a. 3; *Summa Contra Gentiles*, bk. 4, ch. 78. For an account of the development toward Aquinas's position, see Schillebeeckx, *Marriage*, pp. 328-343.

63. See Schillebeeckx, *ibid.*; Innocent III, for example, clearly affirmed the sacramentality of marriage in 1208.

64. The medieval theologians realized, of course, that not all couples could have children because of sterility. But they held that sterile spouses need not repudiate the good of offspring. Such an intention in the exchange of marriage vows would vitiate the marital consent.

65. See Parmisano, "Love and Marriage in the Middle Ages II," *New Black-friars*, 50 (1969), 649-660.
66. See Aquinas, *In IV Sententiarum*, d. 26, q. 1, aa. 3, 4 (=*Summa Theologiae*, Supplement, q. 41, aa. 3, 4); Bonaventure, *In IV Sententiarum*, d. 26, q. 1, a. 3; d. 31, a. 2, q. 1.
67. See, for example, Lombard, *Libri IV Sententiarum*, IV, d. 31, c. 5; Bonaventure, *In IV Sententiarum*, d. 31, a. 2, q. 2; Aquinas, *In IV Sententiarum*, d. 31, q. 2, a. 3 (=*Summa Theologiae*, Supplement, q. 49, a. 6).
68. See texts cited above in Note 66.
69. See *In IV Sententiarum*, d. 32, q. 1, a. 1 (=*Summa Theologiae*, Supplement, q. 64, a. 2).
70. *In IV Sententiarum*, d. 31, q. 2, a. 2 (=*Summa Theologiae*, Supplement, q. 49, a. 4); it should be noted that in the very next article Aquinas states that the third good of marriage — the indissoluble bond — pertains to the essence of marriage and not to its use, and therefore makes marriage to be upright but not the act of marriage.
71. See *In IV Sententiarum*, d. 26, q. 1, a. 4 (=*Summa Theologiae*, Supplement, q. 64, a. 2).
72. See *Summa Theologiae*, II-II, q. 26, a. 11. In *Summa Contra Gentiles*, bk. 3, ch. 123, Aquinas says: "Inter virum et uxorem maxima amicitia esse videtur; adunantur enim non solum in actu carnalis copulae, quae inter bestias quamdam suavem amicitiam facit, sed ad totius domesticae conversationis consortium." In ch. 125, he writes of the great union between spouses which leads them to love each other more fervently. For an account of the various kinds of friendship in Aquinas, and the particular form found in marriage, see Guy Durand, *Anthropologie Sexuelle et Marriage Chez Thomas d'Aquin* (Lyon: Université de Lyon, 1966-1967), pp. 150-172.
73. Etienne Gilson, *A History of Christian Philosophy in the Middle Ages* (New York: Random House, 1955), p. 327.
74. See Alexander of Hales, *Summa Theologica* (=*Summa Fratris Alexandri*), II, 1, Inq. IV, tr. II, Sect. II, q. 2; see Parmisano, "Love and Marriage in the Middle Ages II," 684-685.
75. *Ibid.*
76. See *In IV Sententiarum*, d. 31, q. 2, a. 3 (=*Summa Theologiae*, Supplement, q. 49, a. 6). The view Aquinas rejects here is that of William of Auxerre, *Summa Aurea*, IV, tract. *De Matrimonio*, q. Utrum bona matrimonii excusent. . . (folio 287r of the Paris edition of 1500).
77. *Summa Theologiae*, I-II, q. 31, aa. 1, 2; q. 33, a. 4; q. 34, a. 4; see also Durand, *Anthropologie Sexuelle*, pp. 176-183.
78. John C. Ford, S.J., and Germain Grisez, "Contraception and the Infallibility of the Ordinary Magisterium," *Theological Studies*, 39 (1978), 258-312, at 277-286.
79. The universality of the condemnation of contraception is demonstrated by Noonan, *Contraception*, p. 6.

236

80. See "The Question Is Not Closed: The Liberals Reply" and "On Responsible Parenthood," in *The Birth Control Debate*, ed. Robert G. Hoyt (Kansas City, Mo.: National Catholic Reporter, 1969).

81. "The Question Is Not Closed," p. 76.

82. Michael Valente, *Sex: The Radical View of a Catholic Theologian* (New York: Bruce-Macmillan, 1970).

83. Anthony Kosnik et al., *Human Sexuality: New Directions in American Catholic Thought* (New York: Paulist Press, 1977).

84. Charles E. Curran, "Divorce in the Light of the Revised Moral Theology," in his *Ongoing Revision: Studies in Moral Theology* (Notre Dame, Ind.: Fides, 1975), pp. 77-78; Curran favors the change in Catholic teaching on contraception and proposes that the logical consequences for other areas of sexual morality be frankly admitted.

85. Noonan, *Contraception*, mistakenly supposes that the medieval theologians required procreative intent as a condition for marital intercourse to be wholly good. He praises the position of Martin Le Maistre, a fifteenth-century writer who held that there was no prohibition of intercourse on the part of a husband who is "scarcely master of himself because of the vehemence of the desire of lust." His wife is "given to him for the sake of solace and remedy." This sexist position is clearly opposed to the realistic and balanced position of the medievals who taught that marital relations thus motivated were venially sinful.

86. Parmisano, "Love and Marriage in the Middle Ages I," 603.

87. See J.B. Gury, S.J., *Compendium Theologiae Moralis* (Turin: M.D. Autia, 1852), no. 688. This is an early edition of one of the most reedited and influential manuals of moral theology. Gury taught that spouses may rightly seek marital intercourse out of "the desire of fostering or bringing about decent friendship." See also Dietrich von Hildebrand, *In Defense of Purity* (New York: Sheed and Ward, 1935). For a careful summary and evaluation of Hildebrand's position and that of other influential authors of the twentieth century, see John C. Ford, S.J., and Gerard Kelly, S.J., *Contemporary Moral Theology*, vol. 1, *Marriage Questions* (Westminster, Md: The Newman Press, 1963). This volume makes clear that it had become the common teaching of theologians prior to Vatican II that marital intercourse was morally legitimate insofar as it expressed marital love.

88. Cajetan, *Commentarium in II-II*, q. 153, a. 2: "Unde non debet persona de hujusmodi delectatione recepta dolere, sed potius Deo gratias agere." See Louis Vereecke, C.Ss.R., "L'éthique Sexuelle des Moralistes Post-Trindentins," *Studia Moralia*, 13 (1975), 175-196, at 178-181.

89. See Vereecke, "L'éthique Sexuelle," 182-185.

## CHAPTER 3

1. See Vatican Council II, *Lumen Gentium*, no. 25. Some theologians today — for example, Charles E. Curran et al. (*Dissent in and for the Church*;

237

New York: Sheed and Ward, 1969) and Daniel Maguire ("Moral Absolutes and the Magisterium," pp. 57-107 of *Absolutes in Moral Theology*, ed. Charles E. Curran (Washington, D.C.: Corpus, 1968) — contend that no moral teachings of the Church have been infallibly proposed. From this claim they draw the conclusion that one may reject moral teachings of the Church which have been universally proposed as necessary for salvation if he judges he has good reasons to do so. This radical claim fails to take into account several crucial considerations. First, their contention that there are no infallible moral teachings is highly debatable, even if one takes into account only solemnly defined infallible teaching. It fails completely if one takes into account the infallibility the Church also enjoys in its ordinary magisterium. See John C. Ford, S.J., and Germain Grisez, "Contraception and the Infallibility of the Ordinary Magisterium," *Theological Studies*, 39 (1978), 263-267, for an explanation of the background and theological context of *Lumen Gentium*, no. 25. For a brief account, see Germain Grisez, *The Way of the Lord Jesus*, vol. 1, *Christian Moral Principles* (Chicago: Franciscan Herald Press, 1983), ch. 35. See also *Symposium on the Magisterium*, ed. John J. O'Rourke and S. Thomas Greenberg (Boston: Daughters of St. Paul, 1979).

2. See Grisez, *The Way of the Lord Jesus*, ch. 35, qs. G and F, for a short account of the grounds for religious assent to noninfallible but authoritative magisterial teaching.

3. See *Sacrorum Conciliorum Nova Collectio*, ed. Johannes Mansi (Paris/Leipzig: 1917-1922), 2.1098-1102.

4. See Lateran Council II, Canons, in DS 718; Lateran Council IV, Canon 1, Carl Joseph von Hefele, *Histoire des Conciles*, tr. H. Leclerq (Paris: 1907-1930), 5/2.1325: "Not only virgins and the continent but also the married, pleasing to God by true faith and good action, will be judged worthy of attaining eternal beatitude."

5. Innocent III, "Letter to the Archbishop of Terragona," December 18, 1208, *Ejus Exemplo*, DS 794.

6. Council of Florence, *"Decretum pro Armeniis,"* DS 1327.

7. Council of Trent, Session 24, 1563; DS 1797-1812.

8. Leo XIII, *Arcanum Divinae Sapientiae*, in *Official Catholic Teachings: Love and Sexuality*, ed. Odile M. Liebard (Wilmington, N.C.: McGrath, 1978), nos. 3, 5, 6, pp. 2-3, 4-5. [*NOTE:* Hereafter *Official Catholic Teachings: Love and Sexuality* will be referred to as Liebard's *Love and Sexuality*.]

9. Pius XI, *Casti Connubii*, in Liebard's *Love and Sexuality*, nos. 31, 64, 66, pp. 24-25, 36-37.

10. See Vatican Council II, *Gaudium et Spes*, no. 48. It should be noted that the Council Fathers refer in a footnote at this point in the text to the threefold good of marriage originally articulated by Augustine and long since appropriated by the magisterium.

11. See Pope Paul VI, *Humanae Vitae*, nos. 8-9.

12. John Paul II, *Familiaris Consortio*, no. 11.

13. *Ibid.,* no. 13.
14. See Leo XIII, *Arcanum Divinae Sapientiae,* in Liebard's *Love and Sexuality,* nos. 3, 6, 13, pp. 2, 5, 13; Pius XI, *Casti Connubii,* in Liebard's *Love and Sexuality,* nos. 37-39, p. 27; Vatican Council II, *Gaudium et Spes,* nos. 48, 50; Paul VI, *Humanae Vitae,* no. 9; John Paul II, *Familiaris Consortio,* no. 14.
15. See *Catechismus Romanus, ex Decreto Concilii Tridentini ad Parochos Pii V, Pontificis Maximi Issu Editus* (Regensburg: Pustet, 1907), P. 2, c. 6; see also the sources referred to in the previous note. John Paul II makes clear the connection between these two goods of marriage in an especially compelling way: "In its most profound reality, love is essentially a gift; and conjugal love, while leading the spouses to the reciprocal 'knowledge' which makes them 'one flesh,' does not end with the couple, because it makes them capable of the greatest possible gift, the gift by which they become cooperators with God for giving life to a new human person" (*Familiaris Consortio,* no. 14).
16. Pius XI, *Casti Connubii,* in Liebard's *Love and Sexuality,* no. 84, p. 42.
17. The condemned view is that there is no fault whatsoever in seeking marital intercourse "solely for the sake of pleasure" — that is, without considering the goods to which marriage is ordered. For the condemnation, see "Decree of the Holy Office," March 2, 1679: DS 2109.
18. Pius XII, "Address to Midwives," October 29, 1951, in Liebard's *Love and Sexuality,* p. 119.
19. *Ibid.,* pp. 119-120.
20. Paul VI, *Humanae Vitae,* nos. 12-13.
21. John Paul II, *Familiaris Consortio,* nos. 28-30; the new *Code of Canon Law,* Canon 1061, no. 1, states that an act which consummates a marriage must be an act that is open to the transmission of life, and one in which the spouses become one flesh. The new code was approved by John Paul II on January 25, 1983.
22. Pius XII, "Address to Midwives," in Liebard's *Love and Sexuality,* p. 121.
23. *Catechismus Romanus,* P. 3, c. 7.
24. See St. Leo IX, "Letter to St. Peter Damian," 1054; DS 687-688; "Decree of the Holy Office," March 2, 1679; DS 2109. Sacred Congregation for the Doctrine of the Faith, "Declaration on Certain Questions of Sexual Morality," December, 1975.
25. John Paul II, *Familiaris Consortio,* no. 11.

## CHAPTER 4

1. See Thomas Aquinas, *Summa Theologiae,* I-II, q. 106, a. 1.
2. See Rudolph Schnackenburg, *The Moral Teaching of the New Testament,* tr. J. Holland-Smith and W.J. O'Hare (New York: Herder and Herder, 1971), pp. 15-89.
3. See Germain Grisez, *The Way of the Lord Jesus,* vol. 1, *Christian Moral*

*Principles* (Chicago: Franciscan Herald Press, 1983), for a systematic treatment of the foundations of Christian ethics, which incorporates the teaching of Vatican Council II.

4. See Joseph M. Boyle, Jr., Germain Grisez, and Olaf Tollefsen, *Free Choice: A Self-Referential Argument* (Notre Dame, Ind.: University of Notre Dame Press, 1976), pp. 8-10.

5. See *ibid.*, pp. 11-12.

6. See DS 1521, 1554, 1939, 1941, and 1966; see also Grisez, *Christian Moral Principles*, ch. 2, q. B, and app. 1, for a fuller account of Church teaching on free choice.

7. *Summa Theologiae*, I, q. 83, a. 1.

8. The view that morality is an expression of an arbitrary divine will is called "the divine command theory," or "theological voluntarism." This view is rejected by the great teachers of the Church. Aquinas makes the classical rebuttal in *De Veritate*, 23, 6; for a modern discussion, see William K. Frankena, *Ethics*, 2nd ed. (Englewood Cliffs, N.J.: Prentice-Hall, 1973), pp. 28-30.

9. The view that human choices create the goodness of things can be called "existentialism." This view is associated with the writings of the French philosopher Jean Paul Sartre; a somewhat similar position is developed in the work of English philosopher R.M. Hare. For critiques, see Alvin Plantinga, "An Existentialist's Ethics," in *The Review of Metaphysics*, 12 (1958), 235-256; Henry B. Veatch, *For an Ontology of Morals* (Evanston, Ill.: Northwestern University Press, 1971), pp. 19-84.

10. Aristotle, *Nicomachean Ethics*, 1, ch. 7, provides the classical formulation of the perfectionist account of goodness. Aquinas developed Aristotle's idea; throughout his ethical writing he defines the good as "fullness of being" and as perfection; see *Summa Theologiae*, I-II, q. 18, a. 1. See also Grisez, *Christian Moral Principles*, ch. 5, q. A.

11. The internal quote is from the Preface of the Mass of the Solemnity of Christ the King.

12. See Xavier Léon-Dufour, *Dictionary of Biblical Theology*, 2nd ed. (New York: Desclée, 1973), entries on Justice, Love, and Peace.

13. See *Gaudium et Spes*, ch. 2, and the social encyclicals of the last century, for authoritative teaching on justice and related goods.

14. See Léon-Dufour, *Dictionary of Biblical Theology*, entries on Peace, Truth, and Wisdom.

15. The cowardly, imprudent, or intemperate person does establish a kind of relationship between the various elements of the self. These relations are unstable and profoundly unsatisfactory even by the standards a non-virtuous person might set. This is so because not every kind of self-integration truly contributes to one's perfection as a human being.

16. In Scripture, truth is primarily a matter of trustworthiness; knowledge a matter of intimate experience and fellowship; and wisdom a matter of practical reasonableness or prudence; see Léon-Dufour, *Dictionary of Biblical Theology*, entries on Truth, Knowledge, and Wisdom. Still, knowl-

edge as the grasping of truth, and wisdom as the understanding of reality, are valued in the Scriptures, especially in the Wisdom literature. Until recently the value of theoretical understanding has been expressed more in the life of the Church than in its explicit teaching — for example, in the honor given to thinkers like Augustine and Aquinas, and implicitly to the vocation of the intellectual life they pursued. For recent, explicit endorsements of the pursuit of truth, see *Gaudium et Spes*, no. 15; *Dignitatis Humanae*, nos. 1-2.

17. See Léon-Dufour, *Dictionary of Biblical Theology*, entry on Life.

18. Our listing of human goods is inspired by the list given by Aquinas, *Summa Theologiae*, I-II, q. 94, a. 2. See also Grisez, *Christian Moral Principles*, ch. 5, q. D.

19. See John Finnis, *Natural Law and Natural Rights* (New York: Oxford University Press, 1980), pp. 95-97, for a development of this point. The critique of hedonism is as old as Western philosophy; see Plato, *Philebus*, 20e-22e, 27d, 60a-61b, 67a; Aristotle, *Nicomachean Ethics*, X, 1172b, 10-25.

20. This point is overlooked by many popular criticisms of the Church's teaching on sexual morality; see, for example, the parody of the traditional teaching on sexual pleasure in Anthony Kosnik et al., *Human Sexuality: New Directions in American Catholic Thought* (New York: Paulist Press, 1977), pp. 24-25, 34, 40.

21. See Aristotle, *Nicomachean Ethics*, X, 1174b, 14-1175a, 10.

22. See Aquinas, *Summa Contra Gentiles*, bk. 3, ch. 26, for a statement of the dependence of pleasure on the thing which the pleasure accompanies.

23. See Grisez, *Christian Moral Principles*, ch. 1, qs. D and E, and the literature cited there, for the shortcomings of what Grisez calls "classical moral theololgy."

24. See Garth Hallett, *Christian Moral Reasoning: An Analytical Guide* (Notre Dame, Ind.: University of Notre Dame Press, 1983), p. 46; Timothy E. O'Connell, *Principles for a Catholic Morality* (New York: Seabury, 1978), p. 153; Richard A. McCormick, *Notes on Moral Theology: 1965 Through 1980* (Washington, D.C.: University Press of America, 1981), pp. 354-355; Louis Janssens, "Norms and Priorities in a Love Ethic," *Louvain Studies*, 6 (1977), 214; for a handy collection of proportionalist thought, see *Readings in Moral Theology No. 1: Moral Norms and Catholic Tradition*, ed. Charles E. Curran and Richard A. McCormick (New York: Paulist Press, 1978).

25. See Richard A. McCormick, *How Brave a New World? Dilemmas in Bioethics* (New York: Doubleday, 1981), p. 5; here, McCormick makes clear that he accepts a nuanced account of the human good like the one set out in Part II of this chapter.

26. See Lisa Sowle Cahill, "Contemporary Challenges to Exceptionless Moral Norms," in *Moral Theology Today: Certitudes and Doubts* (St. Louis: The Pope John Center, 1984), pp. 121-135, for a clear, recent statement of the restrictions on the use of the proportionalist method by one who is sympathetic to it.

27. On practical absolutes, see Daniel Maguire, *Death by Choice* (New York: Doubleday, 1974), p. 99; on virtually exceptionless norms, see Richard A. McCormick, *Ambiguity in Moral Choice* (Milwaukee: Marquette University Press, 1973), p. 73.
28. McCormick, *Ambiguity in Moral Choice*, pp. 78-79.
29. For a recent magisterial statement on moral absolutes, see Sacred Congregation for the Clergy, *General Catechetical Directory* (April 11, 1971), no. 63. The importance of moral absolutes for Christian morality is apparent to its opponents; see, for example, the influential article of Jonathan Bennett, "Whatever the Consequences," *Analysis*, 26 (1966), 83-102.
30. Arguments for dissent from authoritative Church teaching are characteristic of the proportionalist movement. These arguments — involving more than appeals to the method of proportionalism — also involve views on conscience, authority, and ecclesiology. These matters will be discussed in detail in Chapter 5 of this book.
31. See McCormick, *Ambiguity in Moral Choice*, pp. 78-79.
32. The most serious attempts by proportionalists to find this mode of moral reasoning in St. Thomas are those of John Milhaven, John Dedek, and Louis Janssens. See Milhaven's "Moral Absolutes in Thomas Aquinas," in *Absolutes in Moral Theology?*, ed. Charles E. Curran (Washington: Corpus, 1968), 154-185, reprinted in Milhaven's *Toward a New Catholic Morality* (New York: Doubleday, 1972), pp. 135-167, 228-236; Dedek's "Intrinsically Evil Acts: An Historical Study of the Mind of St. Thomas," *The Thomist*, 43 (1979), 385-413; Janssens' "Ontic Evil and Moral Evil," *Louvain Studies*, 4 (1972), 115-156, reprinted in *Readings in Moral Theology No. 1: Norms and the Catholic Tradition*, ed. Charles E. Curran and Richard A. McCormick (New York: Paulist Press, 1979), pp. 40-93, as well as Janssens' "Norms and Priorities in a Love Ethic," *Louvain Studies*, 6 (1977), 207-238, and "St. Thomas Aquinas and the Question of Proportionality," *Louvain Studies*, 9 (1982), 26-46. For a critique of the interpretation of Aquinas given by Dedek and Milhaven, see Patrick Lee, "Permanence of the Ten Commandments: St. Thomas and His Commentators," *Theological Studies*, 42 (1981), 422-433. For a critique of Janssens' interpretation of Aquinas, see William E. May, "Aquinas and Janssens on the Moral Meaning of Human Acts," *The Thomist*, 48 (1984), 566-606. For attempts to find proportionalism in past Catholic thought, particularly in the just-war theory, see O'Connell, *Principles for a Catholic Morality*, p. 153.
33. This argument has been developed extensively by Germain Grisez in a number of his works; for a recent summary of the argument along with relevant references to earlier analyses, see his *Christian Moral Principles*, ch. 6, q. F; see also Finnis, *Natural Law and Natural Rights*, p. 115.
34. See Alan Donagan, *The Theory of Morality* (Chicago: University of Chicago Press, 1977), pp. 199-209.
35. See Dan W. Brock, "Recent Work on Utilitarianism," *American Philosophical Quarterly*, 10 (1973), 241-276; Bernard Williams, *Morality: An In-*

*troduction to Ethics* (New York: Doubleday, 1972), pp. 89-107; and Bernard Williams and J.J.C. Smart, in "A Critique of Utilitarianism," *Utilitarianism: For and Against* (Cambridge, England: Cambridge University Press, 1973), pp. 172-209.

36. Richard A. McCormick, "A Commentary on the Commentaries," in *Doing Evil to Achieve Good*, ed. Richard McCormick and Paul Ramsey (Chicago: Loyola University Press, 1978), p. 277. This volume contains McCormick's *Ambiguity in Moral Choice*, already referred to above, along with responses by several moralists, including an important, critical essay by Paul Ramsey and McCormick's responses to the essays.

37. See Grisez, *Christian Moral Principles*, ch. 6, q. E, for an account of various meanings of "greater good" compatible with common sense and the Catholic moral tradition.

38. See *ibid.*, ch. 6, q. D, for a development of this rejoinder.

39. See Williams, *Morality*, pp. 104-105: ". . . . A utilitarian is always justified in doing the least bad thing which is necessary to prevent the worst thing that would otherwise happen in the circumstances (including of course, the worst thing that someone else may do) — and what he is thus justified in doing may often be something which, taken in itself, is fairly nasty. The preemptive act is built into utilitarian conceptions, and certain notions of negative responsibility (that you are as responsible for what you fail to prevent, as much as for what you do) are by the same token characteristic of it. This being so, it is empirically probable that an escalation of preemptive activity may be expected: and the total consequences of this, *by utilitarian standards themselves*, will be worse than if it had never started."

40. This statement of the first moral principle is adapted from Grisez, *Christian Moral Principles*, ch. 7, q. F; for a different formulation, compatible with the one stated here, see Karol Wojtyla (John Paul II), *Love and Responsibility*, tr. H.T. Willetts (New York: Farrar, Straus, and Giroux, 1981), p. 41; Wojtyla calls the basic principle "the personalistic norm" and explicates its meaning by contrasting it with utilitarianism and relating it to the love commandments. "The norm, in its negative aspect, states that the person is the kind of good that does not admit of use and cannot be treated as an object of use and as such the means to an end. In its positive form the personalistic norm confirms this: the person is a good towards which the only proper and adequate attitude is love. The positive content of the personalistic norm is precisely what the commandment to love teaches."

41. See *Summa Theologiae*, I-II, q. 18, a. 4, ad 2; this principle was adopted by later moral theologians and stated in the following pithy formula, which is almost impossible to render meaningfully in a literal translation: "Bonum ex integra causa; malum ex quocumque defectu."

42. See Joseph M. Boyle, Jr., "Toward Understanding the Principle of Double Effect," *Ethics*, 90 (1980), 527-538; and "The Principle of Double Effect: Good Actions Entangled in Evil," in *Moral Theology Today*, pp. 243-260.

43. For a discussion of this denial, see McCormick, *Ambiguity in Moral Choice*, pp. 72-83.
44. See, for example, Josef Fuchs, S.J., "Basic Freedom and Morality," in his *Human Values and Christian Morality* (Dublin: Gill, 1970), pp. 92-111. For references to other statements of fundamental-option theory along with a critical analysis, see Joseph M. Boyle, Jr., "Freedom, the Human Person, and Human Action," in *Principles of Catholic Moral Life*, ed. William E. May (Chicago: Franciscan Herald Press, 1981), pp. 237-266. The articles by Ronald Lawler, O.F.M. Cap., and John R. Connery, S.J., in this volume provide further discussion and references on this matter. See also the remarks on this matter by John Paul II in *Reconciliatio et Poenitentia* (December 2, 1984), no. 17.
45. The self-determining character of a person's choices has been emphasized in the philosophical writings of John Paul II; see Karol Wojtyla (John Paul II), *The Acting Person* (Dordrecht, Boston, and London: D. Reidel, 1979), pp. 105-186, especially pp. 149-151.
46. See Grisez, *Christian Moral Principles*, ch. 2, q. I.
47. See Sacred Congregation for the Doctrine of the Faith, *Declaration on Certain Questions Concerning Sexual Ethics* (Washington, D.C.: U.S. Catholic Conference, 1976), pp. 10-12.

## CHAPTER 5

1. For useful introductions to the literature on conscience, see Philippe Delhaye, *The Christian Conscience* (New York: Desclée, 1968); *Conscience: Its Freedom and Limitations*, ed. William C. Bier, S.J. (New York: Fordham University Press, 1971); *Conscience: Theological and Psychological Perspectives*, ed. C. Ellis Nelson (New York: Paulist Press, 1973); a brief, clear presentation of Catholic teaching on conscience is given by William B. Smith in *Principles of Catholic Moral Life*, ed. William E. May (Chicago: Franciscan Herald Press, 1981), pp. 321-382; for useful magisterial statements, see the Canadian Catholic Conference, *Statement on the Formation of Conscience*, December 1, 1973 (available in pamphlet form from the Daughters of St. Paul, St. Paul Publications, Boston, 1974); Irish Episcopal Conference, *Conscience and Morality: A Doctrinal Statement of the Irish Episcopal Conference*, February 22, 1980 (also available in pamphlet form from the Daughters of St. Paul, St. Paul Publications, 1980).
2. See John Macquarrie, *Three Issues in Ethics* (New York: Harper and Row, 1970), pp. 113-114.
3. The use of "conscience" in the New Testament was apparently limited to the judgment of one's own past acts. See James C. Turro, "Conscience in the Bible," in *Conscience: Its Freedom and Limitations*, ed. W.C. Bier, pp. 3-8; but see Éric D'Arcy, *Conscience and Its Right to Freedom* (New York: Sheed and Ward, 1961), pp. 8-12, for an interesting argument by a philosopher that St. Paul has a directive or legislative sense of conscience as well.

4. See Thomas Aquinas, *Summa Theologiae*, I, q. 79, a. 13; Canadian Catholic Conference, *Statement on the Formation of Conscience*, no. 6; Irish Episcopal Conference, *Conscience and Morality*, no. 2; National Conference of Catholic Bishops, *To Live in Christ Jesus: A Pastoral Reflection on the Moral Life* (Washington, D.C.: U.S. Catholic Conference, 1976), p. 10.

5. See Charles E. Curran, *Themes in Fundamental Moral Theology* (Notre Dame, Ind.: University of Notre Dame Press, 1977), p. 211; Curran mistakenly argues that the traditional view of conscience cannot account for the legitimate role of affectivity in conscience. For a more adequate account, see Germain Grisez, *The Way of the Lord Jesus*, vol. 1, *Christian Moral Principles* (Chicago: Franciscan Herald Press, 1983), ch. 10, q. D; ch. 31, q. E.

6. This is the common teaching of the tradition. See Aquinas, *De Veritate*, q. 17, a. 3; D'Arcy, *Conscience and Its Right to Freedom*, pp. 87-112, provides a commentary.

7. Conscience in this sense is called *"synderesis"* by Aquinas and much of the subsequent tradition; see *Summa Theologiae*, I, q. 79, a. 12.

8. See *Summa Theologiae*, I-II, q. 100, aa. 1, 3, ad 1.

9. *Summa Theologiae*, I-II, q. 100, a. 1.

10. The Abbott translation of *Gaudium et Spes* mistakenly translates "voice of the law" as "voice of conscience."

11. *Gaudium et Spes*, no. 16.

12. Walter E. Conn, *Conscience: Development and Self-Transcendence* (Birmingham, Ala.: Religious Education Press, 1981), p. 205.

13. See John M. Finnis, "Natural Law, Objective Morality, and Vatican Council II," in *Principles of Catholic Moral Life*, ed. William E. May, pp. 113-150, especially pp. 114-121, for an explanation of the teaching of Vatican II on conscience; see also William E. May, "Conscience, the Natural Law and Developmental Psychology," *Communio*, 2.1 (1975).

14. Macquarrie, *Three Issues in Ethics*, p. 114.

15. *Ibid.*

16. Pius XII, "Radio Message on Rightly Forming Conscience in Christian Youth," March 23, 1952, *Acta Apostolica Sedis*, 44 (1952), 271. [*NOTE:* Hereafter *Acta Apostolica Sedis* will be referred to as AAS followed by volume and page numbers — in this case, for example, AAS 44.271.]

17. *Gaudium et Spes*, no. 16.

18. Conn, *Conscience*, p. 205.

19. *Ibid.*, p. 213.

20. See *ibid.*, p. 209f. Conn develops an analogy between ethics and esthetics. He says: "Because the ethical analyst realizes that decisions are made in particular situations according to the subject's best *creative* understanding of the complex concreteness of the situation, he or she does not regard interpretations of general problem areas like abortion as applicable in a *deductive* way to particular cases, any more than a literary critic pretends to

offer the author a formula on how to compose a fine poem or a first-rate novel." In response, it should be noted first that creativity does have a proper role in the moral thinking of a mature and conscientious person; such a person will seek to find ways to carry out all his or her responsibilities so as to best serve human goods and the often conflicting requirements of common life. However, such creativity as is clearly a part of moral life does not exclude rigorous application of moral principles to cases in such a way as to absolutely exclude some kinds of acts. It is a parody of this application, which finds its formal development in casuistry, to say that it is deductive in the sense that it takes no real thinking or creative understanding.

21. For the theological tradition, see the sources cited above in Note 6; for magisterial teaching, see *Gaudium et Spes*, no. 16; *Dignitatis Humanae*, no. 2.

22. Sometimes we arrive at a doubtful judgment of conscience; since it is wrong to be willing to do what might be wrong, one must not follow a doubtful conscience but must instead seek to resolve the doubt. The traditional "moral systems" provide a reflexive device for doing this. In this context, "doubtful" means having a real question as to whether an action is morally good or bad. Its opposite is moral certainty which is not the certainty of strict proof. See Delhaye, *The Christian Conscience*, pp. 213-242, for a summary of the traditional discussion of doubtful conscience.

23. See Timothy E. O'Connell, *Principles for a Catholic Morality* (New York: Seabury, 1978), pp. 91-92; O'Connell says that one's conscience is infallible. This confuses the absolute obligation to follow a certain conscience with the truth status of that judgment. One must follow one's conscience, but that does not imply that its judgment is beyond criticism. Moreover, if one's conscience is in error, and it is one's fault that it is, one is culpable for the error. Thus, one may have an obligation to follow an erroneous conscience and commit sin in so doing, not because one follows conscience but because one has not taken proper care to form one's conscience adequately. One reason why some mistakenly suppose that conscience is infallible is that they misunderstand the teaching that God speaks to persons in the depths of their conscience. The correct sense of this teaching does not imply that what God reveals to people in this way has the infallibility of faith itself, for God thus speaks to us through the natural and fallible resources of our hearts and minds.

24. See Instruction of the Holy Office, *On Situation Ethics* (February 2, 1956), in DS 3918.

25. See *De Veritate*, q. 17, a. 4; *Summa Theologiae*, I-II, q. 19, a. 5.

26. See *Summa Theologiae*, I-II, q. 19, a. 6.

27. *To Live in Christ Jesus*, p. 10.

28. See *Summa Theologiae*, I-II, q. 100, a. 3.

29. *Dignitatis Humanae*, no. 14.

30. See *Summa Theologiae*, I-II, q. 91, a. 2; for Aquinas the natural law is a participation in the eternal law by which God providentially guides the

universe. The divine law is the law of God made known by revelation. This also includes the natural law which is included within both the Mosaic law and the new covenant of Jesus. See also *Dignitatis Humanae*, no. 3.

31. John Henry Newman, *Letter to the Duke of Norfolk*, cited in the Irish Episcopal Conference's *Conscience and Morality*, no. 20.

32. *Conscience and Morality*, no. 11.

33. See Charles E. Curran, *Ongoing Revision: Studies in Moral Theology* (Notre Dame, Ind.: Fides, 1975), pp. 76-87; Curran argues that contraception is now recognized as morally good by married persons themselves, even though officially condemned by the Church. He goes on to apply this same line of reasoning to the indissolubility of marriage.

34. For an analysis of moral dilemmas of this kind, see Germain Grisez and Russell Shaw, *Beyond the New Morality*, 2nd ed. (Notre Dame, Ind.: University of Notre Dame Press, 1981), ch. 12.

35. See *Gaudium et Spes*, nos. 27, 51.

36. *To Live in Christ Jesus*, p. 12.

37. Some specific moral teachings have been defined. The Council of Trent's condemnation of polygamy is a clear case (DS 1802). This Council's affirmation of the indissolubility of marriage also seems to be a solemn definition of a specific moral precept (DS 1805, 1807).

38. See Grisez, *Christian Moral Principles*, ch. 35, qs. D and E, for an explanation of this point.

39. See John C. Ford, S.J., and Germain Grisez, "Contraception and the Infallibility of the Ordinary Magisterium," *Theological Studies*, 39 (1978), 258-312; Marcellinus Zalba, S.J., "Infallibilità del Magistero Ordinario e Contraccezione," *Renovatio*, 14 (1979), 79-90.

40. See Francis A. Sullivan, S.J., *Magisterium: Teaching Authority in the Catholic Church* (New York: Paulist Press, 1983), pp. 148-152, for a recent summary of this position by one who accepts it.

41. Sullivan, *Magisterium*, pp. 148-152, 227-228, does not explicitly accept proportionalism. However, most of the moralists he cites are proportionalists; the list contains well-known dissenters from Church teaching on sexual morality, and no theologians known for support of the magisterium on these matters. For a typical account by a proportionalist, see Philip S. Keane, S.S., *Sexual Morality: A Catholic Perspective* (New York: Paulist Press, 1977), p. 54: "If we accept the notion that the ultimate morality of an action comes from the action in its total concreteness, the Church can never catch up with this total concreteness in such a way as to make infallible or fully absolute decisions on all aspects of concrete or specific moral cases." This argument fails to distinguish between the concreteness of an individual act and the specificity of a kind of act. Every individual act is some kind of act and some kinds of acts have been taught by the Church to be wrong. Thus, the phrase "ultimate morality of an action" is ambiguous. In some sense, of course, a decisive evaluation of an act requires a consideration of all the concrete circumstances of the act.

One who wishes to evaluate fully the entire goodness or badness of an action must take into account not only the kind of act but also the intentions with which it was done as well as all the morally relevant circumstances. But it is not true that one must consider all these features before making *any* decisive judgment about the act. If one knows that a given act was an act of rape or of abortion or a contraceptive act, one knows that this is objectively a gravely evil kind of act and that every concrete act that would be an exemplification of this kind of act is objectively wrong and ought not be done. Such a judgment is not final in the sense of taking into full account every morally relevant aspect of the case. But that does not prevent the judgment from being decisive. Proportionalists, as we saw in Chapter 4, do not accept the traditional teaching that acts of certain kinds are always wrong.

42. See Sullivan, *Magisterium*, pp. 143-145. Here, Sullivan disputes what he supposes to be Ford's and Grisez' effort to demonstrate that the received teaching on contraception is part of the secondary object of infallible teaching. What he says here could easily be applied to other areas of the Church's teaching on sexual morality. On this, see John Paul II, *Reconciliatio et Poenitentia* (December 2, 1984), no. 17.

43. See Germain Grisez, "Infallibility and Specific Moral Norms: A Reply to Francis A. Sullivan, S.J.," *The Thomist*, 49 (1985).

44. Charles E. Curran et al., *Dissent in and for the Church* (New York: Sheed and Ward, 1969), p. 26; in "Ten Years Later," *Commonweal*, 105 (1978), 429, Curran affirmed the more general thesis that dissent can be legitimate with respect to any specific moral teaching.

45. See J.R. Lerch, "Teaching Authority of the Church (Magisterium)," *New Catholic Encyclopedia*, 13.965; Francisco A. Sullivan, S.J., *De Ecclesia*, vol. 1, *Quaestiones Theologiae Fundamentalis* (Rome: Gregorian University Press, 1963), p. 354; I. Salaverri, S.J., *Sacrae Theologiae Summa*, vol. 1, *Theologiae Fundamentalis*, 5th ed. (Madrid: Biblioteca de Autores Cristianos, 1952), p. 708, n. 699; L. Lercher, *Institutiones Theologiae Dogmaticae*, vol. 1, 5th ed. (Innsbruck: Rauch, 1951), p. 297.

46. Sullivan, *Magisterium*, p. 167, one of those who claim that the standard position of the approved authors is to allow dissent from authoritative but noninfallible teaching, cites Lercher, *Institutiones*, p. 297, in support of dissent. What Lercher actually says is this: "If the Roman Pontiff, using his authority but not to its highest degree, obliges all to give their assent to something as true (whether as revealed or as connected with revelation), it does not seem that in principle he is infallible, nor must we say that the Holy Spirit will never permit him to issue an erroneous decree. Certainly, the Holy Spirit will never permit it to happen that by such a decree the Church would be led into error. The way in which the error would be excluded more probably consists in the assistance of the Holy Spirit given to the head of the Church, by which such an erroneous decree would be prevented. However, it is not unthinkable that an error should be excluded by the Holy Spirit in this way: that the subjects recognize the decree to be er-

roneous and cease to give their assent to it." This is hardly a rationale for public dissent.

47. *Lumen Gentium*, no. 25. Sullivan, *Magisterium*, pp. 155-156, provides a recent example of the kind of argumentation to which we refer here. He argues that, because one of the schemata preparatory to *Lumen Gentium* was dropped from consideration by the Council, there is evidence that the Council meant to weaken restrictions on dissent. The schema in question referred to Pius XII's strong rejection of theological dissent in the encyclical *Humani Generis* (DS 3885). However, the very text of Pius XII which Sullivan supposes the Council meant to reject is explicitly referred to in *Optatam Totius*, no. 16. As Avery Dulles, *A Church to Believe In* (New York: Seabury, 1982), p. 124, has said: "The position of Pius XII to this effect [that the decisive judgment of a pontiff ends theological debate] in *Humani Generis* (DS 3885), even though not explicitly repeated by Vatican II, still seems to stand as official teaching, especially in view of its reaffirmation by Paul VI."
48. Richard A. McCormick, S.J., *Notes On Moral Theology: 1965 Through 1980* (Washington D.C.: University Press of America, 1981), p. 667.
49. See, for example, John Paul II, *Familiaris Consortio*, no. 73; *The Code of Canon Law*, (1983), Canons 752-754, 823, 1371.
50. See Pius XII, "Address to Midwives," October 29, 1951, AAS 43.835-854; "Address to the Second World Congress on Fertility and Sterility," May 19, 1956, AAS 48.473.
51. See Grisez, *Christian Moral Principles*, ch. 35, q. F, for a fuller account.
52. Daniel C. Maguire, "The Freedom to Die," in *The New Theology No. 10*, ed. Martin E. Marty and Dean Peerman (New York: Macmillan, 1973), p. 18. Charles Curran argues this position in many of his writings on sexual morality; see *Themes in Fundamental Moral Theology*, pp. 27-80, especially pp. 64-69; *Issues in Sexual and Medical Ethics* (Notre Dame, Ind.: University of Notre Dame Press, 1978), pp. 38-39.
53. See Germain Grisez, *Contraception and the Natural Law* (Milwaukee: Bruce, 1964), pp. 47-53.
54. See Keane, *Sexual Morality*, pp. 52-54; O'Connell, *Principles for a Catholic Morality*, pp. 91-92.
55. See *Gaudium et Spes*, no. 16; see Finnis's commentary cited above in Note 13.
56. Curran uses the terms "hierarchical" and "papal" to describe the Church's magisterium; he calls the teaching office of professional theologians the "doctrinal magisterium," and maintains for theologians a source of teaching authority independent of the papal and episcopal magisterium; see *Ongoing Revision*, pp. 45-48, 75-87.
57. See Grisez, *Christian Moral Principles*, ch. 35, q. A, for a positive account of the sense of the faithful.
58. See Richard McCormick, *Notes on Moral Theology*, pp. 784-786; Avery Dulles, S.J., is the theologian perhaps best known for the position of the twofold magisterium. However, Dulles's remarks are guarded. He rightly

emphasizes that the theologians have a teaching office, and certainly never draws the conclusion which we are disputing. See his *Survival of Dogma* (New York: Doubleday, 1973), pp. 98-108; "The Theologian and the Magisterium," *Catholic Theological Society of America: Proceedings of the Thirty-First Annual Convention,* 31 (1976), 335-346; *A Church to Believe In,* pp. 110-111, and especially his more cautious remarks on the twofold magisterium, pp. 118-132.

59. Maguire, "Of Sex and Ethical Methodology," in *Dimensions of Human Sexuality,* ed. Dennis Doherty (New York: Doubleday, 1979), pp. 139-140. Richard Roach, S.J., provides a critique of Maguire's misuse of probabilism in Roach's review of this volume in *Fidelity,* 2.8 (1983), 23-25. Probabilism was never used to justify dissent from magisterial teaching but was a basis for preferring one from a number of theological opinions on matters not settled by the magisterium.

60. This is implicitly admitted by McCormick in his recent lament in "Notes On Moral Theology: 1983," *Theological Studies,* 45 (1984), 84, that many theologians have rejected the position of dissent and instead follow the magisterium.

61. See Yves Congar, O.P., "Pour Une Histoire Semantique du Terme 'Magisterium,' " *Revue des Sciences Philosophiques et Théologiques,* 60 (1976), 85-98.

62. Aquinas, *Quodlibetum,* IX, q. 8, corp.


## CHAPTER 6

1. See Germain Grisez, *The Way of the Lord Jesus,* vol. 1, *Christian Moral Principles* (Chicago: Franciscan Herald Press, 1983), ch. 23, for an explanation of the concept of personal vocation and its role in Christian moral life.

2. John Paul II, *Familiaris Consortio,* no. 11.

3. See Karol Wojtyla (John Paul II), *Love and Responsibility,* tr. H.T. Willetts (New York: Farrar, Straus, and Giroux, 1981), pp. 45-54; Lucius Cervantes, "Differences of the Sexes," in *Marriage and the Family,* ed. Carle Zimmerman and Lucius Cervantes (Chicago: Henry Regnery, 1956), pp. 127-407.

4. Wojtyla, *Love and Responsibility,* pp. 45-54.

5. Albert Plé, *Chastity and the Affective Life* (New York: Herder and Herder, 1965), p. 117.

6. Thomas Aquinas, *Summa Theologiae,* II-II, q. 32, a. 1, ad 1.

7. See Servais Pinckaers, O.P., "La Vertu Est Tout Autre Chose Qu'une Habitude," *Nouvelle Revue Théologique,* 82 (1960), 387-403; see also Plé, *Chastity,* pp. 118-119.

8. Plé, *Chastity,* pp. 117-119.

9. Aquinas, *Summa Theologiae,* II-II, q. 141, c.1, ad 1; see also q. 151, aa. 1, 2. See also Wojtyla, *Love and Responsibility,* pp. 147-159, 200-210.

10. See Aquinas, *Summa Theologiae*, II-II, q. 142, a. 1; see also Plé, *Chastity*, p. 125.

11. See Aquinas, *De Virtutibus in Communi*, q. 4. a. 4, ad 15; see also Plé, *Chastity*, pp. 125-126.

12. Plé, *Chastity*, pp. 126-127.

13. Pius XI, *Casti Connubii*, in Liebard's *Love and Sexuality*, p. 24. For other magisterial teaching, see DS 1797-1800, for Trent; *Gaudium et Spes*, nos. 47-52; Paul VI, *Humanae Vitae*, nos. 4, 6-8; John Paul II, *Familiaris Consortio*, nos. 11-16.

14. See *Gaudium et Spes*, no. 48; *Codex Juris Canonici* (Vatican City: Libreria Editrice Vaticana, 1983), Canon 1055.

15. The Church has constantly taught that the free consent of the man and woman to live together is what makes their union a marriage. See Edward Schillebeeckx, *Marriage: Human Reality and Saving Mystery* (New York: Sheed and Ward, 1965), pp. 287-302, for a history of this teaching. The Council of Florence taught that "the efficient cause of marriage is the mutual consent duly expressed in words relating to the present" (DS 1327). Pius XI in *Casti Connubii* taught that "each individual marriage . . . arises only from the free consent of each of the spouses; and this free act of the will, by which each party hands over and accepts those rights proper to the state of marriage, is so necessary to constitute the marriage that it cannot be supplied by any human power" (Liebard's *Love and Sexuality*, p. 24).

16. See Walter Brueggemann, "Of the Same Flesh and Bone (Gn 2.23a)," *Catholic Biblical Quarterly*, 32 (1970), 532-542; Brueggemann shows that the formula used in Genesis is a covenantal formula common in the Old Testament. Thus, it has strong connotations of fidelity.

17. John Paul II, *Original Unity of Man and Woman: Catechesis on the Book of Genesis* (Boston: Daughters of St. Paul, 1981), pp. 81-82.

18. See John L. McKenzie, "Toward a Biblical Theology of the Word," in his *Myths and Realities: Studies in Old Testament Theology* (Milwaukee: Bruce, 1963), for a discussion of the "word" in biblical thought.

19. See Aquinas, *Summa Theologiae*, Supplement, q. 48, a. 1, for an account of how marital consent implicitly contains consent to the marital act.

20. The teaching of Augustine on this point is detailed in Chapter 2 of this work. Pius XI, *Casti Connubii*, in Liebard's *Love and Sexuality*, pp. 26-31, says that in Augustine's teaching on the goods of marriage "is contained a splendid summary of the whole doctrine of marriage." *Gaudium et Spes*, no. 48, cites Pius XI and Augustine. Leo XIII, *Arcanum Divinae Sapientiae*, in Liebard's *Love and Sexuality*, p. 9, emphasizes that even the marriages of the unbaptized participate in the goods of marriage and can be called the sacrament of marriage.

21. See Aquinas, *Summa Theologiae*, Supplement, q. 49, a. 3, for an account of the good of the sacrament as the most essential of the goods of marriage.

22. See Augustine, *De Nuptiis Adulterinis*; also Schillebeeckx, *Marriage*, pp. 218-287.

251

23. See Schillebeeckx, *Marriage*, pp. 141-142, for an account of the biblical roots of the patristic and medieval teaching on the indissolubility of marriage. See also John Lucas, "The *Vinculum Conjugale*: A Moral Reality," *Theology*, 78 (1975), 225-230, for an account of the indissolubility of marriage by a non-Catholic.

24. See *Gaudium et Spes*, no. 48. It should be noted that the Church does "dissolve" the marriages of some non-Christians when one partner becomes a Christian and the other refuses to allow the first to carry out the obligations of the conversion, and it dissolves some nonconsummated marriages. In both cases the dissolution is done with the authority of God himself, and by no human authority. In the former case there is no implication that marriage is not naturally indissoluble. Likewise in the latter, for the dissolution is possible only because the marriage is not, as it were, fully completed by consummation. See Schillebeeckx, *Marriage*, pp. 155-168, 287-302.

25. See Council of Trent, Session 7, March 3, 1547, "Decree on the Sacraments, Canons on the Sacraments in General" (DS 1601-1608).

26. See Leo XIII, *Arcanum Divinae Sapientiae*, in Liebard's *Love and Sexuality*, p. 5; *Gaudium et Spes*, no. 48.

27. See Schillebeeckx, *Marriage*, pp. 133-140.

28. See *ibid.*, p. 137: "Experience of marriage 'in the Lord' does not imply any extrinsic addition to secular; that is, the making Christian . . . of marriage, of its natural and human interrelationships . . . is an entirely intrinsic process."

29. John Paul II, *Familiaris Consortio*, no. 13; see also Schillebeeckx, *Marriage*, pp. 167-170.

30. *Gaudium et Spes*, no. 48; see also John Paul II, *Familiaris Consortio*, nos. 13, 49-64. See Michael F. McAuliffe, *Catholic Moral Teaching on the Nature and Object of Conjugal Love* (Washington, D.C.: Catholic University Press, 1954), for a survey of Catholic teaching on this matter.

31. International Theological Commission, *Theses de Doctrina Matrimonii Christiani*, in *Gregorianum*, 3.4 (1978), 453-464, at 450; English translation in *Origins: NC Documentary Service*, 8.12 (1975).

32. See John Paul II, *Familiaris Consortio*, no. 11.

33. *Gaudium et Spes*, no. 50; see also Germain Grisez, "Marriage: Reflections Based on St. Thomas and Vatican II," *The Catholic Mind*, 64 (1966), 5-19.

34. See Aquinas, *Summa Theologiae*, Supplement, q. 49, a. 5, ad 1.

35. See Pius XI, *Castii Connubii*, in Liebard's *Love and Sexuality*, p. 30: "This conjugal faith, which is most aptly called by St. Augustine the 'faith of chastity,' blooms more freely, more beautifully, and more nobly, when it is rooted in that more excellent soil, the love of husband and wife which pervades all the duties of the married life and holds pride of place in Christian marriage. For matrimonial faith demands that husband and wife be joined in an especially holy and pure love . . . as Christ loved the Church."

36. *Gaudium et Spes*, no. 49. See also Paul VI, *Humanae Vitae*, no. 9; John Paul II, *Familiaris Consortio*, nos. 11-14, 20-21, 28.

37. *Gaudium et Spes*, no. 49.
38. See John Paul II, "Analysis of Knowledge and Procreation," in *Original Unity of Man and Woman*, pp. 146-152.
39. See John Kippley, *Birth Control and the Marriage Covenant* (Collegeville, Minn.: The Liturgical Press, 1976), pp. 105-113; Dietrich von Hildebrand, *In Defense of Purity* (New York: Sheed and Ward, 1935), pp. 54-76; Mary R. Joyce, *Love Responds to Life* (Kenosha, Wis.: Prow Press, 1970), pp. 8-26.
40. Paul VI, *Humanae Vitae*, no. 13.
41. John Paul II, *Familiaris Consortio*, no. 16.
42. See Schillebeeckx, *Marriage*, pp. 105-110, 123.
43. *Ibid.*, p. 131.
44. See Roger Balducelli, O.S.F.S., "The Decision for Celibacy," *Theological Studies*, 36 (1975), 219-242.

## CHAPTER 7

1. For the exegesis of these Old Testament passages, see Friedrich Hauck, "Moicheuo, ktl.," in *Theological Dictionary of the New Testament*, ed. Gerhard Kittel, tr. Geoffrey W. Bromiley (Grand Rapids, Mich.: Eerdmans, 1967) 4.730-731; see also John Huesman, S.J., "Exodus," and Joseph Blenkinsopp, "Deuteronomy," in *The Jerome Biblical Commentary*, ed. Raymond Brown, S.S., Joseph A. Fitzmyer, S.J., and Roland E. Murphy, O. Carm. (Englewood Cliffs, N.J.: Prentice-Hall, 1968), 3.50 and 6.20. See also John L. McKenzie, "Adultery," in his *Dictionary of the Bible* (Milwaukee: Bruce, 1965).
2. On this, see Pierre Grelot, *Man and Wife in Scripture* (New York: Herder and Herder, 1965) and Edward Schillebeeckx, *Marriage: Human Reality and Saving Mystery* (New York: Sheed and Ward, 1965), pp. 31-63, 89-91.
3. John Paul II, "Ethical, Anthropological Content of 'Do Not Commit Adultery!'" (address of April 23, 1980), in *Blessed Are the Pure of Heart* (Boston: Daughters of St. Paul, 1983), pp. 26-32. On this matter the observations of Schillebeeckx, *Marriage*, pp. 52-54, 61-62, 89-91, are helpful.
4. An excellent commentary on the significance of lustful desire as a rupturing of the covenant with God and the introduction of the "world" opposed to God spoken of by John (1 John 2.15-16) in place of the "world" of Genesis 1 and 2 that was "good" in the sight of God is provided by John Paul II in his address of April 30, 1980, "Lust, A Rupture of the First Covenant With God," in *Blessed Are the Pure of Heart*, pp. 33-40.
5. On this, see Schillebeeckx, *Marriage*, pp. 141-155. See also Hauck, "Moicheuo, ktl.," and Eugene Maly and John L. McKenzie in their commentaries on the appropriate passages from Mark and Matthew in *The Jerome Biblical Commentary*.
6. This is evident from the fact that Jesus considered as adulterous the union of a person who divorced and remarried. This indeed is the sense in which

the term *adultery* is understood by users of ordinary language. Yet it seems necessary to make this point explicit inasmuch as some contemporary moralists (for example, Richard A. McCormick, S.J., in his "Notes on Moral Theology," *Theological Studies*, 39 [1978], 93) use the term to describe coition with the "wrong" person, leaving open for further judgment whether the "wrong" person is someone who is not one's spouse.

7. Contemporary scholars debate whether Ephesians was written by Paul or not. Even those who believe it to be the work of another writer agree that the teaching in it on the significance of sexual union is Pauline, for it is in conformity with the teaching of 1 Corinthians 6. On the deep significance of Ephesians 5, see Schillebeeckx, *Marriage*, pp. 111-119. See also Hans Urs von Baltasar, "Ephesians 5.21-33 and *Humanae Vitae*: A Meditation," in *Christian Married Love*, ed. Raymond Dennehy (San Francisco: Ignatius Press, 1981), pp. 55-74.

8. See, for instance, 1 Corinthians 6. For an excellent commentary on this central theme in Pauline theology, see George T. Montague, S.M., *Maturing in Christ: St. Paul's Program for Growing in Christ* (Milwaukee: Bruce, 1964). See also Manuel Miguens, O.F.M., "Being a Christian and the Moral Life: Pauline Perspectives," in *Principles of Catholic Moral Life*, ed. William E. May (Chicago: Franciscan Herald Press, 1981), pp. 89-111.

9. For the meaning of *body* in Paul, see John A.T. Robinson, *The Body: A Study in Pauline Theology* (London and Naperville, Ill.: SCM Press and A.J. Allen, 1961).

10. The meaning of the term *skeuos* in 1 Thessalonians 4.4 has been disputed. Literally it means "vessel," "container," or "dish." Some exegetes believe that in this passage it means "wife," whereas others (and these are in the majority) hold that it means one's own "body." For a brief review of the question, see J. Terence Forestell, C.S.B., "The Letter to the Thessalonians," *The Jerome Biblical Commentary*, 48.23.

11. Thus, the reference to adultery in the condemnations of laxism by Innocent XI in 1679 assumes the serious wrongness of adultery and makes clear that the consent of one's spouse does not make an extramarital sexual act nonadulterous. See DS 2150.

12. See Cyprian, *De Ecclesiae Catholicae Unitate*, PL 4.507, who compares the embracing of false doctrine to adultery.

13. Pius XI, *Casti Connubii* (Washington, D.C.: U.S. Catholic Conference, 1969), p. 25.

14. National Conference of Catholic Bishops, *To Live in Christ Jesus: A Pastoral Reflection on the Moral Life* (Washington, D.C.: U.S. Catholic Conference, 1976), p. 19.

15. See text cited above in Note 3.

16. The view that the condemnation of adultery in Scripture, Christian tradition, and by the magisterium is culturally conditioned is advanced by Anthony Kosnik et al., *Human Sexuality: New Directions in American Catholic Thought* (New York: Paulist Press, 1977), pp. 17-29.

17. See the addresses of John Paul II for November 14 and November 21,

1979 ("By the Communion of Persons Man Becomes the Image of God" and "Marriage: One and Indissoluble in Genesis"). The text of these addresses is found in John Paul II, *Original Unity of Man and Woman: Catechesis on the Book of Genesis* (Boston: Daughters of St. Paul, 1981), pp. 70-84; see also the comments of Dietrich von Hildebrand, *Man and Woman* (Chicago: Franciscan Herald Press, 1965), p. 18.

18. *Gaudium et Spes*, no. 50: ". . . It must be said that true married love and the whole structure of family life which results from it is directed to disposing the spouses to cooperate valiantly with the love of the Creator and Saviour, who through them will increase and enrich his family from day to day."

19. John Paul II has written profoundly on the relationship between spousal friendship and the giving of new life within the family. See, in particular, his addresses of January 2, 1980 ("Creation as Fundamental and Original Gift") and of March 5, 1980 ("Analysis of Knowledge and of Procreation"); texts in *Original Unity of Man and Woman*, pp. 99-105, 146-152; see also his analysis in *Love and Responsibility*, tr. H.T. Willetts (New York: Farrar, Straus, and Giroux, 1981), pp. 224-237.

20. *Gaudium et Spes*, no. 49.

21. This case was made famous by Joseph Fletcher, *Situation Ethics: The New Morality* (Philadelphia: Westminster, 1966), pp. 164-165.

22. See Paul Ramsey, *Deeds and Rules in Christian Ethics* (New York: Scribner's, 1967), pp. 145-225, for a detailed critique of Fletcher's consequentialism.

23. This seems to be the view of such writers as Robert and Anna Francoeur and Nona and George O'Neill. See the Francoeurs' *Hot Sex — Cool Sex* (New York: Harcourt Brace Jovanovich, 1974) and the O'Neills' *Open Marriage* (Philadelphia: Lippincott, 1972).

24. For the teaching of Innocent XI, see DS 2150; for John Paul II, see *Love and Responsibility*, pp. 221-222.

25. On this, see, for instance, Herant A. Katchadourian and Donald T. Lunde, *Fundamentals of Human Sexuality*, 3rd ed. (New York: Holt, Rinehart, and Winston, 1980), pp. 486-487; Ashley Montagu, *Sex, Man, and Society* (New York: Putnam's, 1969), ch. 1.

26. Paul VI, *Humanae Vitae*, no. 10; AAS 60.487-488.

27. *Ibid.*, no. 14.

28. It should be noted that the anovulant pills now marketed in the United States may well be abortifacient in addition to being contraceptive. These pills first seek to prevent conception by inhibiting ovulation. Should ovulation, however, still occur, they seek to prevent conception by rendering the mucus of the cervix hostile to sperm. Should some sperm, however, survive and should one fertilize the ovum, these pills then act abortifaciently by changing the lining of the uterine wall, making it reject the developing embryo. On this issue, see Thomas Hilgers, M.D., "The New Technologies of Birth," in *New Technologies of Birth and Death*, ed. Donald McCarthy (St. Louis: The Pope John Center, 1981), pp. 29-55.

29. For an account of this situation, see G.E.M. Anscombe, *Contraception and Chastity* (London: Catholic Truth Society, 1977), pp. 15-17.
30. See Philip S. Keane, S.S., *Sexual Morality: A Catholic Perspective* (New York: Paulist Press, 1977), pp. 43-46, and the literature cited there. One of the best-known statements of this objection is given by Charles E. Curran, in his *Themes in Fundamental Moral Theology* (Notre Dame, Ind.: University of Notre Dame Press, 1977), pp. 27-80.
31. This was suggested by John T. Noonan, Jr., *Contraception: A History of Its Treatment by Catholic Theologians and Canonists* (Cambridge, Mass.: Harvard University Press, 1965), pp. 508-533.
32. Among the many episcopal statements made during this period, the following are representative: Karol Wojtyla (John Paul II), *Fruitful and Responsible Love* (New York: Seabury, 1979) pp. 13-35 (this was an address he gave in Milan in June, 1978, at an international symposium on the anniversary of *Humanae Vitae*); the Bishops of India, "*Humanae Vitae*: Ten Years Later" (a statement of January 17, 1978), *The Pope Speaks*, 23 (1978), 183-187; Cardinal Terence Cooke, "Address to Symposium on Natural Family Planning," New York, May 23, 1978, published in *L'Osservatore Romano* (English edition) (June 27, 1978), 3; the Irish Hierarchy, *L'Osservatore Romano* (March 16, 1978), 11. See also the comments by Bishop T. Stewart of Korea at the conference held in Melbourne, Australia, in 1978, and published in *Human Love and Human Life*, ed. J.N. Santamaria and John J. Billings (Melbourne: The Polding Press, 1979).
33. *To Live in Christ Jesus*, p. 18.
34. John Paul II, "An Address to the U.S. Bishops," October 5, 1979, *Origins: NC Documentary Service*, 9.18 (October 18, 1979), 289.
35. See John Paul II, *Familiaris Consortio*, no. 29.
36. *Ibid.*, no. 31.
37. Paul VI, *Humanae Vitae*, no. 6; AAS 60.484-485.
38. Noonan, *Contraception*, p. 6.
39. It is important to recognize in this connection that the highly publicized statements of various national conferences of bishops which were issued in 1968 and 1969 after the publication of *Humanae Vitae* do not contradict the received teaching on contraception. Some of them do suggest that it is possible responsibly to dissent from this teaching, but they go no further than that; they do not deny the teaching or propose a new teaching. See John Ford, S.J., and Germain Grisez, "Contraception and the Infallibility of the Ordinary Magisterium," *Theological Studies*, 39 (1978), 308-311, for an analysis of these episcopal statements. This is not to deny, of course, that there is considerable dissent among theologians, clergy, and faithful. Although this dissent is very confusing and troubling to many Catholics, it is important to emphasize that it has no normative status. See the analysis in Grisez, *Christian Moral Principles,* ch. 36. q. B.
40. For the first Vatican Council's teaching on the infallibility of the ordinary magisterium, see Session IV (July 18, 1870), Constitution *Pastor Aeternus*, c. 4, "De Romani Pontificis Infallibili Magisterio." See, in particular, DS

256

3069. For the Second Vatican Council's teaching on the infallibility of the pope and of the bishops united with the pope in the ordinary exercise of their teaching office, see *Lumen Gentium*, no. 25.

41. See Ford and Grisez, "Contraception and the Infallibility of the Ordinary Magisterium," 258-312.

42. The argument to be presented here is like that of Germain Grisez in *Contraception and the Natural Law* (Milwaukee: Bruce, 1964), and in "A New Formulation of a Natural Law Argument Against Contraception," *The Thomist*, 30 (1966), 343-361. John Finnis, "Natural Law and Unnatural Acts," *Heythrop Journal*, 11 (1970), 379-387, develops this line of argument by making clear the relation between the procreative and the unitive goods of marriage. Other approaches do not place so much emphasis on the procreative good. Anscombe, *Contraception and Chastity*, p. 21, argues that contraceptive intercourse is not a proper act of intercourse because it is not an act that is the sort of act open to the transmission of life. Thus, it cannot be a true marriage act, and sexual acts that are not true marriage acts are either mere lasciviousness or an inauthentic substitute for marital union. John Kippley, *Birth Control and the Marriage Covenant* (Collegeville, Minn.: The Liturgical Press, 1976), a revision of his earlier *Christ, Covenant and Contraception*, argues that contraception is inconsistent with the marriage covenant. Mary R. Joyce, *The Meaning of Contraception* (Collegeville, Minn.: The Liturgical Press, 1969) and Dietrich von Hildebrand, *The Encyclical Humanae Vitae: A Sign of Contradiction* (Chicago: Franciscan Herald Press, 1969) develop arguments based on the inseparable connection between the unitive and procreative meanings of the conjugal act — a connection emphasized by Paul VI in *Humanae Vitae*. See also Karol Wojtyla, *Love and Responsibility*, pp. 224-237.

43. *To Live in Christ Jesus*, p. 18.

44. *Gaudium et Spes*, nos. 49, 50; *To Live in Christ Jesus*, p. 18; John Paul II, "An Address to the U.S. Bishops," 289, and " 'Stand Up' for Human Life," his homily on the Capital Mall, Washington, D.C., October 7, 1979, in *Origins: NC Documentary Service*, 9.18 (October 18, 1979), 291.

45. On this, see John Paul II, address of January 2, 1980, "Creation as Fundamental and Original Gift," and address of March 5, 1980, "Analysis of Knowledge and of Procreation," in *Original Unity of Man and Woman*, pp. 99-105, 146-152.

46. See Anscombe, *Contraception and Chastity*, pp. 18-19.

47. Thus, Kosnik et al., *Human Sexuality*, point out that fornication in some circumstances can be all right, that "creative adultery" is conceivable, and that homosexual acts between homosexually oriented persons in a stable relationship are also morally permissible. These authors even indicate that bestiality may be permissible when no other sexual "outlets" are available. See pp. 148-149 (adultery), 153ff. (fornication), 186-218 (homosexuality), and 229-230 (bestiality). In his essay, "Divorce from the Perspective of a Revised Moral Theology," Charles E. Curran, in his *Ongoing Revision: Studies in Moral Theology* (Notre Dame, Ind.: Fides, 1976), pp. 77-78, ad-

mits that those were correct who thought, during the debates over contraception, that if contraception were morally permissible, then other forms of sexual activity were justifiable. He, of course, agrees that premarital sex, masturbation, and homosexual activity can at times be morally permissible.

48. See "The Question Is Not Closed: The Liberals Reply," in *The Birth Control Debate*, ed. Robert G. Hoyt (Kansas City, Mo.: National Catholic Reporter, 1969), pp. 74-85. This is one of the documents from the Papal Commission on birth regulation.

49. That contraception leads to abortion hardly needs further proof. In fact, many of the most widely used "contraceptives," especially the IUD (intrauterine device) are not really contraceptive but abortifacient. The pill at times acts in a contraceptive way and at times as an abortifacient. See Note 28 above.

50. Here, it is instructive to note that frequently abortion is described as "post-conceptive" birth control. Moreover, some ethicists — among them David H. Smith ("The Abortion of Defective Fetuses: Some Moral Considerations," in *No Rush to Judgment: Essays in Medical Ethics* [Bloomington, Ind.: The Poynter Center, 1978], pp. 144-148) — argue that if people "responsibly" seek to prevent conception by the use of contraceptives which subsequently "fail," then abortion is morally justifiable.

51. On this, see Anscombe, *Contraception and Chastity*, p. 17.

52. For the connection between the pill and sterilization, see Charles E. Curran, "Sterilization: Exposition, Critique, and Refutation of Past Teaching," in *New Perspectives of Moral Theology* (Notre Dame, Ind.: University of Notre Dame Press, 1976), pp. 207-211. For a critique of Curran, see William E. May, "Sterilization: Catholic Teaching and Catholic Practice," *Homiletic and Pastoral Review*, 72.12 (1976), 9-29.

53. See Curran, "Natural Law," *Themes in Fundamental Moral Theology*, pp. 39-40.

54. It is perhaps worth noting here that *Gaudium et Spes* deliberately refrained from using the traditional terminology of the primary and secondary ends of marriage. This does not mean that Vatican II denied the proposition affirmed in the tradition that procreation is the primary end of marriage; nor do we intend to deny this in affirming that procreation is only one good. The Commission sponsoring *Gaudium et Spes* responded to the requests of "many Fathers" that certain changes be made in the wording of the statements on the origin and properties of marriage. The Commission noted that in a pastoral text there was no need for an enumeration of the juridical elements of marriage. It also noted that the hierarchy of goods within marriage had already been sufficiently stated many times in Church tradition and by the magisterium. The Commission went on to observe that it is possible to look at the hierarchy of goods from a different point of view and then said: "Moreover, in the text of *Gaudium et Spes*, which speaks to the world in a direct and pastoral style, very technical terminology (e.g., the hierarchy of ends) is clearly avoided. In any case the

primordial importance of procreation and education is mentioned at least 10 times in the text, as it often speaks of sacramentality, and fidelity and indissolubility are emphasized at least 7 times in the text" *Acta Synodolia* · *Sacrosancti Oecumenici Vaticani Secundi*, vol. 4, (Rome: Typis Polyglottis Vaticanis, 1978), pp. 476-477. The primacy of the procreative good within marriage is not a primacy of value but of definition; the procreative good is what defines marriage as the kind of community and institution it is and distinguishes it from other forms of friendship. This does not imply that procreation is primary in the intentions of spouses or that it is more valuable than the good of marital love or fidelity. Surely, it does not absolutize the value of procreation as compared with other values in and out of marriage.

55. See Wulstan Mork, O.S.B., *The Biblical Meaning of Man* (Milwaukee: Bruce, 1967), pp. 14-32; Albert Gelin, S.S., *The Concept of Man in the Bible*, tr. David Murphy (Staten Island, N.Y.: Alba House, 1967), pp. 13-24.

56. *Gaudium et Spes*, no. 14.

57. See *Summa Theologiae*, 1, qq. 75-76; see also Germain Grisez, "Dualism and the New Morality," *Atti del Congresso Internazionale Tommaso D'Aguino nel Suo Settimo Centenario*, vol. 5, *L'Agir Morale* (Naples: Edizione Domenicane, 1977), pp. 323-330.

58. See Gabriel Marcel, *Being and Having*, tr. Katherine Farrer (New York: Dover, 1949), pp. 154-175. See also Gilbert Ryle, *The Concept of Mind* (New York: Macmillan, 1949), pp. 11-24.

59. For a more detailed critique of this objection, see Ford and Grisez, "Contraception and the Infallibility of the Ordinary Magisterium," 291-299.

60. See John and Sheila Kippley, *The Art of Natural Family Planning*, 2nd ed. (Cincinnati: Couple to Couple League, 1978); on the reliability of the various methods of NFP, see Hanna Klaus, M.D., "Natural Family Planning: A Review," *Obstetrical and Gynecological Survey*, 37.2 (1982), 128-150, especially Table 6, "Major Use-Effectiveness Studies," 142-143.

61. This is the contention, for instance, of Kosnik et al., *Human Sexuality*, pp. 114, 292-295.

62. Formally this is the fallacy of drawing an affirmative conclusion in a Figure II syllogism; the conclusion does not follow, as the following example shows:

| | |
|---|---|
| From | All crows are birds. |
| and | All eagles are birds. |
| it does not follow that | All eagles are crows. |
| Thus, from | All contraceptive acts are for avoiding pregnancy. |
| and | All use of NFP is for avoiding pregnancy. |
| One cannot validly conclude | All use of NFP is contraceptive. |

63. This is not to suggest that the only way one violates the good of procreation is by acting against it in contraceptive intercourse. Married couples

ordinarily have an obligation to have some children if they can, because marriage is of its nature ordered to the procreation and education of children. To refuse to fulfill this obligation — even by use of NFP throughout one's fertile years — is ordinarily a violation of the procreative good. See Anscombe, *Contraception and Chastity*, p. 19, and William E. May, "Contraception, Abstinence, and Responsible Parenthood," *Faith and Reason*, 3.1 (1977), 46-49; Karol Wojtyla (John Paul II), *Love and Responsibility*, pp. 224-237.

64. For a development of relevant analogies, see Mary R. Joyce, *The Meaning of Contraception*, p. 41; and Anscombe, *Contraception and Chastity*, p. 20. Anscombe asks us to consider two types of protest by industrial workers who have a legitimate complaint against their employer. On one type of protest the workers act violently — for example, by destroying machinery in the factory. In the other they "work to rule," by doing their job at a slow pace within the limits of minimal justice. Clearly there is a moral difference between the cases. If the protest is justified in the first place, the latter strategy is clearly justified but not the former. The use of contraception is analogous to the use of violent protest.

65. It has been objected that the *timing* of these acts functions so as to render them infertile and thus in reality such acts are acts of contraceptive intercourse. Perhaps this objection is based on simply ignoring the distinction between *anti*-procreative acts and *non*-procreative acts. But this objection may be the claim that the timing of the acts of intercourse is just another contraceptive measure, like withdrawal, for example, which puts space between sperm and ovum. This version of the objection fails because it does not analyze carefully enough precisely how the timing of the act affects the agents' understanding and intention. If a couple chooses to have intercourse at times when they are not fertile, they cannot be choosing to engage in procreative activity; they believe that they are incapable of procreating at that time. They cannot have an anti-procreative intention nor can they have a procreative intention given what they know about their own fertility. The procreative good is not, as it were, engaged or at issue in these acts. They cannot be acting against the procreative good when they are convinced that the act of intercourse cannot in this instance be procreative. Thus, they act for the other goods of marriage and they do not act against the good of procreation. In other words, the timing of an act of intercourse cannot be understood as an accidental feature that can be used to distort an essentially procreative activity. The use of contraceptives, by contrast, does involve such a distortion since they are used *only* to prevent what one believes to be a procreative act from having its procreative intent. (We admit that it is possible for couples to use NFP for selfish reasons in order to exclude children from their lives. Such use of NFP is morally wrong, but it is not wrong because it is contraceptive — which it is *not*. It should be noted too that couples can use NFP to increase the chances of pregnancy when they seek to pursue the procreative good.)

66. John Paul II, *Familiaris Consortio*, no. 32.

67. See Germain Grisez, "Natural Family Planning Is Not Contraception," *International Review of Natural Family Planning*, 1 (1977), 123-126; John G. Quesnell, "One Couple Comes Full Circle," *Our Family*, January, 1975; L. and N. Christenson, *The Christian Couple* (Minneapolis: Bethany Fellowship, 1977); Vicente J.A. Rosales, "The Catholic Choice of Rhythm," *International Review of Natural Family Planning*, 2 (1978), 35.

68. On this, see Charles E. Curran, "Sterilization: Exposition, Critique, and Refutation of Past Teaching," pp. 207-211; John Dedek, *Contemporary Medical Ethics* (New York Sheed and Ward, Inc., 1975), pp. 113-120.

69. See, for instance, Bernard Häring, *Medical Ethics* (Notre Dame, Ind.: Fides, 1972), pp. 90-91.

70. See, for example, Paul VI, *Humanae Vitae*, no. 14; National Conference of Catholic Bishops, *Ethical and Religious Directives for Catholic Health Care Facilities* (Washington, D.C.: U.S. Catholic Conference, 1976), nos. 18, 20. See also the July 9, 1980 "Statement on Tubal Ligation" of the National Conference of Catholic Bishops, *Hospital Progress*, 61.9 (1980), 39.

71. A good presentation of magisterial documents and theological analysis of this matter is given by Gerald A. Kelly, *Medical-Moral Problems* (St. Louis: Catholic Hospital Association, 1955).

72. For example, Häring, *Medical Ethics*, pp. 90-91; John Boyle, *The Sterilization Controversy* (New York: Paulist Press, 1977).

73. Martin Nolan, "The Principle of Totality," in *Absolutes in Moral Theology?*, ed. Charles E. Curran (Washington, D.C.: Corpus, 1968). For an incisive critique of this effort to extend the principle of totality, see Paul Ramsey, *The Patient as Person* (New Haven, Conn.: Yale University Press, 1971), pp. 178-181.

74. John Boyle, who agrees that contraceptive sterilization is justifiable on the grounds that it promotes the greater good, provides a good history of this position in *The Sterilization Controversy*.

75. The effort to justify contraceptive sterilization on the grounds of the principle of totality was explicitly rejected by the National Conference of Catholic Bishops in their "Statement on Tubal Ligation."

76. Pius XII, "Address to the Delegates of the Eighth Congress of the World Medical Association," September 30, 1954, AAS 46.587-598.

77. For a typical statement hailing the pill as a revolutionary and liberating discovery, comparable to the discovery of fire and the invention of the wheel, see the rhapsodic hymn to the pill given by Ashley Montagu in his *Sex, Man, and Society*, ch. 1.

78. Thus, Paul VI says in *Humanae Vitae* that any use of marriage must remain open *(per se destinatus)* to procreation. Anscombe, *Contraception and Chastity*, pp. 18-21, makes very clear the conceptual link between contraception and such acts as masturbation and sodomy. Her argument is that if contraception is permissible, then so are such acts as these.

79. See Pius XII, "Address to the Second World Congress on Fertility and Sterility," May 19, 1956; AAS 48.473. The English is from John C. Ford, S.J., and Gerald A. Kelly, S.J., *Contemporary Moral Theology*, vol. 2,

*Marriage Questions* (Westminster, Md.: The Newman Press, 1964), p. 212. Ford and Kelly discuss this and other relevant texts, pp. 188-234.

80. Anscombe, *Contraception and Chastity*, pp. 21-22; see Ford and Kelly, *Marriage Questions*, pp. 224-234, for a judicious discussion of the dangers of hedonism in this area.

81. See Pius XII, "Address to the Midwives," October 29, 1951; AAS 43.835-854.

82. Anscombe, *Contraception and Chastity*, p. 26; Ford and Kelly, *Marriage Questions*, pp. 228-230, suggest three principles for evaluating sexual behavior between spouses: conjugal justice, conjugal chastity, and Christian self-restraint. They make clear how prudent application of these principles helps not only in the avoidance of lustful immoderation but also in the efforts of mutual sanctification.

83. Anscombe, *Contraception and Chastity*, p. 26.

84. Paul VI, *Humanae Vitae*, no. 12.

85. See Pius XII, "Address to the Fourth International Congress of Catholic Doctors," September 29, 1949, AAS 41.557-561; "Address to Midwives," October 29, 1951, AAS 43.835-854; "Address to the Second World Congress on Fertility and Sterility," May 19, 1956, AAS 48.467-474. English translations of the latter two addresses are available in Liebard's *Love and Sexuality*, pp. 101-122, 173-179. On this, also see William E. May, *Human Existence, Medicine, and Ethics: Reflections on Human Life* (Chicago: Franciscan Herald Press, 1977), pp. 45-66, and "Begotten Not Made: Reflections on the Laboratory Generation of Human Life," in *Pope John Paul II Lecture Series in Bioethics*, vol. 1, *Perspectives in Bioethics*, ed. Francis J. Lescoe and David Q. Liptak (Cromwell, Conn.: Holy Apostles Seminary, 1983), pp. 31-60.

86. See also William B. Smith, "Procreation Is Not for the Laboratory," *Human Life Review*, 4 (1978), 42-45; Robert J. Brungs, S.J., "Biotechnology and the Social Order," *Human Life Review*, 5 (1979), 31-50; Paul Ramsey, *Fabricated Man* (New Haven, Conn.: Yale University Press, 1970), pp. 104-160, and "Shall We 'Reproduce'?" *Journal of the American Medical Association*, 220 (1972), 1346-1350, 1480-1485, reprinted in *New Theology No. 10*, ed. Martin E. Marty and Dean Peerman (New York: Macmillan, 1973).

87. Pius XII, in his "Address to Midwives" (translation from Liebard's *Love and Sexuality*, pp. 117-118), criticizes this separation as follows: "To consider unworthily the cohabitation of husband and wife, and the marital act as a simple organic function for the transmission of seed, would be the same as to convert the domestic hearth, which is the family sanctuary, into a mere biological laboratory. . . . There is much more than the union of two life germs, which can be brought about even artificially, that is, without the cooperation of husband and wife. The marital act, in the order of, and by nature's design, consists of a personal cooperation which the husband and wife exchange as a right when they marry."

262

# CHAPTER 8

1. Friedrich Hauck and Siegfried Schulz, "Pornē," in *Theological Dictionary of the New Testament*, vol. 6, ed. Gerhard Kittel, tr. Geoffrey W. Bromiley (Grand Rapids, Mich.: Eerdmans, 1968), pp. 585-586, and Raymond Collins, "The Bible and Sexuality II: The New Testament," *Biblical Theology Bulletin*, 8 (1978), 4.
2. Hauck and Schulz, "Pornē," p. 585.
3. *Ibid.*, pp. 586, 587-588.
4. Collins, "The Bible and Sexuality II," 4.
5. Philo, *Speculum Legis*, III, 51.
6. See Manuel Miguens, O.F.M., "Christ's Members and Sex," *The Thomist*, 39 (1975), 24-48; Joseph Jensen, "Does *Porneia* Mean Fornication? A Critique of Bruce Malina," *Novum Testamentum*, 20 (1978), 161-184, and especially 179-181.
7. The only other mention of *porneia* in the Gospels is in the Matthean divorce texts (Matthew 5.32, 19.9). Current biblical scholars tend to hold that the term *porneia* in these Matthean texts refers to incestuous kinds of relationships, termed *zenut* in Hebrew. See Joseph Fitzmyer, S.J., "The Matthean Divorce Texts and Some New Palestinian Evidence," *Theological Studies*, 37 (1976), 197-226.
8. John J. O'Rourke, "Does the New Testament Condemn Sexual Intercourse Outside of Marriage?" *Theological Studies*, 37 (1976), 478-479, makes it clear that Paul is referring here to extramarital intercourse: "Obviously the Apostle is not speaking of idolatry, nor of marriages prohibited by law, nor of evil in general. He is not speaking of sacred prostitutes, an institution which at one time had flourished in Corinth, but which was most likely nonexistent in a Roman *colonia*. Surely he is not speaking of commercial prostitution. He is not saying that it is likely that a girl who remains unmarried and does not have the special gift which he possesses (see I Cor 7:7b) will become a whore, because the reason that he gives for both a man and a woman is the same: *dia tes porneias*. Thus the only possible understanding in context of *porneia* is illicit sexual intercourse (see also I Cor 7:9, where Paul says of the 'unmarried' [agamoi] and the widows, 'if they cannot exercise self-control, let them marry' [ei de ouk egkateuontai gamesatosan])." See also Jensen, "Does *Porneia* Mean Fornication?" 181-182.
9. See Innocent IV, *Sub Catholica Professione*, March 6, 1254, in DS 835; Decrees of the Holy Office (September 24, 1665, DS 2045; March 2, 1679, DS 2148); Pius XI, *Casti Connubii*, December 31, 1930, AAS 22.558-559; Sacred Congregation for the Doctrine of the Faith, *Declaration on Certain Questions Concerning Sexual Ethics* (Washington, D.C.: U.S. Catholic Conference, 1976), no. 7.
10. John Paul II, *Familiaris Consortio*, no. 11.
11. See Karol Wojtyla (John Paul II), *Love and Responsibility*, tr. H.T. Willetts (New York: Farrar, Straus, and Giroux, 1981), p. 41, for a discus-

sion of what he calls the "personalist principle": "This norm, in its negative aspect, states that the person is the kind of good which does not admit of use and cannot be treated as an object of use and as such the means to an end. In its positive aspect the personalist norm confirms this: the person is a good towards which the only proper and adequate attitude is love."

12. *Ibid.*, p. 30.
13. See *Toward a Quaker View of Sex* (London: Friends Homes Service Committee, 1963); *Sex and Morality: A Report Presented to the British Council of Churches* (Philadelphia: Fortress Press, 1966); United Church of Christ, *Human Sexuality: A Preliminary Study* (New York: United Church Press, 1977). See also Joseph Fletcher, *Situation Ethics: The New Morality* (Philadelphia: Westminster, 1966); John A.T. Robinson, *Honest to God* (Philadelphia: Westminster, 1963).
14. On this, see Paul Ramsey, *Deeds and Rules in Christian Ethics* (New York: Scribner's, 1967), ch. 1.
15. See, for example, Philip S. Keane, S.S., *Sexual Morality: A Catholic Perspective* (New York: Paulist Press, 1977), pp. 92-113.
16. *Ibid.*, p. 107. The principal point is that Keane is here arguing that coition between persons definitely not married (for they only *intend* to marry) can be and is under some circumstances morally good.
17. See Paul Ramsey, "A Christian Approach to the Question of Sexual Relations Outside of Marriage," *Journal of Religion*, 45 (1965), 100-118, at 112. Ramsey places careful qualification on his view in an updated version of the above article in *One Flesh: A Christian View of Sex Within, Outside, and Before Marriage* (Bramcote, Notts, England: Grove Books, 1975).
18. See Anthony Kosnik et al., *Human Sexuality: New Directions in American Catholic Thought* (New York: Paulist Press, 1977), pp. 155-165, for an example of this abuse.
19. On this, see Edward Schillebeeckx, *Marriage: Human Reality and Saving Mystery* (New York: Sheed and Ward, 1965), pp. 37-102.
20. Council of Trent, Session 24, November 11, 1563; DS 1813-1816. The requirement of a canonical form was later incorporated into the 1917 *Codex Juris Canonici*, Canon 1098. In the 1983 revised *Codex* the relevant canon is Canon 1108. Canon 1116 spells out circumstances in which this form is not required. A new canon in the 1983 *Codex*, Canon 1117, declares that Roman Catholics who have by a formal act repudiated their Roman Catholicism may marry validly without this canonical form.
21. The essentially public character of marriage is clearly set forth in *Familiaris Consortio*, no. 11.
22. See Joseph J. Farraher, S.J., "Masturbation," *New Catholic Encyclopedia* (New York: McGraw-Hill, 1965), 9.438, for a general discussion; for a more thorough discussion with several classical definitions, see *Dictionnaire de Théologie Catholique*, ed. A. Vacant, E. Manganot, and A. Amann (Paris: Librairie Letouzy et Ane, 1902-1905), 15 vols., 9.1346-1347. See also Marcellinus Zalba, S.J., *Theologiae Moralis Com-*

*pendium*, vol. 1, (Madrid: Biblioteca de Autores Cristianos, 1958), pp. 771-775, for a modern definition and discussion. Zalba defines pollution as the complete, separate use of the generative faculty. By *complete* he means to orgasm, by *separate* he means outside of sexual intercourse. He goes on to argue that all directly and perfectly voluntary pollution is intrinsically a grave sin.

23. See, for instance, Augustine, *Opus Imperfectum Contra Julianum*, 4, 11, 10 (PL 44.74); 3, 20, 38 (PL 44.72) and *De Nuptiis et Concupiscentia*, 2, 26, 42 (PL 44.460). The penitentials in use from the sixth through ninth centuries strongly condemned masturbation. See, for example, *Paenitentiale Aquilonale* (Canon 2) and *Luci Victoriae* (Canon 8), cited in Josef Fuchs, S.J., *De Castitate et Ordine Sexuali*, 2nd ed. (Rome: Gregorian University, 1960), p. 49. See also the references in John T. Noonan, Jr., *Contraception: A History of Its Treatment by Catholic Theologians and Canonists* (Cambridge, Mass.: Harvard University Press, 1965), pp. 70-77, for a discussion of patristic and Jewish views on masturbation.

24. For medieval thought, see, for instance, Thomas Aquinas, *Summa Theologie*, II-II, q. 154, a. 5. Zalba and Fuchs, cited above in Notes 22 and 23, are representatives of the manualist tradition.

25. It should be noted that not only in the Catholic theological tradition has masturbation been regarded as seriously immoral but also in the whole Christian tradition until relatively modern times. For Protestant thought on this subject, see references given by Derrick S. Bailey, *The Male-Female Relationship in Christian Tradition* (New York: Harper and Row, 1968).

26. See Leo IX, Epistola "Ad Splendidum Nitentis" ad Petrum Damiani, 1054, DS 687-688; Alexander VII, "Errores Doctrinae Moralis Laxioris," September 14, 1665, DS 2044; Innocent XI, "Errores Doctrinae Moralis Laxioris," March 2, 1679, DS 2149; Pius XI, "Decree of Holy Office on Masturbation," July 24, 1929, DS 3684; addresses of Pius XII, October 8, 1953, AAS 45.677-678; May 19, 1956, AAS 48.472-473; Sacred Congregation for the Doctrine of the Faith, *Declaration on Certain Questions Concerning Sexual Ethics*, no. 9; Sacred Congregation for Catholic Education, "Educational Guidance in Human Love," November 1, 1983, no. 98.

27. *Declaration on Certain Questions Concerning Sexual Ethics*, no. 9.

28. On the use of the Onan texts, see the discussions in Noonan, *Contraception*, under Onan in the index.

29. See Fuchs, *De Castitate et Ordine Sexuali*, pp. 47-48; John L. McKenzie, "Onan," in his *Dictionary of the Bible* (Milwaukee: Bruce, 1965).

30. *Declaration on Certain Questions Concerning Sexual Ethics*, no. 9.

31. See, for example, Michael Valente, *Sex: the Radical View of a Catholic Theologian* (New York: Bruce-Macmillan, 1970).

32. See John C. Ford, S.J., and Germain Grisez, "Contraception and the Infallibility of the Ordinary Magisterium," *Theological Studies*, 39 (1978), 263-277, for an exposition of the conditions under which the ordinary magisterium teaches infallibly; these conditions are set out in *Lumen Gen-*

*tium*, no. 25. In the remainder of this article Ford and Grisez apply these conditions to the teaching on contraception; some of this material is directly relevant to the teaching on the morality of masturbation; their analysis suggests that a similar argument can be made concerning the received teaching on masturbation.

33. See Germain Grisez, "Dualism and the New Morality," *Atti del Congressa Internazionale Tommaso D'Aquino nel Suo Settimo Centario*, vol. 5, *L'Agir Morale*, (Naples: Edizione Domenicane, 1977), pp. 323-330.

34. See *Dictionnaire de Théologie Catholique*, "Luxure: Especes," 9.1347-1349, for a critical summary of the theological arguments against masturbation. Plainly these arguments do not assume that procreation is the only legitimate goal of sexual activity.

35. See Kosnik et al., *Human Sexuality*, pp. 219-229.

36. See "Decree of the Holy Office, August 2, 1929," DS 3684; Henry Davis, S.J., *Pastoral and Moral Theology*, vol. 2, *Commandments of God: Precepts of the Church*, 8th ed. (New York: Sheed and Ward, 1959), p. 259.

37. See citations from Pius XII, in Note 26 above.

38. See Kosnik et al., *Human Sexuality*, pp. 227-229; Charles E. Curran, "Masturbation: An Objectively Grave Matter?" in *A New Look at Christian Morality* (Notre Dame, Ind.: Fides, 1968), pp. 200-221.

39. See Charles E. Curran, *Contemporary Problems in Moral Theology* (Notre Dame, Ind.: University of Notre Dame Press, 1970), pp. 159-188; Keane, *Sexual Morality*, pp. 62-68.

40. See Sacred Congregation for the Doctrine of the Faith, *Declaration on Certain Questions Concerning Sexual Ethics*, no. 10: "According to the Church's teaching, mortal sin, which is opposed to God, does not consist only in formal and direct resistance to the commandment of charity. It is equally to be found in this opposition to authentic love which is included in every deliberate transgression, in serious matter, of each of the moral laws."

41. Among the authors taking this perspective are: Albert Ellis, *Sex Without Guilt* (New York: Grove Press, 1965), pp. 10-19; Eleanor Hamilton, *Sex Before Marriage* (New York: Bantam Books, 1970), pp. 6-7, 13-16; James L. McCary, *Human Sexuality*, 2nd ed. (New York: Van Nostrand, 1979), pp. 183-184; Herant A. Katchadourian and Donald T. Lunde, *Fundamentals of Human Sexuality*, 3rd ed. (New York: Holt, Rinehart, and Winston, 1980), pp. 291-308. It is not surprising that these authors regard masturbation in such a casual way because they have adopted an extremely separatist view of human sexuality. They regard its procreative meaning merely as a biological function, and regard sex as simply one way for a lonely individual to break out of his or her prison of loneliness.

42. See the works of Curran and Keane cited above in Note 39, and that of Kosnik et al., previously cited so frequently in these pages.

43. André Guindon, *The Sexual Language* (Ottawa: The University of Ottawa Press, 1976), pp. 251-252, gives a variety of statistics from Kinsey and other sources. See also Farraher, "Masturbation," 438.

44. See *Dictionnaire de Théologie Catholique*, "Luxure: Gravité," 9.1340-1345, for a survey of biblical, theological, and magisterial discussions of the gravity of sexual sin.

45. For a sound, complete discussion on these points, see John C. Ford, S.J., and Gerald Kelly, S.J., *Contemporary Moral Theology*, vol. 1 (Westminster, Md.: The Newman Press, 1969), pp. 174-247.

46. See *Declaration on Certain Questions Concerning Sexual Ethics*, no. 9: "On the subject of masturbation modern psychology provides much valid and useful information for formulating a more equitable judgment on moral responsibility and for orienting pastoral action. Psychology helps one to see how the immaturity of adolescence (which can sometimes persist after that age), psychological imbalance or habit can influence behavior, diminishing the deliberate character of the act and bringing about a situation whereby subjectively there may not always be serious fault. But in general, the absence of serious responsibility must not be presumed; this would be to misunderstand people's moral capacity."

47. See *Summa Theologiae*, II-II, q. 154, a. 4; this is the standard reference for the common teaching of the manuals.

48. See John F. Harvey, O.S.F.S., "Chastity and the Homosexual," *The Priest* 33.7-8 (1977), 10-16, at 12. John R. Cavanagh, *Counseling the Homosexual* (Huntington, Ind.: Our Sunday Visitor, Inc., 1977), p. 38. Cavanagh defines homosexuality as "a persistent, post-adolescent state in which the sexual object is a person of the same sex and in which there is a concomitant aversion or abhorrence, in varying degrees, to sexual relations with members of the other sex."

49. Thus, the definition does not include adolescents in a period of transitional anxiety about sexual identity, nor does it include those who engage in homosexual acts because of the lack of members of the other sex, as in prison or military situations. See Ruth T. Barnhouse, *Homosexuality: A Symbolic Confusion* (New York: Seabury, 1977), p. 22.

50. See Wardell Pomeroy, "Homosexuality," in *The Same Sex*, ed. Ralph Weltge (Philadelphia: Pilgrim Press, 1969), pp. 3-13; see especially Chart 7.

51. See National Conference of Catholic Bishops, *Principles to Guide Confessors in Questions of Homosexuality* (Washington, D.C.: U.S. Catholic Conference, 1973), pp. 5-8.

52. This is the Church's constant understanding of the relevant teaching of the Scripture on this subject. See Pierre Grelot, *Man and Wife in Scripture* (New York: Herder and Herder, 1965), pp. 34-37, and Edward Schillebeeckx, *Marriage*, pp. 14-16, 20-21. See also John L. McKenzie, "Human Origins," in *The Two-Edged Sword: An Interpretation of the Old Testament* (New York: Doubleday, 1966), where McKenzie makes the point that Genesis 1 and, in particular, Genesis 2 — the story of the creation of mankind as male and female and of marriage — is also the story of the creation of marriage. See also the article on sex in *The Interpreter's Dictionary of the Bible* (Nashville, Tenn.: Abingdon, 1966). See also Roger

Shinn, "Homosexuality, Christian Conviction, and Enquiry," *The Same Sex*, ed. Ralph Weltge (Philadelphia: Pilgrim Press, 1969), p. 26: "The Christian tradition over the centuries has affirmed the heterosexual, monogamous faithful marital union as normative for the divinely given meaning of the intimate sexual relationship." Even Charles E. Curran ("Dialogue with the Homophile Movement" in his *Catholic Moral Theology in Dialogue* [Notre Dame, Ind.: Fides, 1972]), who attempts to justify homosexual relations between homosexually constituted persons within a stable relationship on the grounds of a "theology of compromise," acknowledges that this is the normative tradition. This is also acknowledged by Keane, *Sexual Morality*, pp. 87-88.

53. On male homosexuality, see Leviticus 18.22, 20.13; Romans 1.27; 1 Corinthians 6.9-10; 1 Timothy 1.9-10; on female homosexuality, Romans 1.26-27.

54. See *Summa Theologiae*, II-II, q. 154, aa. 11-12; Salmanticenses, tr. XXVI, C. VII, 109; Zalba, 1, pp. 780-781.

55. *Declaration on Certain Questions Concerning Sexual Ethics*, no. 8.

56. James Hitchcock, *Catholicism and Modernity: Confrontation or Capitulation?* (New York: Seabury, 1979), p. 207.

57. See, for example, John McNeill, S.J., *The Church and the Homosexual* (Kansas City, Mo.: Andrews and McMeel, 1976); *Human Sexuality*, pp. 186-218.

58. See McNeill, *The Church and the Homosexual*, pp. 42-53. See also Kosnik et al., *Human Sexuality*, pp. 191-192. For a counterargument that this story definitely includes a reference to homosexuality, see Manuel Miguens, O.F.M., "Biblical Thoughts on 'Human Sexuality,' " in *Human Sexuality in Our Time*, ed. George A. Kelly (Boston: Daughters of St. Paul, 1979), pp. 112-115. It is important in this connection to note that the Epistle of Jude (v. 7) refers to Sodom and Gomorrah, and indicates their sin as unnatural vice.

59. McNeill, *The Church and the Homosexual*, pp. 53-56.

60. See Barnhouse, *Homosexuality: A Symbolic Confusion*, p. 180. See also Miguens, article cited above in Note 58. Joseph Jensen, "The Relevance of the Old Testament," in *Dimensions of Human Sexuality*, ed. Dennis Doherty (New York: Doubleday, 1979), p. 8, points out the failure of biblical writers to distinguish between homosexual activity and homosexual orientation. Still, he notes that this provides no suggestion that the biblical condemnation of the former is based on anything beyond "the nature of the act itself."

61. *Declaration on Certain Questions Concerning Sexual Ethics*, no. 8.

62. On this, see John M. Finnis, "Natural Law and Unnatural Acts," *Heythrop Journal*, 11 (1970), 384-385. (See also Chapter 6 of this book.)

63. Guindon, *The Sexual Language*, 339.

64. See Paul Cameron, "A Case Against Homosexuality," *The Human Life Review*, 4.3 (1978), 17-49. Cameron is a psychologist and argues effectively on the basis of the empirical data that homosexual activity undercuts the

values required for stable family life and society because of its direction to immediate sexual gratification. See also Samuel McCracken, "Are Homosexuals Gay?" *Commentary* (January 1979), 19-29, for further convincing documentation of the almost exclusive orientation toward pleasure on the part of most homosexuals, and of their consequent irresponsibility; two quotes from homosexuals are most revealing: ". . . Gay people have more fun than your average married guy in a home with two or three kids. You have more time and money. You don't have the responsibilities. . . . I can lavish . . . presents . . . on my nephews and take them to the zoo and have a great old time. When they get tired and cranky I take them back to mommy and dad — you know, dad has just finished paying two hundred bucks for their teeth." ". . . It's so hard to be a straight man, harder than to be a faggot, because the rewards are so stupid — the rewards that you are told you can have. Whereas if you're a faggot, I guess you can make up your own rewards. . . . It's more fun to be a faggot because nobody expects anything of us."

65. McCracken, "Are Homosexuals Gay?" 20-21, shows convincingly by a critical analysis of data published in pro-homosexual books that the claim that homosexuals are as happy as other people has not been established; in particular, he points to data which show that suicide attempts are significantly higher among homosexuals than among others — for example, 3% for white non-homosexual males, 18% for white homosexual males.

66. *Ibid.*, 22, cites the following statistics: 14% of homosexual males studied and 38% of females lived in an equivalent of a "happy marriage." But 84% of the males studied "cruised" at least once a month, 42% at least once a week. Half the males in the study cited had at least five hundred sexual partners.

67. *Ibid.*, 27: "The fact is that homosexuality generally entails a renunciation of responsibility for the continuance of the human race and of a voice in the dialogue of the generations. This is a renunciation made also by some heterosexuals and indeed by some married heterosexuals. There is, however, a still greater renunciation made by homosexuals, and that is of the intricate, complicated, and challenging process of adjusting one's life to someone so different from oneself as to be in a different sex entirely."

68. See *Dictionnaire de Théologie Catholique*, 14, 4.1350, for an elaboration and explanation of this definition.

69. See A.C. Kinsey et al., *Sexual Behavior in the Human Male* (Philadelphia: Saunders, 1948), pp. 667-673; *Sexual Behavior in the Human Female* (Philadelphia: Saunders, 1953), pp. 502-509.

70. See Leviticus 18.23, 29; 20.15-16; Exodus 22.19. See the commentary on these passages in *The Jerome Biblical Commentary*, ed. Raymond Brown, S.S., Joseph A. Fitzmyer, S.J., and Roland E. Murphy, O. Carm. (Englewood Cliffs, N.J.: Prentice-Hall, 1968), pp. 60, 78-79.

71. See *Summa Theologiae*, II-II, q. 154, a. 12, ad 4; Marcellinus Zalba, S.J., *Theologiae Moralis Compendium*, vol. 1, pp. 781-782.

72. Kosnik et al., *Human Sexuality*, pp. 229-230.

73. For a standard statement of the Catholic position, see Zalba, *Theologiae Moralis Compendium*, vol. 1, pp. 765-766.

74. See *ibid.*, and Bernard Häring, *The Law of Christ*, vol. 3, (Westminster, Md.: The Newman Press, 1966) p. 300.

75. See Sharon L. McCombie et al., "Development of a Medical Center Rape Crisis Intervention Program," *American Journal of Psychiatry*, 133.4 (1976), 418-421, at 418: "It is the fastest rising violent crime in the United States: the FBI reported a 68% increase in rape (from 31,000 to 51,000 cases) between 1968 and 1973, and police records in Boston show a 43.5% increase between 1972 and 1973." It is common knowledge also that many cases of rape are not reported. See L.S. McGuire et al., "Survey of Incidence of and Physicians' Attitude Toward Sexual Assault," *Public Health Report*, 91.2 (1976), 103-109.

76. Here the words of Dietrich von Hildebrand, *In Defense of Purity* (New York: Sheed and Ward, 1935), pp. 12-14, are instructive: "Sex . . . as contrasted with other departments of bodily experience is *essentially* deep. Every manifestation of sex produces an effect which transcends the physical sphere and, in a fashion quite unlike the other bodily desires, involves the soul deeply in its passion. . . . It is characteristic of sex that in virtue of its very significance and nature it tends to become incorporated with experiences of a higher order, purely psychological and spiritual. Nothing in the domain of sex is so self-contained as the other bodily experiences, e.g., eating and drinking. The unique profundity of sex . . . is sufficiently shown by the simple fact that a man's attitude toward it is of incomparably greater moral significance than his attitude to the other bodily appetites. Surrender to sexual desire for its own sake defiles a man in a way that gluttony, for example, can never do. It wounds him to the core of his being. . . . Sex occupies a central position in the personality. . . . Sex can indeed keep silence, but when it speaks it is no *obiter dictum*, but a voice from the depths, the utterance of something central and of utmost significance. In and with sex man, in a special way, gives himself."

77. For a standard statement of the permissibility of using such procedures after rape, see Zalba, *Theologiae Moralis Compendium*, vol. 1, pp. 765, 888. For an accessible discussion of some of the contemporary issues and literature on this point, see Benedict Ashley, O.P., and Kevin O'Rourke, O.P., *Health Care Ethics: A Theological Analysis* (St. Louis: Catholic Hospital Association, 1978), pp. 293-297.

78. See Ashley and O'Rourke, *Health Care Ethics*, pp. 293-297.

79. See *Summa Theologiae*, II-II, q. 154, a. 9.

80. Keane, *Sexual Morality*, pp. 58-59, misses this important point. He says, ". . . It can thus be said that in most cases sexual thoughts and fantasies do not deeply involve the average person; they are not very significant as an area of moral concern." This statement is ambiguous; he may be saying that most sexual thoughts are such that they never become an object of choice. This is contrary to common experiences; sex is important, and when a person is self-consciously dealing with sexual matters deliberation

270

is triggered and choice is required. Keane may, of course, simply mean that sexual thoughts are not a morally serious matter. We have argued otherwise, and his position is simply inconsistent with the common teaching of the Church and with ordinary common sense.

81. For a fuller account, see *Dictionnaire de Théologie Catholique*, 9.4, "Luxure," 1352-1354, for the standard classification. See also Zalba, *Theologiae Moralis Compendium*, vol. 1, pp. 786-789. For an account in English, see Henry Davis, S.J., *Pastoral and Moral Theology*, pp. 218-221.

## PASTORAL CONCLUSION

1. The fundamental principles of pastoral theology are exemplified in the pastoral visits John Paul II has regularly made to many nations. Pastoral theology has an integrative and immediately practical thrust: in sincere charity it seeks to understand the situation of those to whom the Gospel is taught; it offers encouragement and assistance; it is compassionate in the face of weakness but firm in its concern to proclaim the saving truth in its fullness, and to hearten the faithful to follow Christ generously. The American bishops outlined the fundamental principles of a pastoral approach to moral questions in two recent pastorals: *To Teach as Jesus Taught* and *To Live in Christ Jesus: A Pastoral Reflection on the Moral Life* (Washington, D.C.: U.S. Catholic Conference, 1975 and 1976).

2. John Paul II, *Familiaris Consortio*, no. 31.

3. Thus, John Paul II stresses how important it is to offer practical assistance in observing the moral precepts that express the requirements of love in *Familiaris Consortio*, no. 35, and in his concern to help pastoral leaders to see how great are the problems they must help the faithful to overcome (see Parts I and IV of *Familiaris Consortio*).

4. The Church insists that her teachings on morality are not merely authoritative declarations or rulings but express the truth entrusted to the Church by God; see Vatican Council II, *Dei Verbum*, ch. 1; John Paul II, *Redemptor Hominis*, no. 12. In his recent apostolic exhortation *Reconciliatio et Poenitentia* (December 2, 1984), John Paul II speaks of the duty of all teachers in the Church to avoid subjective views and seek to proclaim in moral matters the truth found in the word of God as interpreted by the magisterium (cf. no. 25).

5. The primacy of the duty of teaching the faith, including its moral aspects, is clear in the recent teaching of the Church. See Vatican Council II, *Lumen Gentium*, no. 25; *Christus Dominus*, nos. 12-13; on the right of the faithful to have the whole of the faith proclaimed to them, see John Paul II, "Address at Catholic University to Presidents of Catholic Universtities and Colleges," October 7, 1979, in *Pilgrim of Peace* (Washington, D.C.: U.S. Catholic Conference, 1979), pp. 166-167. See also *Code of Canon Law* (1983), Canons 747, 760.

6. See the moving appeal of John Paul II to theologians in *Familiaris Consortio*, no. 31. See also Paul VI, *Humanae Vitae*, nos. 28-30.

7. John Paul II reminded American bishops that this duty remains foremost for bishops, even when it becomes painful: "The bishop must announce to the young and the old, to the rich and the poor, to the powerful and the weak the fullness of truth, which sometimes offends, even if it always liberates. . . . Precisely because he cannot renounce the preaching of the Cross, the bishop will be called upon over and over *to accept criticism*, and to admit failure in obtaining a consensus of doctrine acceptable to everyone." See "The Bishop — A Living Sign of Jesus Christ," September 5, 1983, in *Ad Limina Addresses: April 15-December 3, 1983* (Washington, D.C.: U.S. Catholic Conference, 1984), p. 18.

8. This is an insistent theme in contemporary Church documents in catechesis and pastoral theology, confronting tendencies to be silent about authentic teachings that some scholars reject, or to present a vision of the faith that fails to proclaim the excellent and saving but demanding requirements of the Gospel. See Paul VI, *Humanae Vitae*, no. 29; *Evangelization in the Modern World* (December 8, 1975), no. 78.

9. See Sacred Congregation for the Doctrine of the Faith, *Declaration on Certain Questions Concerning Sexual Ethics*, nos. 9-10.

10. See Pius XII, "Address to Psychotherapists," AAS 45.278-286; see also *Declaration on Certain Questions Concerning Sexual Ethics*, no. 10.

11. See *Declaration on Certain Questions Concerning Sexual Ethics*, no. 10. For a presentation of "fundamental option" theories in accord with authentic Catholic teaching, and a critique of extreme views, see Ronald Lawler, O.F.M. Cap., "The Love of God and Mortal Sin," and Joseph M. Boyle, Jr., "Freedom, the Human Person, and Human Action," in *Principles of Catholic Moral Life*, ed. William E. May (Chicago: Franciscan Herald Press, 1981), pp. 205-215, 237-266. See also Germain Grisez, *The Way of the Lord Jesus*, vol. 1, *Christian Moral Principles* (Chicago: Franciscan Herald Press, 1983), ch. 16, qs. B through E.

12. See Grisez, *Christian Moral Principles*, ch. 17, q. A.

13. See *ibid.,* ch. 17, qs. C through F.

14. John Paul II in *Familiaris Consortio*, no. 33, quotes this passage from Paul VI, *Humanae Vitae*, no. 29.

15. Thomas Aquinas, *Summa Theologiae*, II-II, q. 141, a. 8.

16. See *ibid.,* II-II, q. 153, a. 5.

17. See John Paul II, *Familiaris Consortio*, no. 37.

18. *Ibid.,* no. 6.

19. That some of the most popular forms of birth control, notably IUD's and most contemporary forms of the birth control pill, permit conception (and so the coming-to-be of a new human being) and then cause the destruction of that person is well known. See Kevin Hume, "Latest Research Findings: The Pill and the I.U.D.," *Proceedings of the First International Congress for the Family* (Madras: Office of the Congress, 1983), pp. 86-95. For a theological reflection on these facts, see Germain Grisez, *Abortion: The Myths, the Arguments, and the Realities* (Washington, D.C.: Corpus, 1970), p. 344.

20. John Paul II, *Familiaris Consortio*, no. 32.
21. *Ibid.,* no. 35.
22. On education for chastity, see *ibid.,* no. 37.
23. *Ibid.*
24. See *ibid.,* nos. 77-85.
25. Aquinas, *Summa Theologiae*, I-II, q. 107, a. 4.

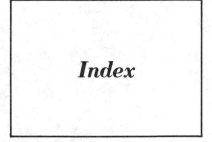

# Index